The Wonder of Boys

Also by Michael Gurian

The Wonder of Boys

What Parents, Mentors and Educators
Can Do to Shape Boys
into Exceptional Men

Michael Gurian

JEREMY P. TARCHER/PENGUIN
A MEMBER OF PENGUIN GROUP (USA) INC.
NEW YORK

For Gail, Gabrielle, and Davita

JEREMY P. TARCHER/PENGUIN
Published by the Penguin Group
Penguin Group (USA) Inc., 375 Hudson Street, New York, New York 10014, USA • Penguin Group (Canada), 90 Eglinton Avenue East, Suite 700, Toronto, Ontario M4P 2Y3, Canada (a division of Pearson Penguin Canada Inc.) • Penguin Books Ltd, 80 Strand, London WC2R 0RL, England • Penguin Ireland, 25 St Stephen's Green, Dublin 2, Ireland (a division of Penguin Books Ltd) • Penguin Group (Australia), 250 Camberwell Road, Camberwell, Victoria 3124, Australia (a division of Pearson Australia Group Pty Ltd) • Penguin Books India Pvt Ltd, 11 Community Centre, Panchsheel Park, New Delhi– 110 017, India • Penguin Group (NZ), Cnr Airborne and Rosedale Roads, Albany, Auckland 1310, New Zealand (a division of Pearson New Zealand Ltd) • Penguin Books (South Africa) (Pty) Ltd, 24 Sturdee Avenue, Rosebank, Johannesburg 2196, South Africa

Penguin Books Ltd, Registered Offices: 80 Strand, London WC2R 0RL, England

First trade paperback edition 1997
Copyright © 1996, 2006 by Michael Gurian
Title-page photograph © Black Box, Index Stock

Most Tarcher/Penguin books are available at special quantity discounts for bulk purchase for sales promotions, premiums, fund-raising, and educational needs. Special books or book excerpts also can be created to fit specific needs. For details, write Penguin Group (USA) Inc. Special Markets, 375 Hudson Street, New York, NY 10014.

The Library of Congress catalogued the first trade paperback as follows:

Gurian, Michael.
    The wonder of boys : what parents, mentors and educators can do to shape boys into
exceptional men / Michael Gurian.
        p.   cm.
    Includes bibliographical references.
    ISBN 0-87477-887-5
    1. Boys.   2. Boys—Psychology.   3. Child rearing.   I. Title.
HQ775.G83   1996   95-42188 CIP
649'.132—dc 20
    ISBN 1-58542-528-1 (paperback reissue)

Printed in the United States of America
20   19   18   17   16   15   14   13   12

BOOK DESIGN BY CHRIS WELCH

Contents

Preface to the Ten-Year Anniversary Edition

Ten years ago, I was thirty-eight, a teacher, therapist, new father of my second child—and my fourth book was just coming out. This book, about what boys needed in contemporary life, had been rejected by twenty-six publishers. "Girls' books are what we're looking for," the editors had said. It was hard to blame them. Numerous bestsellers had come out in the early to mid-nineties about the issues that girls face. A controversial book on the issues that confronted boys—this was untried, risky on many levels, including the possible political fallout in gender politics. Also, my book was science-based (based in neurobiology). That, too, was risky, since the biological sciences of gender had not yet been applied to child development in this way. Neither my editor nor I knew what would happen when the yellow book with three boys smiling on the front cover was officially published. We held our breath.

Fortunately, when *The Wonder of Boys* came out in September 1996, the risks paid off. Some reviewers attacked it immediately for political reasons, some even arguing that boys' issues meant very little. But just as immediately, something started happening. Mothers and fathers wrote me letters (no e-mail yet) telling stories of raising boys in today's world. A teacher wrote that "the struggles of boys in school today are much larger than people realize." People began writing from all around the world, agreeing that boys needed as much careful attention as girls.

A decade has passed since the publication of this risky book about "the other half." Thanks to readers, the book has reached hundreds of thousands of families. In a ten-year period, several boys' issues have continued to find the light. A number of other powerful books on boys have also been published. The school shootings in the late nineties showed us how dark the male soul can become when a civilization neglects to care for its sons. A national think tank called the Boys Project has recently emerged in our culture—its mission: to alert academics and the government to boys' issues.

I have continued to write new books about boys (and girls) and continue to receive daily mail (now it's mainly e-mail) regarding this work. In all this correspondence, the affection shines through, of parents, grandparents, researchers, and many others who care for all children, and who are saying, "Our boys DO need our help. We know it. We care deeply." Since *The Wonder of Boys* was first published, America went to war. The ripple effect of this on the lives of boys is just being understood.

Also, since the book's original publication, the Internet has become a major media factor in the lives of both adults and children. There is now a heightened need for guidance and mentoring of boys and girls as they navigate the free-for-all cyberworld. The section of this book titled "Teaching Boys Values Through the Media" has taken on new meaning as boys spend hours every day (sometimes up to seven or eight hours) on the Internet, watching television, playing video games—and they start using computers as young as two and three years old. Indeed, everything our boys do today requires vigilance, for many of the new things they are doing affect their ability to live with wonder. Wherever I go now to give talks or meet with communities, I am thrilled to see a constantly growing understanding of all the issues boys face.

The response to boys' issues over the last ten years shows me that our boys have inherited from us adults not only a great deal of our mettle, our tenderness, our drive, and our accomplishments—but also our insecurities and unresolved conflicts, the weight of our questions, passed down through the generations, that are now coming to difficult confluence:

What is a man?

How should boys become men?

How should boys and men show their love and be loved?

In what way do males have a sacred role in this life?

Answers to these questions are being lived and fought for by boys, girls, women, and men. These were the primal questions that drove *The Wonder of Boys* into words and action. I am nearly fifty now, my children teenagers, and I am still working to answer these questions.

A reader, a grandmother in her eighties, wrote this to me recently: "I got *The Wonder of Boys* for my granddaughter when she had her first son. Now I've given a copy to one of my great-granddaughters. She's also having a boy." There is no better feeling for a writer than to know he has touched several generations.

As I read again the words and research and stories I presented ten years ago, I feel most of all honored to continue to be part of a timeless effort in our civilization to help our sons—one family, one neighborhood, one generation at a time. I thank you for reading this book and letting it help you love and care for your children. Our children, much more than any single book, are the real risk worth taking and, indeed, the reason for our living.

Writing this book and also this preface has been an honor for me. I hope that as you read this anniversary edition, you experience much more than just my feelings and insights and observations. I hope you'll receive a deep understanding of the needs, hopes, dreams of your sons, for they are filled, I know, with the wonder of boys.

—Michael Gurian
February 2006

Introduction

Pinocchio! Oh Pinocchio!
You're a boy!
A real boy!
                                        —*Geppetto*

When I was a boy I joined millions of other children in experiencing Walt Disney's version of the Pinocchio story. I watched Geppetto, the carpenter, fashion a boy from wood. I watched the Blue Fairy come down from the starry sky to promise Pinocchio that if he were brave, truthful, and good, he'd be transformed into a real boy. Bravery, I learned, made a boy real. Truth and goodness made a boy come alive. Without them, he was an inferior model of a boy—he did not quite exist.

Hungry to be real myself—hungry in my small weakling body to be brave, hungry in my young spiritual mind to be truthful, hungry in my boy's search for love to be good—I watched Pinocchio set out on numerous adventures, with Jiminy Cricket as his conscience. I watched this wooden version of myself, who did not know who he was and did not feel important, learn how to be brave in the whale's belly, how to be truthful when his nose grew so long, how to be good by suffering the painful consequences of being bad. I cheered happily when the Blue Fairy made Pinocchio real. In that moment of transformation, I was like every boy who identified with Pinocchio—I felt just a little closer to becoming who I wanted to be. I felt real.

When I was growing up in the late fifties and throughout the sixties, cultural attitudes toward boys had begun to shift. Part of why I identified so utterly with the simple, basic Pinocchio story was my own confusion about how and why to grow up, a confusion I gained from a confused culture. By the time I was a young man, my culture's attitudes toward me had shifted utterly, more than once. I was not unique. Just about all of us were caught up in this whirlwind.

In those turbulent years, styles of discipline swung like pendulums from day to day. Rigid rules for boys gave way in many households to experiments in permissiveness. Sometimes we received abusive discipline when we needed empathy, sometimes we were coddled when we needed clear consequences.

Attitudes toward what kinds of families best served boys also changed with the surge in divorces. As our parents struggled to hold their marriages together, some of us kids withdrew into private and scared worlds.

Values—which exist in large part as ways to teach children how to feel worthwhile in a complex world—became almost completely individualistic, so that each of us who learned one set in our home learned another next door.

Meanwhile, political perspectives squashed dialogue about biological tendencies in boys and girls. Our parents and communities were not allowed the simple information our ancestors had always known—that boys and girls have been wired differently for millions of years and need special, gender-specific attention. A lot of common sense about raising boys was not passed on.

By the time I had become a young man, I did not know what being brave, truthful, and good looked like. Nor did most young people. War—the great initiator of young men—had become a place not of bravery but of shame. Truth had become an icon of stodgy old men—we young people knew that truth, once deconstructed, became naivete, and naivete rarely led either to social change or, once we had kids to support, to profits and social success. Traditional morality had become a bastion not of goodness but of stultification.

Unable to tolerate the confusion, the culture divided in the late seventies and early eighties. Part of the culture continued its passionate search for new models (needing a label, we call these people liberals and radicals, depending on their vehemence). Another part of the culture cried out, "The simple story is the only story, the last thirty years have been devil's work" (we call these people conservatives and reactionaries). These two cultural forces now clash in our schools, legislatures, homes, streets, prisons, books, magazines, movies, and newspapers. Everywhere you turn, our culture is being defined by a melodrama even more simplistic than Pinocchio, a melodrama some boys watch with sad fascination, others with morbid pessimism, others with outright fear of abandonment, others without any way to reach out except rebellion, and others with a predatory eye toward revenge.

Pinocchio's Journey

If we do not teach boys how to be brave, truthful, and good, they will not feel real. They will manifest their feelings of woodenness by becoming cowardly in their relationships with intimate partners, dishonest in their relationships with family and friends—hiding their true feelings—and amoral, even antisocial, in their dealings with their community. How shall we help boys feel real—alive, complete, loving, wise, powerful? How shall we teach them to find these qualities in themselves without falling into the extremes with which our culture entertains itself: the "there is no truth" extreme, which allows anything into a boy's growing mind, no matter how dangerous; or the "there is only one truth" extreme, which fears the present so completely, it must pray over the corpse of the past?

The Wonder of Boys seeks to combine the best of past knowledge of how to raise boys with the best of the present. This book will answer questions about teaching boys healthy sexuality, discipline, values, respect, intimacy, and self-reliance. It will challenge you as parents, educators, policy-makers, and community members to change your very culture through day-to-day efforts of raising, mentoring, and educating healthier boys. Its vision of boyhood grows from the many boys and adults around the world with whom I've worked in my years as a therapist, community consultant, teacher of male development, researcher, and father. Wherever I've gone, I've heard people saying, "Yet another advice book on how to raise boys is not enough.

Yet another book saying how difficult boys are is not enough. We need a new vision."

What I present to you in these pages is a new (and at times old, forgotten) vision of how to love boys. This vision gleans wisdom from other cultures as well as our own, and asks American communities and culture—not just American two-parent families, but schools, media, workplaces, neighborhoods—to alter themselves as they need to, so that boys can grow up physically and emotionally healthy.

Some of this book may make you uncomfortable, for it may ask you to alter parts of your lifestyle, political ideology, methods of disciplining yourself and your kids, ways of relating to boys, even attitudes toward your own son. Reading this book may, at times, feel like a difficult journey, but I hope you'll find it well meant, and worthwhile. It grows, above all, from a great love we all have for boys, a love that has been fearfully, confusingly and incompletely expressed to them over the last few decades.

MOVING BEYOND FALSE MYTHS

As I was growing up, innocently watching *Pinocchio* and learning who to be, like many of you I kept hearing how there were old myths about "gender" we had to debunk. By the time I went to college, I understood what all this was about and joined, I'm proud to say, in the debunking of some myths:

▼ that women should be barefoot, pregnant and in the kitchen;
▼ that men deserved more money than women for the exact same work;
▼ that women were intellectually inferior;
▼ that men were entitled to more social power than women;
▼ that men should be allowed to beat their wives.

In my efforts to right social wrongs against some women I helped create some new myths:

▼ that all women, as if in one gender body, agree with a single party line of feminism;

▼   that men have inherently more power on this earth than women;

▼   that masculinity is responsible for the world's ills and femininity is the world's salvation;

▼   that men are the only dangerous ones;

▼   that males and females are only different because they're socialized to be different.

It was well into my professional life that I began to see through not only the old "patriarchal" myths but also the new "gender" myths. It was only about ten years ago that I began to see the danger of some of these new myths in the lives of boys. It was only about five years ago when I was able to see how little actual study was going into boys' lives. Over the last quarter century, I realized, we had done a lot of catch-up on learning about girls and women. Unfortunately, some three decades of scientific and social growth came and went during the process with very little state-of-the-art research devoted to boys. The direct results of this mistake are now being seen in the tens of thousands in juvenile or adult prison, the thousands in gangs, the millions of boys who, as they try to be real boys and grow into real men, simply feel lost.

I hope that *The Wonder of Boys* will give you a look so deep into boy's lives that you'll feel comfortable reassessing not only the old myths but also many recently forged myths about boys, masculinity, and navigating boyhood effectively. Here are some major contemporary myths this book will counter:

Girls, our new myths tell us, have life much worse than boys. In-depth research shows that girls and boys each have their own equally painful sufferings. To say girls have it worse than boys is to put on blinders. What we say in this book about the difficulties boys face is not to detract from the privations girls suffer. Yet we cannot be helpful to boys if we do not notice the following facts: Parents talk to, cuddle, and breast-feed their boy infants significantly less than their girl infants. Male infants also suffer a 25 percent higher mortality rate than female infants; boys are twice as likely as girls to suffer from autism, six times as likely to be diagnosed with hyperkinesis, and more likely to suffer birth defects. The majority of schizophrenics are boys. The majority of retarded children are boys; emotionally disturbed boys outnumber girls 4 to 1. Learning-disabled boys outnumber girls 2 to 1; boys are twice as likely as girls to be the victims of physical abuse. Twice as many boys as girls are injured and die from physical abuse at the hands of parents and caregivers; by age nine, most boys have learned to repress all primary feelings except anger. For many boys, rage becomes the principle conduit for repressed pain, fear, sadness, and grief. For others, suicide is the response to repression. Boys are four times as likely as girls to commit suicide; even when rape and incest are figured into the statistics, boys are three times as likely as girls to be victims of violence. Today, an African-American boy in an urban area is more likely to die of a gunshot wound than was an African-American male who served in the Vietnam war; of the millions of "boys" who went to Vietnam, 59,000 were killed. During that war millions of those boys became "men." Over 60,000 of these veterans have committed suicide since the war, more than died in the war itself. Many more have become alcohol- and drug-addicted. These boys grew into emotionally powerless men; boys drop out of high school at higher rates than girls. As kids get older, girls seem to have more opportunity and more encouragement than boys to get advanced education. In recent years, females outmatriculated males in both college and graduate school.

If we care for our boys, our social progress depends on debunking the superficial stereotypes in which boys lead "more privileged lives." A more accurate picture is one with two children in it, a boy and a girl. Where she has privilege—more nurtured feelings, personal protection, a longer lifespan—he does not. Where he has privilege—more physical power, more and various job opportunities—she does not.

For the last few decades our cultural microscope has focused on the oppression of girls and women. That focus has led us to many gains in public consciousness, national policy, and private life. Now the lens must focus on boys too. For every boy who feels powerful at home or in his neighborhood there is another boy who feels lost. For every football star there are far more male drug addicts, teenage alcoholics, high school dropouts, and juvenile delinquents. Boys are in pain.

Boys, our new myths tell us, are not born boys—we make them boys. These myths also tell us there's little scientific evidence that boys and girls are born, or "wired," differently.

In reality, there's overwhelming scientific evidence. It's some of the most interesting and challenging material around. Much of what you'll read in this book is based in that research. The material presented will convince you, I hope, that boys are wired a certain way, and need to be dealt with as boys. When boys are understood and guided as boys, we help them become the men we want them to be much more effectively than when we assume socialization is most of the picture, try to force boys to "change," and then feel frustrated toward boys who "don't change."

Mom and Dad, our myths tell us, are responsible and ought to be responsible for almost all of the important raising of the son. When something goes wrong with the boy it's the parents' fault.

In reality, we are the only culture on earth that raises its sons in such a vacuum of conscious influences. This book presents another view of a boy's life. Just as raising Pinocchio was the responsibility of his many guides, *so too is every boy the responsibility of every adult in his life.* Anthropologists have generally agreed that it takes a whole village to raise a child. While parents begin, in most cases, as the most powerful influences on a boy, many others in the "tribe" must become equally important. Think how different your life and the lives of your children would be if that vision held more sway. Communities would be responsible for their own. The media would have to become more accountable. In this book you'll be challenged to build community spirit around the task of raising boys. You'll see models of communities around you that are having success with boys because they are finding ways for the whole "village" to raise them.

Boys, our new myths tell us, are inherently flawed creatures. They commit crime, they are predators, they just want sex from girls, they're too competitive, they don't listen, they're too physical, they're feelingless. At a dinner table conversation a couple years ago, Christina Crawford, author of *Mommie Dearest,* and I got into a very heated argument after she said, "Males are basically destructive and females are basically constructive." My respect for Crawford's work with abuse victims runs deep, but statements like hers by national leaders of some factions of the women's movement, by politicians, by scholars, by wives, by husbands themselves, even by children, indicate an unwritten national consensus:

Males destroy, females create; males stand in the way of positive spiritual/social values; males are inherently violent.

The book you are reading argues that there is no inherent flaw at the center of masculinity. Neither boys nor men are intrinsically defective. Those who fear masculinity have often let their fear turn to hatred rather than understanding, but they need not consume our cultural vision of boyhood.

My vision in this book intends to take nothing away from the feminist research and thinking of the last thirty years that has rightfully delineated abuses of male empowerment and the tendency of some masculine social systems to perpetuate violence. However, I differ from some of the conclusions reached by some of these thinkers as to how we should deal with problems the male world needs to address. For me, condemning boys' natural proclivities, debasing masculinity, separating boys from men, and enmeshing male development with a female culture in transition have not served boys well, nor, ultimately, culture as a whole.

As we progress through the book, we'll explore how dangerous the new gender myths have become not only for boys but for our society; and we'll explore the much more positive, inspiring reality that boys, like girls, are inherently blessed, and if nurtured properly, provide the world with indomitable spirits, humble hopes, courageous love, and unflagging energy. The fact is, masculinity, if appropriately parented, mentored, and educated, is one of life's most nurturing and creative forces.

How to Love a Boy

"Why does my boy love sports so much?" asks one mother.

"Why does my boy sulk so much?"

"What can I do about getting my son to listen better?"

"Why does my son seem to hate his father right now?"

The boys in your lives present wonderful and difficult challenges. As you begin this book, I hope you'll bring all those challenges to your reading. As you read, you'll find practical answers to practical questions.

"Why do boys' conflicts turn violent so quickly?"

"If I'm getting divorced, how can I make it easier for my son?"

"Why don't boys play with dolls no matter how much we try to make them?"

"Why don't the boys in my class sit still!"

You'll learn a lot about testosterone and its effects on boys. You'll also get a look into the male brain.

"What are effective ways to discipline boys *at different stages of their life?*"

"Are there ways to teach boys about sex that work better than others?"

"My son is gay. How did this happen? What should I do?"

"How do you define sexual abuse of a boy? Don't most boys go through a stage of sexually playing with each other?"

The Wonder of Boys will ask and answer hard questions. You may disagree with some of the answers I provide. That's part of our commitment to work together to raise our sons. I hope you'll write me with your disagreements. I don't have all the answers. I hope to give you enough information so that, when you disagree with me, or think of things I haven't covered that affect the boys in your life, you'll have resources to consult.

Once a mother of two sons in a parents' cooperative put this question to me:

"You men like bottom lines," she quipped, "so I'll ask you for a bottom line. In twenty-five words or less, what does a boy need?" Unprepared to give her an answer in so few words, I tried an old teacher's trick. "You all have the wisdom," I joked back, pointing to the group. "You tell me!"

After a long and fruitful dialogue, here's what we came up with:

1. nurturing parents/caregivers
2. a clan or tribe
3. spiritual life
4. important work
5. mentors and role models
6. to know the rules
7. to learn how to lead, how to follow
8. an adventure, and a best friend to have it with
9. lots of games
10. an important role in life

As a starting point, that's a pretty good list. One of the fathers in the group added, "It's kind of like the old Boy Scouts' saying:

"Boys need to know the objective, know the rules, and know who's in charge."

Simple "bottom lines" are not all there is to it, but they hold a great deal of wisdom. You'll find as you read this book honor paid to the suggestions of the many boys, parents, caregivers, grandparents, mentors, and teachers like yourselves who have learned how to guide the boys in their lives, and have shared that wisdom with me.

Why Boys
Are the Way
They Are

chapter 1

Where It All Begins: The Biology of Boyhood

The past is prologue.
—*Shakespeare,* The Tempest

I n Israel, at a social gathering, I met an emigré from India, a physician. I've never forgotten what he said.

Educated at Texas A & M, he had returned to India to work in Madras, then moved with part of his family to Haifa. Standing together at a party in Haifa, Dr. Jagdish Kulanapoor and I reminisced about India, where I had lived as a boy. We got onto a nature-versus-nurture conversation, which led him to the importance of ritual. Ritual, he said, is how children learn and adults flourish. When I got us onto the topic of boys' rituals, we agreed that American male rituals emphasize material acquisition and social education at the expense of spiritual growth.

He said: "Of course it would be this way in America. You have turned completely away from the primacy of biology. You pretend that human socialization, not natural inheritance, is the prime mover of the human animal. You pretend that human beings and human societies have so much power they can make boys and girls what they are. Believing this, what need have you for pervasive ritual whose job it is to honor nature's course?

"In my culture, we do not have this arrogance. We know that boys and girls are made very differently. We know and respect this even before birth. Not to do so, we believe, is to bring trouble upon us. We make separate spiritual rituals for each sex's natural and predetermined being."

This conversation took place in the early eighties. At that time in my life, I assumed, as did the vast majority of my colleagues, that nurture—"human beings and human society"—was most of why boys are boys and girls are girls. The "nature" view—that biology determined male and female behavior—had resulted, many of us could see, in women being oppressed for centuries.

So I smiled politely at Dr. Kulanapoor, and the conversation moved on.

But more than ten years later, I've realized how wise Jagdish was—not just wise in his commonsense knowledge that boys and girls are naturally different, but wise in his ability to connect biology to spirituality. For boys, no matter the tribe or culture, that link has been essential to healthy maturity. That link is missing in our families, schools, and culture.

Nature Versus Nurture

Camilla Benbow and Jullian Stanley, of Johns Hopkins University, studied 100,000 boys and girls, paying close attention to sex-different approaches to learning and living. In the late eighties, they let their results be known: "After fifteen years of looking for an environmental explanation and getting zero results," Benbow said, "I gave up." Benbow became popular on talk shows. But in many of the places she went to show her evidence that biologically inherited brain and hormone differences basically control the way males and females operate, she was treated with suspicion.

Now, in the mid-1990s, she and researchers like her have been more than vindicated. Researchers like Roger Gorski have discovered marked differences in physiological structures between the male and the female brain. Researchers at the University of Pennsylvania have measured, with brain-scan equipment, what parts of the brain males and females use during different kinds of stimulation. Amazing things have been discovered, which we'll look at in this chapter.

It requires pretty effective blinders these days to think as I did in the early 1980s—that boys are boys and girls are girls predominantly because of environmental forces. It's more accurate to say that much of who we are is determined by body chemicals, brain differences, hormones, and by society's efforts to honor this biology through its socializing influences.

Society has the choice of whether to fight our natural and inherited abilities or channel them effectively. With males especially, the "environment is the prime mover" view to which I adhered more than a decade ago has backfired. Boys as a group have not changed, despite decades of trying to make them. Not only have they not changed, they've gotten more randomly aggressive and more antisocially dangerous, the very things we thought, decades ago, we could nurture out of them by demeaning masculine culture and elevating feminine culture.

This chapter lays out information toward this view: that a boy is, in large part, hard-wired to be who he is. We can't, in large part, change who he is. We can teach him how to develop who he is with confidence, and toward a direction that contributes to our world. In this view, our best choices in nurturing him revolve around *knowing who and what he is,* then *channeling his energy in ways appropriate to him—* not to what or who we believe politically he ought to be.

Saying this does not deny the importance of environment and socialization on boys. They are important factors. Nor does it deny the importance of individual personality, both genetically driven, then individually developed, on a boy's life experience. However, as I will present in this chapter and elsewhere throughout the book, I believe that helping boys to grow up well, and helping culture to progress, requires us to do some informed generalizing about a boy's nature, and requires us to put socialization and environmental influences in perspective. When we return to the common sense of nature in our upbringing of boys, we work with boys, give them the structure, discipline, and wisdom they, in particular, need. When we accomplish this, we don't create more random violence, we ensure less of it; we don't make boys into men who victimize women, we ensure less victimization of women. In our lives as parents, mentors, and educators, we stop feeling as if we're fighting against boys and masculinity; we start realizing how to work with boys and maleness. Consequently, our homes, schools, streets, and bedrooms start looking very different.

The Prime Mover: Testosterone

Marti, a mother of a now-grown son, recounted something many mothers in a workshop could identify with: "No matter what I did, Artie was just more aggressive than his sister. When Artie was four, five years old I'd try to get him to play with dolls. He'd play with them, sure, just not the way I meant. He'd take the biggest one, make it into a gun, and blast away at the others!"

Sheila Moore and Roon Frost, authors of *The Little Boy Book*, recalled this comment by a mother:

"The biggest things in my daughters' lives right now are Barbie dolls and nail polish . . . Jonathon—he walks like the Incredible Hulk, shovels down his food, and wrestles with every boy he sees— and he's only three and a half!"

Don and Jeanne Elium recounted the words of Sam, father of a ten-year-old, in their book, *Raising a Son:*

"My son is quiet and sensitive. He doesn't go in for rough-and-tumble play with the other boys. But he is like a madman when he turns on his computer."

Because of their dominance by the hormone testosterone, aggression and physical risk-taking are programmed into boys. It's important to distinguish between "aggression" and "violence." As psychologist Aaron Kipnis has put it, "Violence is not hard-wired into boys. Violence is taught. Aggression is hard-wired."

Aggression will show itself quite overtly, as with Artie and Jonathon, or it will mask its predominance, as with Sam's son, until one of its channeling activities—like a debate or a computer video-game—begins. The quality and quantity of aggressive behavior in a boy always depends on the boy's age and how he has been taught to channel it. Boys who are mentally ill, have attention deficit disorder (hyperactivity), are genetically female, have a female brain, are homosexual, or are by personality describable by parents as "more sensitive" than most may prove to be more or less aggressive than "the average boy." Yet, still, one of the best ways to deal with a boy is to focus on his aggression and risk-taking—his domination by the hormone testosterone.

The effect of testosterone on a boy in the twentieth century has millions of years of history. Going back as far as four million years ago, males needed more testosterone than females in order to be able to reproduce. That testosterone created more body-muscle than body-fat, and that it made males more aggressive, were probably secondary functions four million years ago. Now higher levels of male sex drive than female (on average), higher levels of muscle mass, and higher levels of aggression all seem to be primary functions of testosterone.

Millions of years ago males produced trillions of potentially fertile sperm in a lifetime but were required to mate with human females who created a few hundred potentially fertile eggs—approximately one per month between the age of puberty and either death or menopause. Humans, in this male/female difference, are like most primates. In order for a male to fulfill his predominant biological imperative—to reproduce himself—he had to constantly mate with females. Back then, all a male knew was that a female was ovulating "estrous" (even now, in the 1990s, timing isn't sure). He had no way of knowing when the fleeting moment of egg-in-its-place would occur, or whether one particular ejaculation of his semen would connect with it. He was also in constant competition with other males and their sperm for the female's egg. The male's sperm competition and need for constant arousal and mating required high sex drive.

It required high testosterone.

Things have not changed much since the first humans started walking about the African savannah. Males are still in competition for females and will do nearly anything to get females to have sex with them, and love them. Females still decide (except in the case of rape) with whom they will mate based on how the males around them compete to win their affection. Males still need higher sex drives than women and still possess them, through their higher levels of testosterone. Testosterone is still the defining agent of whether a fetus will be male or female, even more lasting in its impact on the child than the chromosomal fusion that occurs in egg and sperm, for if a boy is created chromosomally but not enough testosterone exists to make him a boy, he will come out of the womb looking like a girl.

Here's how it works.

First, genetic fusion occurs between the sperm and egg to make a chromosomal boy (XY). Then the hormone testosterone surges through the chromosomally male fetus early in the pregnancy, making a boy's genitals drop. Then, in the middle months of the pregnancy, testosterone surges again, giving the boy a male brain. If, during the pregnancy, traumatic stress on the mother, for instance, inhibits testosterone release, an XY genetic boy may be born without male genitals and/or without a male brain. He may also be born homosexual without realizing it until later in life. Many external factors—traumatic stress on the mother, a mother's intake of drugs or alcohol—and many internal causes, the exact shape of which neurobiologists are still not certain, affect testosterone release in the womb.

TESTOSTERONE AND AGGRESSION

If you have a "normal" boy—meaning, he is an XY boy whose body and brain were created male by appropriate testosterone surges—he will himself be dominated by the hormone that made him what he is.

As an infant and little boy, he will show on average more aggressive tendencies than girls. Studies done with six-month-old infants have shown that when boys and girls both pull a string to get a happy result, like a smiling image on a screen, and then testers take the image away, the boys will keep pulling and pulling, more stubbornly and aggressively. Girls will, within a few pulls of not getting the image, put the string down and cry out for help.

It also shows in a boy's motor activity. From infancy, a boy's motor activity is more vigorous than girls', but the duration of each motor act is shorter and the peak of the motor act happens more quickly. So a boy will push his arm out in a jab and bring it to rest quickly, where a girl might bring her arm out more slowly and smoothly.

From infancy, boys tend to be more irritable. A factor that adds to this natural tendency might be the higher incidence of prenatal and birth complications in boys.

A little boy (on average) will turns toys into guns or swords with more frequency than girls will. He will hit more. He will try to one-up more. He will tend less toward empathic first-responses to others' pain and more toward provocative first-responses. He will be generally more competitive than his sister and especially in the few activities in which he perceives the potential to dominate over or be superior in. He will assess his potential to dominate based on his understanding of his personality, talent, and skill strengths. He will seek rough-and-tumble play or, if he perceives himself as physically weak, another outlet for aggression. Later we'll explore how to help boys navigate their excesses of aggression toward siblings by helping them find healthy ways to be aggressive with friends and in boyhood community.

TESTOSTERONE AND INDEPENDENCE

Boys, especially after the toddler years, often navigate independence differently than girls—some of this relates to testosterone and continues throughout a male's life. One mother, Mary Beth, said to me: "My husband and I were together until Casey was five. At about two, Casey was independent and just stayed that way, unlike his sister who was always more attached to me. Then when we divorced, Casey started clinging to me. Which one is more 'Casey'? The independence or the clinging?"

Mothers like Mary Beth often report having "independent boys," and just as often, seeing that independence change when a divorce occurs. Boys, dominated by testosterone, often feel compelled to gain independence earlier than girls, but only when they feel safe and confident that they are not losing a parent's love. If a parent misunderstands this equation—holds onto the boy longer than he wants to be emotionally controlled; or disrupts his sense of safety through a circumstance like divorce—his natural and very testosterone-controlled urge to separate and force himself into the world is disrupted.

Often single mothers will say things like, "I liked the clinging my son did with me after the divorce. It made me feel like I could have more influence on him. But at the same time, I knew there was more going on for him." They are wisely sensing the complexity of a boy's response to his sudden loss of confidence in becoming independent. They often find that loving him appropriately means getting him—with, hopefully, the divorced father's help—back on his independent feet again.

The more we study testosterone in a boy's life, the more explanation we have for boys' hitting, playing style, physical risk-taking, flirtations with danger, desires for independence, and general difficulty from many parents' points of view. Again, of course, we're talking averages. Some parents will say, "Are you kidding? My boys were easy. It was my girls who drove me nuts!"

TESTOSTERONE, PUBERTY, AND BEYOND

When a boy hits puberty, the influence of testosterone on his body and brain increase manifold. His testosterone level itself will increase in quantities ten to twenty times more than girls. His genitals will increase to eight times their previous size. His body will process anywhere between five to seven surges of testosterone per day. You can expect him to masturbate continually, bump into things a lot, be moody and aggressive, require a great deal of sleep, lose his temper, want sex as soon as he gets up the emotional guts to propose to a partner, have a massive sexual fantasy life, and so on. And this is just during adolescence.

When he becomes an adult, you can expect him to be more aggressive and competitive than the average woman—remember, we are again speaking of averages—more ambitious about workplace superiority; more prone to one-up in conversation; quicker to react physically to external stimulation. He will be more likely to hit when he feels accosted, and to seek rough-and-tumble play, competitive sports, or any physical or motor activities through which he can release tension, take risks, and show competitive prowess. Often he will show his prowess only to himself, and often that is enough. He will be more likely to force his way up the corporate ladder.

Testosterone so influences aggression and even assertiveness that studies done on women have shown an increase in both qualities when women have been injected with testosterone-like androgenic hormones. They take more risks, discover more ambition within themselves and in the workplace, and feel more assertive in everyday life.

TESTOSTERONE AND TENSION

Testosterone also affects the way boys, male youth, and men release tension. This in turn affects vast portions of male life. Don and Jeanne Elium, in *Raising a Son,* put it well:

"The instant when the hunter makes the kill, the thrill of the long touchdown pass, and the closure of a big sell are all moments that live in the dreams of men from prehistoric times through today. Central to these moments is a powerful cycle of energy, fundamental in the makeup of a man: a short buildup of tension followed by a quick, gratifying, and decisive release. This short-term, immediate-gratification cycle prepares a male's body to act."

Understanding how a boy's (and man's) energy works is fundamental to loving him. That energy, propelled by testosterone, and guided by the specific structure and workings of the male brain structure, is the primary cause of three behavior patterns you've probably noticed in boys:

1. the search for instant or quick gratification, whether in eating quickly, jumping from activity to activity, or quick sexual conquest;

2. the tendency to move quickly to problem-solving, even in emotionally complex experiences;

3. the tendency to find activities through which his body will build physical tension—like sports or other concentrated, single-task experiences—then release the tension with an "Ahhh."

The male sex act is the best metaphorical and literal way of seeing this tension-release cycle with clarity. The male's reproductive job, unlike the female who will carry the child, is to plant the seed in a female, then find another female to plant it in, and so on: quick sexual tension and release, and as often as needed. We teach boys to do much more, of course, but their bodies are still built on the basis of their sexual biology.

As we continue through this book, we'll explore hundreds of ways to nurture boys for who they are, and in so doing, help them find healthy and socially adaptive ways to release tension, get gratification, and be happy. We will also explore ways to teach boys to do more than just release tension and get the kind of gratification their bodies need. But we won't do the latter without first doing the former. To try to teach boys to "rise above instant gratification," "become more like girls," "be more sensitive," "not like sports as much," and so on without first teaching them personally fruitful and socially acceptable ways to do all those things is to shoot ourselves in the foot. Boys don't believe adults who don't understand boys.

How a Boy Thinks: The Male Brain

"What we are and how we live," say Anne Moir and David Jessel in *Brain Sex,* "is largely dictated by the messages that mould and inform our brains."

Centuries ago—even just a few decades ago—when people talked about "the male brain" or "the female brain" they often did so in order to prove that one—usually the male—was superior to the other. When it was discovered, for instance, that the weight and volume of the male brain is ten to fifteen percent greater than the weight and volume of a female's brain, social thinkers were quick to say, "You see, the male brain is bigger and therefore men are better—smarter, more capable of doing the most important jobs." In this and so many other ways, brain "science" was used to put women down. As a result, talk about male and female brains has been avoided and even called "dangerous" in the last quarter century. In this absence of neuroscience in our political and social dialogue, we've avoided one danger but replaced it with another. We have constructed a late-twentieth-century society that specifically tries not to tailor child-raising techniques to boys and girls themselves. In the absence of this tailoring, boys whose brains work one way are told they're not okay; and girls whose brains work another way are also told they're not okay.

Nevertheless, brain research has been going on throughout our social changes so that now its evidence of male/female brain differences is so vast that responsible parents, mentors, educators, and social thinkers cannot avoid it if they are going to do right by children. Thankfully, research has advanced beyond the "my brain is smarter than her brain" stage. Now we are able to see differences between a boy's brain and a girl's without saying, "So this means girls can't do what boys can do and boys can't do what girls can do."

Brain research does not mean biology is destiny. It means biology is proclivity. The brain is so wonderful a mechanism that anyone can be most anything, given the drive, skill, and right nurturing. Opportunity need not be curtailed to anyone based on sex or gender. At the same time, because biology is proclivity, when our children are young, we must do everything we can to help boys and girls feel comfortable in the development of their own separate ways of doing things. Not to do so is to teach them that their core self is inadequate by nature and will not be nurtured by society. Our children, brought up this way, will take their revenge.

STRUCTURAL DIFFERENCES IN THE BRAIN

If we had X-ray glasses and could look into our childrens' heads, what are some differences we would see?

We would notice, as Laurie Allen, brain researcher at UCLA has pointed out, that in at least seven of the measured brain structures there are structural differences between female and male brains.

We would notice a difference in size—the boy's brain at least ten percent larger than the girl's.

We would also notice that within the smaller girl's brain is a larger corpus callosum than in the larger boy's brain. The corpus callosum is the bundle of nerves that connects the brain's right and left hemispheres. Moore and Frost have summarized how this happens:

"During fetal life when the brain and nervous system are being organized, the female cortex (brain) develops in advance of the male cortex. The left half of the cortex (the part of the brain that controls thinking) develops somewhat later than the right (the part that works with spatial relationships). In males, though, there is an even greater lag. 'As a result,' one neurologist says, 'when the right side is ready to hook up with the left side (by sending over connecting nerve fibers), in the male the appropriate cells don't yet exist on the left. So (the fibers) go back and instead form connections within the right hemisphere. You end up with extremely enriched connections within the right.' "

One of the results of this structural difference is increased focus in the male brain on spatial relationships and activity. Little boys, much more so than little girls, manipulate objects like blocks to see how they use up space.

Because the female cortex develops faster than the male, it is able to create the larger corpus callosum, and because that bundle of nerves is larger, it is able to enjoy more cross-talk between the left and right hemispheres of the brain than does a boy's brain. Boys in general do less well in reading than girls—one reason is the smaller corpus callosum. The brain that will read better is the brain that can draw more heavily on both sides of the brain *at once,* which is what reading requires. The smaller corpus callosum in boys is also one of the reasons boys find it more difficult to identify with accuracy the emotions on another person's face. That, too, is an activity that is better done when more of the brain is being used.

If we could look with our X-ray vision even deeper into the brain, we would identify a neurotransmitter, serotonin, which inhibits aggressive behavior, and which exists in higher levels in girls than boys. Serotonin works with hormones secreted in the hypothalamus of the brain, hormones like testosterone. A boy's brain secretes more testosterone than a girl's *and* transmits less serotonin. Boys become all the more aggressive, girls less aggressive.

If we could continue our X-ray journey into the brain we would notice, as has Rubin Gur at the University of Pennsylvania, structural differences in the way girls and boys use their left and right hemispheres. Gur uses brain-scan equipment to generate computer photographs of brains in use. He hooks males and females (college age and older) to the equipment, then gives them tests. The scanning equipment photographs the brain in different colors, each color showing a different degree of intense cortical activity. So the photographs end up looking like those maps we studied as children, where different heights each got their own color—mountain ranges different from plateaus, plateaus from deserts, deserts from oceans.

When males and females are asked to do a spatial task—like figure out how two objects fit together in space—most of the male's right hemisphere lights up in various colors representing various degrees of right hemisphere intensity. Much less of his left hemisphere lights up with higher degree colors. The colors and their intensity are pretty much equal on both sides of the female brain. This very visual and state-of-the-art process for putting our X-ray glasses into the brain gives us clear visual evidence of why males of all ages (except the very old) do on average better than females in spatial tasks—from complex use of blocks as children to architectural design as adults. The male brain is set up to be intensely spatial, the female brain is not.

On the other hand, Gur has shown through his process how the male brain is not set up to be verbal but the female is. When verbal skills are tested, much less of the male brain is used than the female, and the intensity of activity in the left hemisphere is increased in the female over the male.

Overall, brain research has shown how the female brain is at work in more sections than the male *just about all the time.* It is on call in a way the male is not. To use an analogy: the male brain turns on, like a machine, to do its task, then turns off; the female brain is always on. This is an exaggeration, of course, for parts of the male brain are also always on, but when Gur compares the two brains in non-active states, the difference between the constantly "on" female brain and "on/off" male brain is startling.

This difference is a primary reason males are so "task-oriented," testing out as less able than females to do a number of different kinds of tasks at once; and why males react to interruptions in their thinking with more of a sense of invasion than females tend to, and combined with testosterone-based aggression, more forcefully.

BRAIN DIFFERENCES AND *YOUR* CHILDREN

Once I was speaking to a school group about brain differences. Sally, a mother of one boy and two girls, told me:

"My son is just like his father. He spreads things all over the floor, taking up more space than his sisters. It's like having a huge dinosaur living in the house. His sister can draw in a neat stack on the table, not Sandy. He's got to pretend the whole world belongs to him. Does this stuff about space relate to the way his brain works?"

Sally hit the nail on the head. Boys tend to use up far more space than girls. When my daughter was in daycare, our friend and daycare provider once complained to me about three brothers, ages five through nine, she looked after. They were always active, always throwing things, "uncontrollable." I suggested she send them outside more. As I said it, she realized what common sense it was. It had crossed her mind too, but she hadn't acted on it. "I just wish they'd do what I say in here. Why should I have to give them special treatment?"

Yet her daycare space was very small. When she did make more space for the antsy boys, both inside her house by converting another basement room for "the boys," and by letting all the kids go outside more (supervised, of course), she discovered that her discipline problems decreased.

So often the boy's brain cries out to us like these boys did: "Give me more space!"

The boy's brain tries to recreate itself in the outside world by creating and playing games—like basketball, football, etc.—that fill large spaces and challenge the male brain to hone its skill at moving objects through space. The girl's brain tries to recreate itself in the outside world by creating situations and playing games—like house, doll life, imagined community life—that use lots of verbal skills, require lots of one-on-one communication between actors, and involve overtly complex emotional behavior.

Here are a few other behavioral differences you might notice between boys and girls—differences that begin in the brain.

From infancy, boys look at objects for shorter but more active periods than girls do. Girls pay attention longer than boys. This tendency continues throughout a boy's life. When parents complain that boys don't pay attention, part of the reason is innate. One thing parents find helpful in getting boys to pay attention is to wrap the activity or theme they want attended to around a concomitant activity involving objects moving in space—whether in a game, on the computer, or in a physical job.

Boys and men take in less sensory or "proximal" data than girls and women. They smell less, taste less, get less soothing and input from tactile information, hear less, and see less.

Let's take hearing as an example. Girls complain that boys don't listen, women complain that men don't hear, people don't feel heard by boys and men. This begins from the very beginning of life, in the brain. Males in general hear in one ear better than in the other. Females in general hear more data and hear equally well in both ears. All the way through life, males hear less than females say, which creates profound problems in relationships. Boys from very early on are reported to ignore voices, even parents' voices, more than girls do. In some of these cases, they are simply not hearing. Boys also do less well than girls at picking out background noises. Boys, quite simply, hear less background noise and differentiate less. This is one of the reasons parents and anyone around a boy often report having to speak more loudly to the boy than to a girl.

When parents or educators feel unheard by boys, some of the frustration needs to be replaced by an understanding of how the boy's brain is working. If he's not hearing, try another sense—especially the visual, which is the boy's best sense on average. Also try to get the message to him through stories, games, objects that move through space. Start by learning which is his better ear.

It probably comes as no surprise to anyone that girls and women want prolonged touch more than boys and men. The brain has set us up this way. Boys, especially as they get older, often feel demanded upon when they are forced to hug, etc. Simultaneously, girls often feel diminished and unloved when they don't get a higher amount of prolonged physical touch. Much of this is hard-wired by the brain.

Boys do better with visual problems and interpreting visual information when it is presented to their left eye—the one that feeds the right hemisphere, their strongest hemisphere, the hemisphere that specializes in spatial relationships. Girls do equally well with visual information no matter which eye it's presented to. Even in infancy, boys gaze at their mothers one half the amount of time girls do. Often mothers feel they are doing something wrong with their boys, or feel unloved because the boy doesn't seem to attend to their face for as prolonged a period of time. The real reason for his quick visual fix, then eye movement to whatever objects are in the room, lies in his brain's need to move quickly from object to object in space.

Television, videogames, and the whole computer culture is very much a creation of the male brain. It is predominantly a visual means of communication, providing lots of quick moving images and objects moving through virtual space. Televisions and computers can, of course, be used too much, at the expense of a boy's development of other senses. But still, it is important to realize that when a boy channel surfs and a girl wants him to stay on one program for a longer period of time, or when a boy seems preverbal unless he's at his computer: rather than say to ourselves, "Let's change that boy," we'd be better off saying, "Let's help that boy expand who he is through the skills he already enjoys."

Boys have three times more reading difficulties than girls. Preschool boys often come into their verbal skills up to a year later than girls. On the other hand, they test out on average better at math than girls. The brain holds the key. Math is an abstract, spatial construct of the right hemisphere. Boys will on average do better at it. Verbal skills originate in the left hemisphere. Girls on average do better at them.

These brain differences continue robustly throughout male and female life. Females tend to choose ways of relating, people to relate to, and jobs that utilize their verbal and empathy skills and thus will make them feel comfortable. When the hormonal and emotional drive to mate takes over, they will often choose mates who do not verbalize well, have lower empathy skills, and so on. But for the most part, girls pick girls to relate to. By the same token, boys pick boys to relate to.

This is not to say romance and other kinds of social life can't lead a man and woman or boy and girl to gain the skills of the other sex, or that parents and educators can't teach children and adults the skills of the other brain, or that boys relating to girls and girls to boys is somehow antineurological. Those sorts of interpretations are over-reactions. A rich community life means relating to as many people as are helpful to community spirit. Brain information is a pathway to a child-raising system in which boys and girls discover who they are in large part by seeking out the people, both peers and elders, of the same sex with whom they feel comfortable, and innately at one.

HOW THE DIFFERENT BRAINS WERE CREATED

When we talked about testosterone we talked about how our male and female ancestors adapted to life and brought their very different hormones along with them. They did the same with the brain.

Until about 10,000 years ago, when we shifted to agriculturally based societies, we spent millions of years hunting and gathering. Females carried and birthed the babies, took care of home and local governing, and "gathered" food and nesting material from the local agricultural environment. Males inseminated females, formed intra-local alliances, and hunted over millions of years. The female brain developed to do well at what survival required it to do; the male brain did the same.

It is no wonder, then, that the female brain should be better at sensory data. It needed to hear, smell, touch, taste, and see more minutely and effectively than the male because childrens' cues are more subtle than a lion's or a deer's, and because gathering roots and tubes, and figuring out which ones are poison, needs more sensory excellence as well.

It is no wonder, too, that the female brain developed better handling of emotive data. Kids and local community life required more emotive processing strength than did large or very isolated hunting parties, which were single-task focused rather than multi-task focused.

It is no wonder the male brain developed better spatial capacities. Hunting needs a very acute sense of dimensionality, depth perception, and distance.

It is no wonder the male brain developed better abstraction skills. Hunting, then large-population society building and edifice building, required an acute sense of abstract design.

Given, too, the daily necessity of the male to kill animals and, in war or other protection activity, humans, it is no wonder the male brain de-emphasized emotive and verbal skills, as well as empathy skills.

These different brains developed so our ancestors could survive. These brains are still in us. They will not change biologically or structurally for countless years. If we train these brains well, they can help us not only survive but spiritually flourish. Through our understanding and nurturing of these aspects of a boy's nature, we can take better care of life itself.

Often people who are aware of the evolution of brain differences will worry that if we nurture boys according to how their brains and hormones work, we'll be saying, "Boys will be boys." They fear that in saying this we'll be nurturing more violence, destructiveness, less intimacy with spouses and children, and more sexual stereotypes that will keep women out of architecture, engineering, and police work and keep men wary of social work, daycare, and primary parenting. This does not need to be the case. Knowledge of the evolution of brain differences teaches us that societies are capable of creating intimate and fruitful human relationships that nurture *both* the best of the female and best of the male brains. Our mistake is not in letting "boys be boys"; it's in letting boys be boys without the proper care, love, and discipline.

Essential also as we adapt our growing knowledge of brain differences to our own parenting and living is to look at how we have defined intimacy between people, especially women and men. Perhaps the single most important influence on our boys is how they see their parents be intimate. We live in a time and culture that defines how people should be intimate through the X-ray vision of the female brain—most self-help books are about how men are too absent, too incapable of intimacy, and how women know how to be close but men don't. *The standard most of these books use is the female brain's standard.* Our marriages, and thus the way we raise our kids, will change significantly for the better when we develop a standard that honors both the male and the female brain. Thoughts along this direction are the focus of books like John Grey's *Things Your Mother Couldn't Tell You and Your Father Didn't Know,* Harville Hendrix's *Getting the Love You Want,* my own *Love's Journey,* and videotapes for couples put out by Gary Smalley, Barbara DeAngelis, and The Learning Channel, on Brain Sex.

The Way Boys Feel: Feelings and the Brain

Once at a training I was doing for Big Brothers and Big Sisters, a case worker shared this story with me. She had been working with a single mom whose son had been a "crier," her word for a boy who cried on her chest when he was hurt, like any little boy would. But then sometime around seven or eight he stopped crying. "He changed," the mom reported. "He used to be honest with me about his feelings, but around eight he started keeping to himself more, he wanted more fighting, he kind of turned away from me. Once he told me I was no good to him. I just nagged him and wouldn't let him be."

Many mothers notice changes between five years old and ten years old in the way their sons process feelings and take care of their emotional needs. This mom's observations caused her pain, yet what was happening to her son was normal. Even given the other external factors in their lives—the father's departure from the home, the mom's return to work, an elder brother's exit from the home to live with dad—still, the eight-year-old boy's way of processing feeling was forming into a way he would use throughout his life.

The male brain and hormones give a boy a natural tendency toward processing feeling and emotion in a very "male" way. This way becomes quite clear by the age of ten, or if not by then, certainly by the time puberty hits.

There is a great deal of cultural misunderstanding of how boys process feelings, just as there are huge cultural expectations of the way some people want boys to process feelings. Boys are in their way "sensitive" and "compassionate." That is a given. Every person has this capability. And boys can always be trained to become more sensitive and empathic toward others than they are. These are givens. But still, their testosterone and brain wire them naturally to process their feelings and react emotionally in some boy-specific ways, and it is traumatic to try to make a boy change the very way he processes his own feelings. They are his, no one else's, and he needs to be able to do them his way.

HOW BOYS EXPERIENCE THEIR FEELINGS AND EMOTIONS

Here are eight internal processing methods favored by males. You'll notice as you read them that they grow logically out of things we've learned about testosterone and about the brain.

1. *The action-release method.* Boys process and release feeling in quick bursts of displayed energy. Often they angrily yell at us, or "fly off the handle," or slam a door, or hit their fist into a table, or "turn us off" and bury themselves in some activity, like a videogame. They are processing and releasing feeling through action. Sometimes this feels like rejection to us because they are processing the feeling through actions that seem to isolate us or even seem dangerous.

2. *The suppression-delayed reaction method.* Males are wired for a certain degree of delayed reaction. The male brain is very much a problem-solving brain, so it delays emotional reactions in order to solve a problem. It is very common to see boys who do not come to their parents with problems they've had in school until a week or more later. The boy is irritable or "a little off kilter" for a week, then finally allows us to help him get at what's bugging him, then in expressing it realizes it has been bugging him. Often the boy never even realized he had experienced emotional pain or trauma. Our best strategy when we see a boy in suppression-delayed reaction is to be patient, let him know we're there, and as always with boys, show him that a safe

structure exists for him to continue living his life despite his twisted insides.

3. *The displacement-objectification method.* Let's say a boy I'm with is angry but won't talk about it. We happen to walk by a car that's dented. I say, "I'll bet that car is pissed off to have been smashed up that way. Look how pretty that chrome was, look how someone waxed that car up, and now some putz trashed the car. Sometimes I feel like that. I feel like I've done my best and I just get trashed anyway. I know you feel like that sometimes . . ."

This is a strategy we use that acknowledges the boy's tendency to make objects even of emotions, to project emotions into outside space, and to displace emotional responses from original sources to safer, inanimate receptacles. If I can get the boy to put his emotional experiences into a story on a movie screen or a piece of mythology or a personal story involving objects around him, he is more likely to be able to talk. This often works much better than saying to him, "What's wrong, tell me, I'm sitting across the table from you, talk to me," and meaning "I've got only a few minutes, so just talk already." Boys often need us to give them more time than girls need, and they often need us to connect their feelings to objects in the outside world.

4. *Physical-expression method.* Boys will experience, express, and expel their feelings physically to a greater degree than girls (on average). This is, of course, common sense to everyone. In order to facilitate this method of expression, we must give boys enough physical space, enough disposable objects, and enough training in boundaries of physical space and disposability. The father who puts a punching bag in the basement and says, "This is your space. Come here when you need to, punch the bag when you need to" is wisely giving the son an object and a space. Simultaneously, he must teach the son that punching bags and having physical space is not to be confused with giving the boy carte blanche to punch anything or anyone. Just the opposite: by providing the boy with space and receptacle, the father is showing the son the proper boundaries for his feelings. "When they overwhelm you," he is teaching, "you bring them here. They will be contained here. When you return to the company of others, you'll know how to bring your feelings appropriately back to others because you've felt them cleanly here."

5. *The going-into-the-cave method.* Boys on average do not process feelings as quickly as girls. The social anthropologist Jennifer James

told me of a study that showed males can take up to seven hours longer than females to process "hard emotive data"—in other words, stimulation that requires complex emotive responses. Boys often feel overwhelmed by a mother's swirl of feelings, sisters' myriad verbalizings of feelings. They often need time away, just time in the cave of their room, or a fort, to get away from the stimulation.

With boys who go into the cave a lot, it is essential that caregivers hold them accountable once they come out. That is, if we let the boy walk away while we're trying to get him to process emotional material, we must make sure we have his general agreement that once he's processed it, he'll bring the insights back to the family, the relationship. Boys often need us to show them that it's okay to go into the cave and it's essential that the boy feel good about coming out of the cave, (and we'll be waiting) to be reaccepted and refined by his insights.

6. *The talking-about-feelings method.* Most parents have noticed how hard it is, once the boy is seven, eight, or older to get a boy to process his feelings by talking about them. It's a lot easier to ask him later what he felt; at the time the experience is happening, he often just does not know what he feels and feels invaded when we force him to say what he does not know.

Because the two halves of the male brain are connected by a smaller group of fibers—the corpus callosum—than in the female brain, we can expect males in general to have greater difficulty than females expressing feelings. Information flows less easily from the right side of the brain to the verbal, left side. As the male and female brains mature in the first decade of life, then through the hormonal adjustments of puberty, we see boys getting less and less able to connect feeling and verbal information in comparison to girls. So, often, talking about feelings with boys does not work like it works for girls.

On the other hand, we have to keep trying. We have to pick and choose the right moment to ask him, "How do you feel?" Or "How was that (experience) for you?" Timing is everything here. We may need to wait until he's in a place where he feels emotionally safe. We may need to ask once, wait a few moments, then let it go—letting him come to us on *his* timing. Boys who are constantly asked how they feel will, for a while, feel good that their caregiver cares so much; but soon, if we just keep prodding the boy to talk about his feelings and he won't, what he's doing inside is building up resentment.

7. *The problem-solving method.* Often boys do not invest as much

emotive energy in certain low-level problems as we think they do or think they should. For boys, the solving of a problem often releases the emotive energy of the experience. With men, of course, this is frequently true as well. This is one reason males in general move to problem-solving as quickly as they can. Yes, part of it is that they've been trained that way, but most of it begins in their hormones and brains—they see a problem, it agitates them, once they solve it they feel much better.

8. *The crying method.* In his classic story of boyhood, *The Little Prince,* Antoine de Saint-Exupéry wrote: "It is such a secret place, the land of tears." For boys, especially as they get older, it is secret indeed.

Boys, by the time they are school age, will cry only under very stressful and very safe circumstances. As their brains form more completely and testosterone dominates them more fully, they feel unsafe in the activity of crying especially toward puberty. It is about the most vulnerable a boy can be. That vulnerability, in his natural composition, is frightening not only because culture teaches him not to cry but because in order to cry he must be processing hard emotive data at such a fast and confusing rate—something his brain, unlike the female's, is not as well wired to do—he feels he is losing himself.

Part of why boys (starting at about four or five) don't tend to cry as much as girls, or men as much as women, is certainly that we have taught them not to. Much of that teaching, however, has been a result of centuries of human understanding and acceptance of the male brain. Boys process a lot more of their feelings through other methods than tears—through action, through problem-solving, through displacement. As much as possible, we need to help boys perfect these methods because these methods are natural to them.

At the same time, we must realize that the danger in male biology is its tendency to repress feeling. "I don't know what I feel," a boy (or man) will say. "I just don't know, help me." This is a terrible problem for males. Thus, many of our cultural efforts to help boys and men feel more, even cry more, are worthwhile. Yet emboldening the male-specific methods might be more fruitful than some of the methods for sensitivity training in which we try to get males to talk about their feelings and cry on call. This is often unnatural for them, whether they are a boy or a man.

From Biology to Culture

Wherever we turn we see the biology of boyhood at work. We drive by the park and see boys playing football: developing self-image by moving an object through space in a highly organized way, following highly complex rules of spatial conduct.

We walk past the street B-ball court and see boys, shirtless, sweating, and dissing each other: moving an object through space in a competitive way while verbally one-upping each other.

We walk past a building and watch men constructing the building from ground up, first having abstracted the spatial dimensions, then designed them onto paper, then organized a team of people to build the building into the local geography of the land.

We enter the information age—its e-mail, computers, televisions, videophones—and find the visually and spatially oriented male brain manifesting its best functioning onto computer screens.

We also face increased antisocial violence every day, by males, as the male brain and its recently untrained, undisciplined testosterone do increasing damage in the world.

Everywhere we turn we see male biology at work. Usually, though, we say to ourselves, "There's those boys again, forming their boy society, their boy culture. Look how they've been socialized. If only we could change it." We say, "That masculine culture has got to go. It trains males to stare at TVs, keep women out of the workplace, play violent games, and make war." We say, "Male culture and female culture—they'll never get along. Let's change one or the other."

What about boy culture? What can we do about it? Or, more helpfully, what can we do for it? It will form whether we like it or not because the male brain will create it. The question we must answer as parents, mentors, and educators is: Will we guide it, or turn away from it in confusion and fear?

The Culture Boys Create

*My parents and teachers don't understand
the first thing about me. They just don't
take the time. They put me in a little box:
He's a boy. Either he'll be president, or he'll
screw up.*

—*Loren, fourteen*

K arol in Tucson wrote this letter to my newspaper column:
"I'm a single mother with three sons, from fourteen to
eight, and one daughter, eleven. As I watch my boys grow up I see
how confused they are, how confused I am. My fourteen-year-old
'hangs' with a group of four boys. When people see them walking
together, dissing each other, and wearing their baggy jeans, you can
tell the people are worried. My son, just because he's got his little boy
peer group, looks like a criminal.

"My ten-year-old came back from school one day and told me his
teacher told him he was going to grow up in prison—my son's a good
student, good grades. I called the teacher and she said, 'It was just a
joke, trying to show Nathan he better watch out, better hold onto
himself before that boy world twists him all around.'

"My eight-year-old still loves to hug his mama, but he's already
moving away from me and I'm letting him go. Then there comes my
own confusion, because even though I know my boys are going to do

what they're going to do, I get afraid for them. I don't get afraid for my daughter so much because I understand her. I understand how girls do things with each other. But the boys, they live on the edge and even though I think I love my sons, I know I pull and push at them not to be boys sometimes.

"I'm not sure what my question is. I guess I just wanted to be honest about how hard it is to raise boys. I thought I knew what attitude I should take toward them, but I'm just not sure. Years ago I was sure the thing to do was give them dolls. That worked with my oldest for about thirty seconds. After he tore it apart, my gender politics fell apart. I guess for over a decade my husband and I, and now pretty much just I, have been trying to figure out boy culture. Have you got it figured out?"

My answer to Karol was "I'm getting there, let's work together and we'll figure it out." That letter, and others like it over the years, have inspired me to write this book. One of the things I've had to wrestle with as I work with parents, boys, and communities is our bipolar attitude toward boy culture. We love it and we hate it. We respect it and we're terrified of it. We like to be entertained by its violences until those violences touch home. Most of all, we wish it would change into something other than it is. Some people have devoted their lives to changing the core personality of male culture. Others, like John Stoltenberg and Andrea Dworkin, have called for the end of masculine culture altogether.

Yet, in the end, these individuals have made little dent in male culture. Male culture never changes significantly because it is ruled by male biology. As we explore male culture we have two choices: start out our assessment with the assumption that it is inherently flawed and must be changed; or start our assessment with the assumption that it is inherently sacrosanct and must be nurtured better than we've done. If we start out with the latter point of view, we create strategies to better love boys and, in so doing, temper the excesses and abuses of male culture. This kind of strategy is very important these days because for a few decades we've missed the interdependence between nurturing male culture adequately and properly protecting our overall culture.

Boys are wired to need a culture which creates special guidance, discipline, and structure. If that culture is demeaned, if we attempt to change its core personality, or if we don't give it structure, we not only fail at loving our boys, we also condemn our overall and shared culture to increased violence, sexism, homophobia, and other dangers.

Even if this assumption sits badly with you now, I ask you to join me for the next few chapters. We will be looking at boys as biologically hard-wired human beings who seek to be trained by society through good software. The intention of this whole book is to build a kind of software program for boys that plugs right into a boy's culture, family, community, and society. I have spent years observing and helping boys and reading thousands of pages of research on boys. Just about everything I've learned teaches me that our recent "socialization-is-what-makes-boys" philosophy is a social experiment without precedent. It indicates our arrogant belief that it is possible for human beings to create society that is not driven primarily by nature. As far as I know, we are the only culture that has believed this idea, even if only for a few decades, and now, finally, we are again seeing more clearly through this fog. Culture has always been very much the communal refinement of biology, the practical expression of nature. Even our complex network of socializing influences are created as outgrowths of biological imperatives. We create sports structures for boys, boys create gangs for themselves, more boys go into science than girls, boys communicate through certain male-specific verbal patterns—the list of boy-specific "cultural" patterns is very long, and few, including male violence, do not begin in brain and hormonal biology.

So my approach is to be realistic—as Dr. Kulanapoor said, "spiritual"—and that means humble: I don't believe any of us can change a boy's nature, nor even the basic principles of boy culture, but we can guide boy culture to its best fruition. Once we remove our parental, mentorial, political, and educational energy from changing boys into _____ (fill in the blank with whatever you've heard lately), and put it back where it belongs—on helping boys be boys—we will be directing them, supervising them, structuring their lives, disciplining their energies, and loving their society and culture in the ways it needs.

Boy culture is based in certain principles. Most of them, I'll argue, are good for boys if they're handled without fear.

Principle 1:

Competition, Performance, and Skill-Building

Boys need to compete and perform well to feel worthy. What will we do with this principle of boy culture? A boy who is not being taught skills, shown how to compete successfully, and given praise for his success, feels lost.

BOYS AND COMPETITION

Boys and men often gain a great deal of their self-image by putting others down. "Hey you little shit, how you doin?" one will laugh. The other will reply, "Okay, peckerhead, how you doin?" I am often told by moms how much they hate this practice. Yet they know there's not much they can do about it. One mom told me, "My fifteen-year-old can't talk to his friends without them cursing at each other. When I'm around they don't do it as much, I suppose because I'm an adult or because I'm a woman, but, my God, when I overhear them, it's just so alien to me."

Boys compete verbally and physically and base some relationships on competition. Competition, for boys, is a form of nurturing behavior. They have formed cultural and linguistic constructs in which to gain self-image through this strategy. We can always expect them to put others down more than the average girl does. We can expect them, on average, to experience their lives through different and subtle forms of "hierarchal" systems—systems in which there is competition for positions in the power pecking order. We can expect them to form collaborative relationships when the collaboration feels safe for them—i.e., they feel that a structure exists within the collaborative organization by which they will not be intrinsically one-upped.

Often, game and sports activities are good examples of boys coming together to grow and nurture through competition. The boy on the sidelines is not only less likely to be asked into the game by his male playmates than the sidelined girl by her female playmates, but he himself is more likely to spend greater time observing the situation to see if he can compete. Thus it will often appear he is "left out." If he has a physical size or skill advantage, or knows he has a social advantage—based on previous experience with this same group of kids—he may jump right in. But without one of these advantages, he'll tend to hold back.

Nurtured competition is crucial to male development and self-image, so crucial that studies show boys who play organized sports are less likely to do drugs, join gangs, and become antisocial than boys who do not. Boys must find ways to compete and see themselves as performing well. If they do not, if society does not provide them with these opportunities, they'll compete against society itself, abusing their community and themselves.

Yes, competition can itself be abused. Some fathers can obsess about it so much they only see their sons as competing machines. Some boys grow into men who know no other relationship style. Competition can feed patterns of male violence, as Myriam Miedzian has pointed out in her study of male violence, *Boys Will Be Boys.*

But those negatives apply to a minority of boys. Most boys don't abuse competition, they just live it. Whether it is a desire to excel at a physical sport, or to be the smartest in the class, or to be a champion at chess, or engage in sibling rivalry that won't quit, or to paint or play a musical instrument better than someone else—a major priority of anyone who observes boys and helps shape male culture must be to help each boy find the arena in which he can compete.

COMPETITION, AGGRESSION, AND ANGER

There is a definite correlation between competition and aggression, and then also between these and anger—a correlation that previous cultures, when they trained soldiers, understood. In Roman culture, for instance, a soldier's anger was part of his sacred energy, and that anger needed to be encouraged in him so he could be more aggressive in battle. By the same token, when Roman culture initiated boys into manhood, the elders, fathers, and teachers taught the boys where and when the anger was to be appropriately expressed. In other words, the boy didn't just learn competition and aggression in male culture; he also learned "anger management."

When we participate in male culture, it is essential we manage competitive experiences and give structure to the aggression our males generate. Without using every opportunity within those experiences to teach anger skills, we are setting ourselves up for randomly aggressive boys who abuse their power.

In Part II of this book we'll see how to provide boys, especially high-testosterone boys whom you observe to be especially competitive and aggressive, with disposable or inanimate objects—couches, sticks, beds—on which to work out anger, and concomitantly to teach them the difference between expressing anger toward living things and non-living objects.

This kind of teaching becomes more and more important as our cultural values change so that fewer and fewer boys get trained, from very early on, to be soldiers. In our ancestral past, it was assumed a boy would become a soldier one day. It was assumed he would develop through his culture into a boy or man who would potentially sacrifice his life for a greater cause. From infancy he was being taught by both male and female culture the skills, the spiritual and political focus, and the discipline of his feelings, including anger, necessary for him to be the protector of life. He knew what was important, what life needed protecting, and whether he needed sacrificing.

Our boys most often lack this sacred teaching and often lack the anger management training that was intrinsic to it. With the dominance of military systems waning, we need nonetheless to deepen our adult sense of how competition can nurture, and then pass that on to kids in the form of anger and competition management training.

Our boys often lack the ability to separate living and nonliving things in their attempts to work out feelings, because they are not taught the value of one versus the simple utility of the other. In fact, many of us, afraid of male energy, teach boys not to be angry at anything, including nonliving things. This is impossible for a boy, given his hard-wiring and the soft-wiring of his culture.

A good practical tool for understanding the worth of competition in a boy's life is to observe whether the boy is gaining or enervating self-confidence through his competitive structure—his sport, his chess playing, his studies, his dissing and verbal one-upping of his friends. Is the boy you know gaining more self-confidence than he's losing by becoming better at his skill and the verbal or (well supervised) physical combat he is engaging in? If he is, he's on track. If he's not, he needs help from the adults: help finding situations, structures, and friends who won't beat him down so severely with their superior one-upping skills; help finding games, skills, and equipment that will put him in a position to compete; and, of course, help learning that there are other ways to trust yourself besides linguistic and social competition.

PERSONAL EXCELLENCE

The bottom line here is that wired into boys and their culture is the search for the sense of personal excellence that comes with competitive skill-building. *Boys need to compete and do combat, they need to feel tested in the physical and interpersonal world. Our job is to help them navigate—not squash—this need.*

We are afraid of this philosophy because it smacks of war. War means that we lose our sons to death and we lose the planet to possible destruction. We must push through this very limited view of the "warrior" that each boy has in him. Yes, that warrior may be trained to make war, but it can be trained for myriad other skills, competitions, and performances too. If we don't help train the boys to gain self-image through competitive experiences we can share with them— like doing sports with them or dissing them ourselves—they will take that energy somewhere, often into places we don't like.

MODIFYING OUR VICTIM PHILOSOPHY

Understanding boy society and its love of competition and performance ultimately requires us to give less weight to our victim-based relationship philosophies. The victim philosophy says, "I'm set up to be a victim, so let's train everyone else not to victimize me." This has sometimes occurred in the philosophy that "females are set up to be victimized by male power, so let's do what we can to eliminate male power." This I've-been-abused philosophy impedes our ability to raise sons. It forgets that each of us, female or male, is responsible for learning to protect and care for ourselves. Especially as I grow up, no one else is responsible for me.

If the "victim standard" rules our approach to boys, we will only see competition and combat as a bad thing. Therefore we will do worse by our boys and they will, in turn, victimize us. If we say,

"Competition and combat are bad because someone gets hurt. I don't want my boy hurt, and we must certainly protect girls (and women) at all times from males. So let's not teach boys to be competitive and combative," we set boys up to retort, "You don't understand that for me love is often in the toughness and the hardness, it's in the discipline and the competition, it's in the risk-taking and getting shot down and getting up again, it's in the physical and psychic woundings that occur, the broken bones and broken hearts. I grow because I'm forced to grow by others who care enough to compete with me. If you won't bring this part of my needs into your parenting and socializing, I'll grow up twisted, and act that out against you."

PROGRAMS AND PROJECTS

Midnight basketball, youth sports associations, intramural sports of all kinds, karate and other martial arts—getting your son into the right competitive program gives him a structure in which to flourish. Getting him into that program also requires you and your community to spend more time with him, practicing with him, helping him to be the best he can be at whatever is his sport or competitive game. Frisbee competitions may bore you, but you still may need to throw that Frisbee. To put him into a competitive program which will severely test him, then to abandon him to those tests is very dangerous to his self-image.

Adapting your personal relationship style to include more playful competition will probably help the boys you know. Dissing can be overdone and can become psychically dangerous if it's done by an adult as a technique to get power over the boy; it can also be painful if the boy isn't able to diss back. But playfully "dissing" your son, getting him to act "better" not by telling him to but by joking provocatively with him—"You're going out looking like that? You stink, man. Where were you brought up?"—these communication techniques honor the boy in a way that may seem alien to you at first, but do help the boy feel he's growing more powerful, more sturdy.

Reaching out to a boy through a project that builds his skills—stamp collecting, model building, playing the French horn, baseball—is often a better way to reach a troubled boy than trying to talk directly to him. Male biology and culture emphasize the "parallel play" form of human interaction, sometimes called "shoulder-to-shoulder contact." Males of all ages tend to relate most comfortably when playing a game or doing a project together, working side-by-side. This is especially true when a male feels emotionally troubled.

A single woman told me recently about her son, Noah, with whom she had decided to, in her words, "become more shoulder-to-shoulder." She and Noah, eleven, were in conflict a lot over little things, especially the fact that he had become sullen, preoccupied. She couldn't get him to talk about it. On advice from a counselor she decided to get him into running, which she enjoyed every morning. For a while he resisted, but one day he relented. As the two of them ran side by side she found him more talkative. As he enjoyed the skill and challenge of running, it felt to her "like a new door was opening for him, for us."

Principle 2:
Task-Specific Empathy

Boys are empathic but often in very different ways than girls. Boys tend to produce *performance* energy as their first-response to an exigent circumstance unless the emergency inherent in the circumstance is severe enough to make *empathy* a necessary first-response. You can observe this in games played in your neighborhood. Watch boys playing street hockey, for instance. At face-off, one boy's hockey stick wallops another's—the walloped boy cries out, the boy who succeeded in getting control of the puck looks back, ascertains in an instant how hurt the boy is—i.e., whether his task must switch from making a goal to taking care of a hurt friend—decides he's not hurt enough to warrant stopping, and so goes on to push through defenders toward the goal, his first task. Emphasis on task, especially performance tasks, is more often than not a boy's first-response to small crises that take place on the street, in his home, school, or garage.

On the other hand, boys tend to produce empathy as a first-response to another's physical or emotional stress when that empathy is felt, by the boy, to serve a problem-solving purpose. If the game can't continue without empathy becoming a first-response, the boys will certainly make sure the hurt party gets empathy. Or if the boy has

committed himself to a high social tenet—protecting someone, helping someone, fighting for a cause or any other tenet he feels is paramount—and if within his work toward this tenet he must choose, for
instance, between performing a specific task and dropping that task to
give empathy to someone he is supposed to protect, help, or assist in
the cause, he will leave the specific task or game to give the empathy.
Boys also often use empathy as a nonmalicious form of manipulation.
They ascertain that someone who holds something they want will be
more likely to relinquish it if they give empathy to that person. Instead of choosing performance, they choose empathy.

If the boy sees no problem-solving, social, or self-serving purpose by
being empathic, he will probably respond to another's hurt not with
evocative aid but with provocative challenge. "Get up, man, you're not
hurt." This is not true of all boys, of course. One mother said to me,
"My son is much more empathic than my daughter. He'll come to
anyone's aid even when they don't really need it." Even despite the
exceptions, a good way to understand boys and their culture is to
watch how they attach empathy to tasks—the task of watching out for
his sister, the task of watching out for mom (or dad), the task of
hunting, through which, if he's well mentored, he learns compassion
for the very thing he kills, and compassion for the shiver he has sent
through the natural world by killing it. Perhaps the primary reason
male culture, not only among humans but among other animals as
well, has carried the task of "protector" throughout its history is because "protecting" is a task through which males can channel their
empathy in a structured, disciplined, goal-oriented way.

How boys use empathy gets more complicated when they play with
girls. Here are two sentences from the same boy:

"Get up man, you're not hurt."

"Are you okay? Here, let me help you."

The first sentence is the more likely sentence from a boy when he
sees another boy fall in a game. The second sentence is more likely
when the boy sees a girl fall in a game. Eleanor Maccoby of Stanford
University has done pioneering studies in which she observed how
much more empathic boys are in cross-gender culture than in boy
culture. She interpreted this tendency to be gender-based, i.e., boys
have more empathy for girls than for boys. Yet there are interesting
exceptions to this rule. A boy will tend to be as empathic toward
another male as to a female when he has been instructed to protect

that male or when that male is someone whose leadership in an organizational system the boy has sworn to protect. Again, the boy's empathy depends on his inner ability to see the empathy as central to his
task—protecting, following a leader, doing his part to uphold an organizational system.

The key to understanding "empathy training" and "sensitivity
training" for boys lies in realizing that boys respond with empathy
when empathy is a required part of a task; male biology and male
culture restrain male empathy severely in comparison to the more
free-floating empathy natural to female biology and female culture.

When a boy sees someone get hurt, what should we train him to
do? We can train boys to be more sensitive to others' hurt, but we
should also expect them to show empathy in other ways. Most specifically, boys will show empathy noninstantaneously, i.e., as delayed reaction after the game or task is complete ("You took a pretty big fall
back in the third quarter, how you doing?") or by offering a hurt
person something that does not, on first appearance, seem to pertain at
all to the hurt person's earlier pain ("Hey, man, you want a ride?").

The flaw in much of our recent empathy training for boys has been
our attempt to get them to say at the moment of pain: "Gee, I'm sorry,
are you all right?" A boy's culture has formed around not saying this,
for his biology and culture both require the competitive task or system
the boy has joined to continue despite the hurt of one of the cogs in
the system. When we try to get boys to be "as empathic as girls," this
translates as our trying to get boys to stop the workings of a whole
system in order to pay attention to the minor pain of a cog; they'll
resist this and rebel against us. The better strategy is to teach boys
what empathy is and its huge range of possibilities, including delayed
empathy and task-attached empathy.

"If someone gets hurt," we might teach a boy, "and you don't at
least ask about him when the game's done, then you've missed an
opportunity to be a better friend." This a boy can learn and apply
without feeling he's being forced to change his core tendency. "If so-
and-so gets hurt and you were a part of it, you make sure to do
something he would like before today's over (or weekend's over)."
Teaching a boy this gives him time to be in control of what he'll do to
make up to the hurt person. This works better than railing at the boy
that he's been insensitive.

Instead of trying to get boys to change their initial responses, *we need to help them see empathy as a task, a sacred task even, that they have the resources and time to fulfill.* Saying this in no way denies their responsibility to aid someone substantially hurt; all boys must learn basic empathy. But boys are already wired to give emergency aid, recognize severe injury, and give immediate, problem-solving assistance. Their culture and we who influence it need to nurture these instincts but also do the more subtle teaching of the more complex, boy-specific empathic responses.

Principle 3:
Large Group Preference

It is a sociological truism that boys more often prefer to socialize in larger groups than girls, and that girls more often prefer to socialize in dyads and triads than boys. Its biological basis is confirmed by its tendency even in primates. Its sociological consequences have been observed by linguists like Deborah Tannen and anthropologists like Victor Turner.

In the Ndembu tribe of Zambia, Turner confirmed what he had noticed in numerous other tribes: distinct differences in the way male and female culture created groups for both sexes. Boys, for instance, were initiated through passages in their lives in large groups, whereas girls were taken by individual elder women and initiated individually. Turner called this difference a difference between the "collective nature" of boy culture and "individual nature" of girl culture.

Deborah Tannen's book *You Just Don't Understand* notices a similar pattern in North American males and females. Males develop language and social relationship styles as an outgrowth of ever-larger social groups; girls get more practice in one-on-one relationships and "speak" accordingly.

The collective nature of a boy's cultural experience is consistent with biological construction. Large groups create a larger circle of energy and influence through which the boy can exercise his need for more space and more physical activity. Large groups are also a better place for a being with a brain that does not process hard emotive data too quickly—the large group allows that brain to shut off and turn on as needed, whereas a dyadic relationship requires the emotional faculties of that brain to be on constantly. A large group, moreover, provides the boy with a place to have wide and varied competition/acceptance experiences. The more people who notice the boy, the more empowered he feels; he is not as content to find one powerful human being to notice and empower him (except in developmental relationships, like parental, mentorial, and mating relationships). He prefers a large culture around him to do that.

Boys gravitate toward and form their culture around large groups. A boy without a "peer group" feels very lost. One of the many reasons boys join gangs is the search for the group in which he can relax, have a task, feel powerful as a part of a collective, yet not feel constantly invaded by emotional stimulation.

When I teach this material about boys, people sometimes say, "You're limiting boys, you're pigeonholing them, they're more than that." That's absolutely true. Yet they have that tendency. We must honor it. We have been trying to individualize their experience over the last few decades to such an extent that they often do not feel comfortable. As one sixteen-year-old boy put it, "I just want to be with the guys. My mom always wants her piece of me, my sister, my aunt. They always want to sit me down and talk to me. I just want to get away from them."

In Chapter 3, "Boys Need a Tribe," we'll look closely at how essential it is for all our communities to come together and honor, in very practical ways, the way male culture forms its groups. Most specifically, we as adults help mold this aspect of male culture by supervising our boys' already tribal activities.

One new program in psychological services that understands the collective nature of boy culture is something called WrapAround Care. When a person (boy or girl) is having trouble in school, acting out sexually, depressed, excessively combative, or causing enough stress that the parent seeks a counselor's help, the counselor trained in WrapAround Care does not go the normal route of just calling the parent and child in for one-hour weekly sessions. While these may occur, the counselor's larger task is to help the parent form extended family and community alliances among neighbors and friends. The counselor helps the parent create a collective atmosphere out of friends and family who are, without the parents realizing it, waiting in the wings. The counselor gets these people connected and even helps train them in how to help.

This kind of program honors the need for community involvement in any family's life; it especially honors the group sensibility boys carry in their biology and culture.

Principle 4:
The Search for Independence

One father told me, "I've tried very hard to be different than my father was. He rarely hugged me, maybe I remember two hugs my whole life. My mom used to say, 'From day one he thought you could be independent and conquer the world on your own.' I'm not speaking ill of the dead when I say dad just didn't get it. With my son, I'm huggy and always wanting him to be included. I'm noticing some changes recently, though. He's eight now. He's not as huggy, he pulls away more. Sometimes I think I'm forcing myself on him. I'm in a men's group and the guys are saying to me, 'Maybe you're trying too hard not to be your dad. Maybe your son just wants to be left alone.' "

Just about anyone who has raised a son has noticed how the boy often changes over the years from a huggable bear to a stiff tree. There are many reasons boys become standoffish as they grow older— your boy may not get standoffish till he's eighteen, but it will probably happen at some point. It's more than just a dad trying too hard. There are biological and cultural imperatives at work.

Studies of boy culture show us how boys mold cultural lives to fulfill biological imperatives. They need large groups in which to flourish, yet at the same time they need space, a comfort zone, an amplified sense of not being threatened. One reason males use quick sex as a way of being intimate—and shy away from cuddling or long intimate conversations before and after sex—is that the vulnerability of the sex act is quick, structured, and cathartic. Making intimacy into a two- or three-hour affair is often more threatening to the male.

What we have called "a male's need for independence"—a need that's been analyzed in many books like Lillian Rubin's ironically titled *Intimate Strangers*—is a biological need intensified by male acculturation. That acculturation says to the male, "When you don't want someone in your face or touching your body, you have a right to push that person away." Male culture, more than female, gives boys and men this right, which they exercise often better than females. Jeannie Corkill, a marriage and family therapist, told me, "When I'm counseling a single mother who just doesn't know how to get men to respect her needs, I tell her to watch how her sons set boundaries. They've been setting boundaries and gaining independence from the very beginning."

There's a great deal of wisdom in this advice. Think of how so many boys just refuse to do things, rebel so early, "won't let anyone walk all over them." Think of the boy who will not go for help when attacked by a bigger boy but, instead, decides to "take care of it myself." Think of the boy who joins a group but rises up one day and says, "Heck with this, I'm outta here." Many girls are very independent, many boys are not—so Jeannie Corkill was generalizing. But still, boys learn quickly that being part of a group does not mean one has to lose one's independence, and being part of a couple need not mean that either.

Of course, the biological and cultural proclivity toward independence can be abused and abusive. A boy can be raised to believe "independence" means "irresponsibility." That acculturation means danger for him and for his community. Some cultures watch this very closely. When a boy is initiated into manhood in Eastern Turkey, for instance, he is taught to balance "freedom" and "responsibility." He is free to be a man, but in gaining this freedom he has gained the responsibilities of a man. Those responsibilities are outlined in the Koran. For most of our recent human existence, our male ancestors were trained to be both independent and interdependent in this same way. There were three entities involved—the boy/man, his community, and a sacred text that outlined his role.

In our society, boy biology still creates a boy culture in which males are given more "independence" than females, and encouraged to seek more adventures of independence, but that culture does not have at its disposal a sacred text, a set of sacrosanct traditions by which to teach men (and women) what the male's role within his independence will be. Lacking that, and adequate intimate role models in general, our boys grow toward independence without knowing how to keep it honest and intimate—they often grow up irresponsible and uncertain about how to be joyfully intimate and committed with mates.

We've seen this problem in male culture for a couple of decades and have attempted to "fix it" by asking female culture to tell us what a boy should learn about dependency, independence, and interdependence, then how a man should act in regard to these. This has been useful but much of it has come from a "females are victims/males are villains" stance, impressing more guilt and shame on males than helping them grow. When a boy is taught that his most important task is to protect the weaker female from himself, it will not take him long to realize that this task-teaching assumes he is inherently defective, something he knows at some deep level to be untrue.

Over the last few years, male culture has re-entered the social dialogue. One reason is that women have begun to ask for mens' help again. Women have seen their sons growing up and needing more of male culture. Many mothers have told me how hard it is to raise a boy, especially single mothers who raise boys alone. These women realize that they cannot make their sons into men. They can't speak, as one mom put it, "to that masculine part of him that's always pulling away."

Helping a boy navigate freedom and responsibility is very difficult in a culture that does not define boys' lives and mens' responsibilities by the use of a commonly accepted sacred text. Throughout much of human history, male culture has been taught the tasks of how to live by stories and books, like the Bible. These "sacred texts" provide male culture with tradition, sacred tasks, ways to measure commitment, rules, objectives, and spiritual certainty. Most of our boys are raised now without male culture having committed itself to a Bible or Koran or other guiding mythology. So our task, in navigating a boy's desire for independence, yet compelling him to give that independence over, when necessary, to interdependence, is a very difficult one.

Fathers, male mentors, mothers, and female mentors who can adjust to male culture without fear of masculinity are even more essential in our culture than in Eastern Turkey or in biblical times. These fearless parents, mentors, and educators do the hard work not only of parenting, mentoring, and educating, but also of providing power, presence, rules, objectives, and spiritual certainty that the Bible used to provide male culture. These people know only too well that without nurturing by acceptance, discipline, role-teaching, natural and acculturated tendency toward independent activity, and personal freedom within group functions, we will raise boys for whom independence becomes emotional isolation, male silence becomes not soulful solitude but tragic loneliness, and freedom becomes irresponsibility. Part II of this book specifically and practically details ways to teach boys such a balance.

Principle 5:

Personal Sacrifice in the Collective Experience

"What we do for ourselves dies with us," said Albert Pike. "What we do for others is immortal." The principle of personal sacrifice is instinctual for any human being. It is also a primary principle of male culture. Males often bond with each other through their mutual commitment to a mission of sacrifice. In carrying out a mission of sacrifice they find independent prowess and receive independent praise, yet simultaneously befriend each other, and feel useful, even essential, to the great cycles of spiritual and human life.

Former President Woodrow Wilson wrote a book in 1901 called *When a Man Comes to Himself.* Its insight into the best we want for boys carries wisdom for us today. He advises us to raise boys to become the kind of man who realizes that, in Wilson's words, "[He] *is* the part he plays among his fellows. . . . Men are in love with power and greatness . . . but if they use power only for their own ends, if there be no unselfish service in it, if its object be only their personal aggrandizement, their love to see other men tools in their hands, they go out of the world small, disquieted, beggared, no enlargement of soul vouchsafed them."

Wilson is speaking the age-old tradition of male culture, in which boys are shown that at some point their adventures of independence must be connected to missions of sacrifice. Their individualistic search for power must be united with their sense that others, as a collective body, need that individual power and energy if that collective is to flourish and, in flourishing, make the world better for the individual.

In Alabama a boy becoming a man, Kahlil Baker, was recently honored with a Swearer Student Humanitarian Award for his work in the Partners in Prevention program. The PIP program is a volunteer effort that involves older black students as tutors and mentors to younger African-American youth. Baker is one of many boys and young men who have discovered their own power and energy to affect the world by sacrificing individualism for a common or collective good.

When we work with boys, we do them and ourselves a great service by opening up to them an equal measure of *adventure* and *mission*. Their individual lives must become an adventure in which they discover, experientially, who they are and, in that discovery, get "hooked up" with their own power. Simultaneously, they must search for a mission or missions which permit boys to fully bond with their fellows, fully discover who they are, fully embrace and be embraced by their culture, tribe, or nation, and fully discover themselves as spiritual beings who are united with all things.

Whether we realize it or not, boys are ready, at any moment, to sacrifice themselves for a principle they can believe in. They do this even when they join gangs, sacrificing their lives for principles that seem shadowy to us but essential to them—care of the hood, protection of boundaries and territory, initiation into the group. How will we as parents, mentors, educators, and policy-makers tap back into the primal force of sacrifice within each boy? Each of us needs to look at the lives of the boys around us and figure out how to bring his desire for adventure together with a sense of mission. When we show him how his mission can become his adventure, we have hooked him up. Sometimes we'll discover a series of small tasks, including taking out the garbage and mowing the lawn, but contextualize them into the mission of "making the family home comfortable." Drilling the mission—the context—into the boy's mind, not just the chores, gives him more reason to cooperate. Sometimes the sacrifice will be the need to get a job after school instead of play—the mission is survival of family. Boys who are given everything and for whom everything is done learn little adventure and little mission.

For many boys, war and soldiering was a very dramatic way to hook adventure up with mission—individual effort with collective good. It was the way to say to a boy, "Your life gains ultimate meaning by its sacrifice." Today, most boys do not grow up learning this way. In just a few decades, that cultural component has changed. But the boy's desire for something like it has not changed. This is one of the reasons so much of video, game, and sport culture is still so warrior oriented.

Besides sports there is perhaps no common social component like war and conquest/exploration in which to hook adventure with mis-

sion. Even sports are not comparable with war, conquest, and exploration because though the warrior structure is similar, the mission of
scoring a goal or basket is not sacred in the same way warriors knew
their mission was sacred.

We must find, within our families and communities, small and
large tasks—from fixing things around the house to protecting neighbors through programs like PIP—to provide boys with and, in providing them, interpret with boys as both adventure and mission. "When
you do such-and-such," we need to teach boys, "you are gaining individual power or 'juice' in such-and-such a way, *and* you are gaining it
in this other deeply spiritual way—you are finding a mission that will
reward you by rewarding your community. I think you're old enough
now to understand how this kind of spirituality works."

Boys will understand it when they see that sacrifice is not just about
loss—it is about gain. It is not "Do this because I tell you to, if you
don't I'll make you feel guilty." Or "Do this because *I* say it's *right.*"
Boys need to see how their sacrifice of themselves ultimately helps
them find themselves.

Principle 6:
Male Role Models

Without male role models, boy culture feels lost, and human culture in general is put in danger. Perhaps the biggest mistake our
culture has made in its history has been its forgetfulness of the essen-
tiality of both the father and the male role model. Without these, we
risk the loss of a huge portion of our humanity.

David Blankenhorn's *Fatherless in America* is just one of many fine,
recent writings on this phenomenon. My own training video, *The Role
of the Mentor,* published by Big Brothers and Big Sisters, emphasizes
the practical aspects of male role modeling. In chapters of books, in
articles, in newspaper magazines everywhere we are seeing a culture
reawaken to the necessity of these models in human life.

Boy culture that is not mentored by spiritually vital elder males is
more a gang than a culture. The elder males provide it with intergenerational magic, discipline, and direction.

The elder males teach the boys how to honor and respect girls and women. "What kind of boy hits a girl?" the elder snaps at the irresponsible boy. The boy hears him. The boy can learn from empathy what effect his hit has had on the girl, but without the deep voice of that elder—which is in some magical way an echo of the deep voice he is trying to form within his young self—he won't learn that hitting is not power.

The elder males teach boys how to develop healthy boundaries with girls and women, so they don't become the kind of men who agree to what women want, resent the women, and then leave them. "A man listens to others, to women, to girls," the elder teaches. "He hears, he talks, he stands up for himself without putting her down, he seeks agreements, not control—neither control by her, nor by him."

The elder males teach boys how to navigate changes in their bodies, minds, and souls. They help boys find a mission, they help boys gain the skills for their adventure. They teach boys how to contribute to the world through sacrifice, not self-destruction.

If we are to do right by our boys, female culture in general must end its bitter feud with male culture by holding out the olive branch to the elder males. As much as men have neglected their duties as elder men, women have pushed them away from those duties. As divorced mothers give their sons (and daughters) to fathers, as divorced fathers fight for their rights to their children; as mothers help their sons bond with other males, as males step forward to make these bonds; as women rise out of their victim role, as men rise out of their villain role—children will gain infinitely, for men will themselves feel healthier, more spiritually vital, more alive, and they will become entranced again with the hard but magical work of loving boys into men.

Boys often send us "role-model signals" we don't recognize. A boy might come home and say, "Mr. Crane, my biology teacher, is pretty neat." This may be a moment in which the boy is saying, "I think Mr. Crane could be a role model for me. I'm shy, I'm nervous, help me approach him." It's essential we recognize these moments and follow up by calling Mr. Crane, talking to him about mentoring, role-modeling; asking him his values, sharing our own; and, if possible, bringing him deeper into the life of the boy's family. Even a few decades ago, neighborhoods, families, and communities were closer knit, so boys found role models more frequently, close to home, with less parental effort. A boy bonded with a friends' father, or his own godfather, or his own uncle or grandfather, or others in a small town who taught him work or other skills. Now our boys have less natural routes to the role models, so we must facilitate the discovery of these models much more than we used to.

There are, of course, "bad" or unhealthy or shadowy role models out there. These we will always guard against. Yet one of the first steps each of us can take toward rebuilding healthy aspects of male culture is to realize that those shadowy figures are not the norm, and even more important, if we take a healthy part in helping our boys find "good" role models (which means imperfect ones), our boys will be less likely to gravitate to the unhealthy men who have always and will always assert their shadowy place in any culture.

Principle 7:
Making Sport of Life and Life of Sport

When a boy hears, "Be on our team, you're one of us," he feels at home. Not all boys like sports or are cut out for them, but between in-school and nonschool sports, most boys are involved to some degree. More than twenty million children—the majority of them boys—play institutionally organized sports outside of school grounds—Little League, youth soccer, etc. It is estimated that more than that number play nonorganized "street" sports—basketball, tennis, soccer, football, and other sports involving groups thrown together spontaneously. It is impossible to estimate how many boys watch their friends play sports and wish they did it as well. And, of course, it is impossible to estimate the effect that sports figures—the Michael Jordans, the Joe Montanas, the Ken Griffey Jr.'s—have on boys.

Boys often make life into a sport and give sports so much life observers marvel at how completely a boy can make a sport his focus. The therapist, Terry Trueman, a father of two sons, once said something to me I've never forgotten: "There's a time in a boy's life when his body grows into his spirit, and vice versa, and sports and athletics are the way that happens." For Trueman, sports are a wholistic experience—physical, mental, spiritual.

Boys are wired, of course, to find structures in which to perfect the aggressive movement of objects through space. Parents, coaches, and role models are charged with the duty of providing male aggressiveness with structure, skill, and focus. Boys who have little elder contact will, nonetheless, create street sport structures to find space for their aggression.

Male culture has refined its sense of the physicality, mental challenges, emotional/self-image rewards, and spiritual magic of sports to make male sports one of the two or three defining activities of American entertainment life. The downside of this is that many males spend dangerous amounts of time devoted to playing and observing sports. Many males become more aggressive, not less, by playing sports. A great deal of social wealth may be unfairly spent in rewarding a few sports figures, "who do nothing but move a ball around."

Far too many parents, mentors, and educators obsess about boys' performances in their athletics. As psychologist Thomas Tutko, co-author of *Winning Is Everything and Other American Myths,* has put it: "Good athletes are scarred by injury or burned out psychologically by the time they are fifteen because they are unable to meet the insatiable needs of their parents, their coach, their fans, or their own personal obsession."

Because sports systems are competition based, they must be supervised very carefully. Many parents and coaches do not fulfill this burden, whether from lack of emotional and psychological training, an imposition of their own adult agenda, or a simple inability to perceive what kids are going through with compassion. Countless boys suffer from their sense of failure in sports—their self-esteem drops far lower than it was before they tried the sport, they turn away from involvement in physical activity, they learn to despise authority figures, they become hostile.

Despite the negative possibilities inherent in sports activities, it remains nonetheless one of the most profound and potentially useful socializing forces in boys' lives. Nancy Ruppel, a pastoral minister and mother of two boys, fourteen and sixteen, once said to me, "Boys just need to be dumped together and figure things out. That's what the swim meets are really about. They're not about winning an Olympic gold medal. They're about giving these boys a place to find themselves. It's what churches used to do a lot of. They don't do it as much anymore, but it's sure going on in my boys' sports programs." I cannot say how many times I've heard a boy talk about how good he feels when he plays sports, how comfortable. His physicality is honored, his ability to compete is challenged, his sense of self has the potential to grow, he feels part of the large group, he has a role within the organizational system, he knows what the objective is, he sacrifices his body and even at times his position if it's necessary for the team, he receives praise when he's done or critique and new skills. If the sport has a coach, he also has the potential to bond with a model and mentor.

Sports activity can also provide a second family to a boy. Eric, a fifteen-year-old who had no siblings, said to me: "Football gives me brothers. I like them some times and hate them other times. I guess that's what it would be like if we were real brothers." Tim, thirteen, plays on a U-14 soccer team. "Sometimes I feel better when I'm playing soccer than I do maybe even when I'm with my own family." The family and team feeling boys get from sports gives them a secure base to develop and grow.

Sports activities provide a place for emotional development, a place to be empathic when need be, a place to find that one "best friend" everyone looks for, a place to find a group with whom to talk, in that veiled way boys often talk. Sports activities are partially responsible for making boys into men. They give boys a kind of frame in which to develop into manhood. If they are handled by effective mentors, the sports activities will teach a boy that growing up means equal parts playfulness and responsibility.

We've explored seven principles of male culture, but I'm humbled by how many principles are left unexplored. Hopefully, this exploration will inspire you to make a list of the other principles of male culture you've noticed, and in making that list explore them in the adult communities to which you belong. Having explored them, perhaps you will bring the information and wisdom you develop to the many boys in your care, discussing outright with them the culture in which they belong. If not this, at least you can become more conscious of the virtues and vices in the boy culture around you, enhancing the former and retraining the latter. And as you explore boy culture in your communities I hope you won't be tempted to shame or throw out parts of it—causing boys to resist, with a vengeance, your efforts—just because they scare you in some way.

I'll never forget one family whose son wanted to play football once he entered high school. He was very athletic and his father didn't mind his choice, but his mother refused to let him. In the end, this boy benefited from his mother's refusal, for though it was based initially on her fear of potential injury, she did not operate solely from this fear. She said, "Look, you can play basketball and soccer. You like both these anyway. You won't gain anything in football you can't gain in these." The son argued that only football players received certain attentions in school. The family worked on this issue for almost six months. The mother always made her arguments and always listened to her son patiently. By the time tryouts came around, the father saw his wife's logic, the son was being swayed, and time had taken care of some of the urgency. The boy was really getting more into basketball, now that the door to football was, perhaps, closing. In the end, he played basketball and soccer and went to college on a soccer scholarship.

In navigating this decision, the parents negotiated a crucial life decision with the boy, showing him that they respected his body and soul yet still wanted to help him find just the right niche for it. Sports activities, handled this way, can become a part of a boy's blessed future.

The Stages of a Boy's Life

As we have talked about boy biology and boy culture we've used the word "boy" as if boys are the same no matter their age. Let's pause a second and note the importance of seeing boys' development in stages, especially in regards to how boy culture carries them along the river of life. The stages of a boy's life don't change his biology per se—he came into the world testosterone-driven, skull full of a male brain, and chromosomally male. But the way those innate qualities get accepted or rejected by culture at certain times of his life deeply affect his growth. And more concretely, just knowing what to expect from a boy at the various stages of his life can relieve parents, mentors, and educators of terrible guilts and confusions.

We will not present here a month-by-month or year-by-year explanation of the stages of male development. For that kind of information, you might read *The Little Boy Book* by Moore and Frost, or the year-by-year series put out by the Gesell Institute for Human Development, authored by Louise Bates Ames and Frances L. Ilg, entitled *Your __ Year Old* (fill in the blank with a year). The subtitle, for instance, for the book on four-year-olds is *Wild and Wonderful*. Aren't four-year-old boys both of those and more! Brazelton and Kramer's *The Earliest Relationship* is very helpful. The Princeton Center for Infancy and Early Childhood has also put out a series of books beginning with *The First Twelve Months of Life* by Frank Caplan, which takes readers year by year through a young child's life. And the American Academy of Pediatrics has put out *Caring For Your Baby and Young Child: Birth to Five Years.*

All these books give you an in-depth look at the stages of your boy's life from pregnancy to infancy, infancy to toddler years, toddler years to school years. Books that specifically focus on stages of a boy's life from school years through adolescence are harder to come by, which is why we will spend more time on the second decade of a boy's life.

Key elements to focus on as you watch your boy move through the stages of life are how he emotionally attaches and separates from parents, mentors, and educators. Even when he seems ornery and completely detached, you might want to notice how he is in fact attached to you but navigating his psychological separation in search of independence.

THE EARLY YEARS

In his infancy, a boy may seem less attached to you than his sister because he looks you in the eye less and seems more easily distracted, but he is very attached and needs to be nurtured as such. Parents cuddle male infants less than female, mainly because of the diminished eye contact and the greater physicality of the boy. He needs to feel safe, even if that means wrapping him real tight in a papoose-like blanket. He needs to be carried around a lot more than perhaps one would think. Again, our cultural impression is, often, that boys need less carrying and cuddling than girls, but it's not true.

The frontal lobes of the brain, which handle many social and cognitive functions, mature more slowly in the male brain than in the female, therefore in boys than girls. This is all the more reason to resist whatever cultural programming you may have about "leaving little boys alone." Their infant brains, some researchers argue, make them even more emotionally fragile than their sisters, needing even more close care.

It is a truism in infancy studies that you cannot spoil a baby. Only when a child is around eighteen months old does he truly begin to understand the rigors of discipline. To withhold affection from him, or to be substantially disciplining him before this time, is to confuse and perhaps do damage to his growing brain.

At approximately two years old the boy enters full-force the drama of individuation—his first major separation and search for independence from his primary caregiver. It is essential that his caregivers open up more emotional and physical space for the child, and not take personally things the child does that seem "angry at mom," or "anti-dad." The child is experimenting with independence. The parent who squashes this child's experiment, who makes the child feel guilty for pulling away, who suspects the child—or in some other way acts on her or his own fears of abandonment and anxieties about being a bad parent—risks "impinging" on the child's development of his core self. His core self is his personality, temperament, and other innate tendencies. Some of them show up more clearly between the ages of two and five than ever before. When parents and caregivers squash them, they risk giving the child a personality disorder that will wreck his life. By squash I do not mean discipline; I mean try to change the pull toward independence, try to alter the extroverted or introverted personality type; I mean keeping the boy attentive only to the caregiver and not to other loving people in the world to whom he is seeking to attach; I mean seeing a boy's talent emerging and trying to kill it.

By the time a boy enters kindergarten, he will probably have asserted another massive pull toward separation, individuation, and independence. Parents' abilities to "let him go," yet show they are always there for him, pay off throughout the child's life and, if they remain attentive parents, in adolescence. Studies show that boys whose parents divorce or who suffer ongoing trauma or whose parenting style changes significantly—i.e., becomes inconsistent—during the first decade of a boy's life, will be more likely to significantly rebel against parental values and become antisocial in the second decade of life.

PUBERTY AND ADOLESCENCE

Another huge transition in a boy's life takes place, of course, at the onset of puberty and adolescence. For many primary caregivers—so often, moms—puberty is especially difficult because so often boys pull so far away, getting involved in peer groups and male culture that often seem alien and dangerous. The pulling away is normal separation and needs to be encouraged carefully. My book *The Prince and the King* explores the father's and adult male culture's role in taking the boy from boyhood to manhood. We will further explore the practical details of this process in Part II of this book.

A mother's "letting go" of her son does not mean the mother and son love each other less. It simply means she psychologically releases him from dependency on her and herself from dependency on him. This letting go is difficult, especially for single moms who do not have a community of emotionally healthy men around them, or who have unreasonable emotional and social expectations of ex-husbands and other men, making it difficult for them to let their sons go into male culture. In her book *The Courage to Raise Good Men,* Olga Silverstein analyzes the tough position of single mothers of sons. For some single mothers, Silverstein argues, there is no practical way to let the boy go, so the mother must keep him close, and try to help him navigate adolescence without loving, wise, and powerful men to help her. Any mother who does not let go of a son risks that the son will grow up through adolescence punishing her or saving her feelings and punishing women and society later in his adult male life.

In Part II we will explore how to navigate the terrible pain of a boy's adolescence in our culture so that it can be—for the boy, the mother, the father, and the community—a joyful time. The stage of a boy's life we call adolescence does not need to be a time of abject rebellion. We are the only culture I've observed that assumes, "He's an adolescent, he's going to rebel and hate me, that's just the way it is." Adolescent boys are not biologically required to rebel as substantially as they sometimes do—to become as dangerous to us, to themselves, and to others. A culture that accepts rebellion as the primary method of a boy's journey through the second decade of life abandons boys to adolescence, throwing them into the second decade with little guidance, structure, and discipline.

Boys will be boys no matter what their stage in life. What kind of man a boy becomes depends much more than we realize on how we form community relationships, service projects, and kinship systems for boys in the stage of life many people fear: the boy's adolescence.

Can Boys Be Boys and Feminists Too?

I was doing a radio talk show and a woman called in. "Out of one side of your mouth," she said, "you sound supportive of feminism and gender equality. Out of the other side I hear you talk about male biology and how boys will be boys. I don't see how you can believe both. If boys will be boys, then they want power, they're acculturated to have power over me. That's why I've spent years working to change male culture in my sons' lives and in my husband's life. Now you're saying boys can be the very boys I've been trying to change—competitive, stuck on performance, bad listeners and violent—and they can be feminists too? I don't buy it."

As we discussed in the first chapter, aggression and physical risk-taking are hard-wired into a boy. It is culture that teaches the boy violence.

Competition is hard-wired into a boy. Culture can teach the boy to forget the spiritual balance that comes from finding noncompetitive worlds and relationships.

Quick problem-solving is hard-wired into a boy. Culture can teach a boy to live so out of balance that he perfects no other methods of dealing with pain.

Boys will tend to communicate more confrontatively in certain situations than girls and tend to care less than girls about whether mo ment-by-moment group functioning is maintained. It is culture that helps the boy to adjust his confrontation when group functioning needs the adjustment and to be more inclusive of others who appear more powerless than he is.

Feminism is not by definition misandrist—male hating, anti-male—though some feminists (and non-feminists) are. Feminism is not, by definition, an enemy of male culture, or a tyrant trying to ruin boys. Boys can be boys and feminists too if feminism is not anti-male, accepts that boys are who they are, and chooses to love them rather than change their hard wiring. I work with many feminists who join me in trying to change parts of masculine culture that are out of balance toward the extremes of competition, nonempathy, sexual harassment, and emotional isolation. I also work with many feminists who join me in trying to change parts of feminine culture that are out of balance toward extremes of victim-based thinking, villainization of males, political myopia, and emotional tyranny. Books by these colleagues include Christina Hoff-Sommers's *Who Stole Feminism,* Aaron Kipnis and Liz Herron's *Gender War/Gender Peace,* Warren Farrell's *The Myth of Male Power,* Katie Roiphe's *The Morning After,* and Camille Paglia's *Sexual Personae.*

The great lesson I've learned from observing and working with boy culture is that our whole culture's future depends, in large part, on our raising and mentoring our boys in more boy-appropriate ways than we do.

Most crime is committed by young males. Ninety-one percent of *violent* crime is committed by males. Our cultural response to this crisis is to lock the young males up. As damage control, the merits of this practice can be argued.

But lock-up strategies miss the deeper message boys are giving us by their criminal behavior. They are acting out against society and parents because neither is providing them with enough modeling, opportunity, and wisdom through which to act comfortably within society and feel, in that social inclusion, empowered.

"We want more from you," boys are crying. "We deserve more from our parents. We need more from our mentors, media, and community. If we don't get more from you, we'll take more for ourselves. Our biology influences us to be aggressive, and we will be. Get used to it, or learn the lesson."

My study of boy culture, then, has taught me that it's not boy culture that's inherently flawed; it's the way we manage it. In Part II, we'll look at ways to manage it better.

II

What Boys Need

Boys Need a Tribe

Train up a child in the way he should go:
and when he is old, he will not depart
from it.

—*Proverbs 22:6*

The second of two boys, I was born in the fifties, in Honolulu, Hawaii, to a mother and father who were New Yorkers, she an anthropologist and homemaker, he a sociologist and writer. Living in Hawaii is like living in fifteen different kinds of family systems— Caucasian, Hawaiian, Samoan, Japanese, Chinese, Filipino, African-American, Southeast Asian. My birth in Hawaii began an odyssey through family systems, tribes, and clans I couldn't see coming, for during my boyhood my New Yorker parents would take me to live in India, Wisconsin, Wyoming, Colorado and other places where I would experience different ways of being a boy and being raised as a boy.

In India, for example, I was raised in the early 1960s by my parents, but also by "extended family" members—Aiya, Mahmoud, and other "aunties" and "uncles"—who treated me as their own child. In India, the idea of a nuclear family—mom and dad raise the child and every-one else stays out of the way—was considered craziness. My brothers' and my boyhoods were changed forever as we experienced this communal upbringing. In India my parents adopted my sister, so our lives were changed by that experience, too.

After life in a major Indian city—Hyderabad—my family moved to a small city in Wisconsin—La Crosse. From there we moved back to Honolulu, then to Laramie, Wyoming. I became, over this time, a creature both of small towns and big cities, experiencing boyhood from both vantage points. Then, early in my adolescence, we moved to Durango, Colorado, so my father could work on the Southern Ute reservation in northern New Mexico. I came to the reservation experience after living in Laramie, Wyoming, where family systems with which I interacted were very insular, often very nuclear. On the reservation, as in India, family systems extended to include more nonparental influences. And many Native family systems paid special attention to the specific needs of boys and girls as they entered adolescence—needs for special mentoring and initiation.

By the time my father worked on the reservation, my boyhood had established two patterns I wouldn't understand until decades later. One was the movement between small communities and large cities. The other was more subtle: I moved from one culture that emphasized extended family traditions to one that emphasized nuclear family traditions and back again, over and over—from Hawaii to Minnesota, then from Minnesota to India; from India to La Crosse, Wisconsin, then from Wisconsin back to Hawaii; from Hawaii to Laramie, then from Laramie to the Southern Ute reservation.

I would only see the patterns in my boyhood experiences when, as an adult, I began to commit much of my life to studying boyhood. Over the years since, I've experienced kibbutz life in Israel, studied village life in Turkey, and researched tribal ways from around the world. Combining those experiences with my clinical work, I've come to the conclusion that boys need three families to raise them. Trying to raise them in one family is not enough.

The Three Families

My basic vision of how to love a boy always returns to the insight that *three families—not one—raise a healthy boy to healthy manhood:*

▼ Family 1. Birth or adoptive parents, including grandparents who raise kids (the "nuclear" family);

▼ Family 2. Extended families—blood relatives or nonblood "friends," day-care providers, teachers, peers, and mentors;

▼ Family 3. Culture and community—media, church groups, government, other institutions and influential community figures.

Together, these three families comprise a boy's tribe.

When the three families do not coordinate efforts, do not build communal values together, and do not make child-raising the primary purpose of culture, children feel unsafe and unloved and the boys will, in turn, develop into subgroups, much like we have today, such as one subgroup that is antisocial—i.e., violent criminals, gang subcultures, sexual predators; one large subgroup unable to commit to long-term relationships with mates; one large subgroup emotionally unskilled to raise healthy children to adulthood. Thus we will have a majority of males living without a life-defining or confident sense of spiritual purpose.

The nuclear family alone, in which dad, or mom and dad both, work away from the children, cannot, in general, raise boys to fulfill the four basic goals of socially and personally responsible adult life, which are: contribution to society, commitment to mates, responsibility for children, and ongoing spiritual growth.

This, then, is the foundation of the second part of this book. As we discuss how to discipline boys, how to give them a spiritual life, how to teach them about sex and love and so on throughout the rest of this book we'll focus on more than how one or two parents can do these things; we'll look at how all three family elements can be responsible for raising children and we'll provide all three units practical tools to help them fulfill their responsibilities. It will take us the whole rest of the book to develop the advantages and practicalities of this three-family vision in depth, but by the end of *The Wonder of Boys* I think you'll see wisdom, even absolute necessity, in dividing the labor among these three units, especially for adolescent boys.

THE DEMISE OF THE THREE-FAMILY SYSTEM

Most of our ancestors, no matter where they came from in the world, were brought up in some form of a three-family culture. Most of our own American predecessors lived close to their grandparents, aunties, uncles, or lived in small neighborhoods. When they moved to another city, they usually moved to another family member's neighborhood and thus felt, soon enough, that they belonged in more than one family, and their kids would be raised by far more than one adult.

This, of course, has changed radically. By the 1950s, but developing for a long time in our individualistically oriented and geographically massive culture, we inculcated the "nuclear family system." If better jobs existed away from our childhood homes, we moved ourselves and our children to them, giving up friends and family, emotional safety, and bonds with the natural landscapes and social communities in which we were raised. We didn't move to our cousin's community. We "had to find our own community." We "moved there with nothing and no one and fended for ourselves." For many people, of course, this kind of move was idyllic. Giving up family bonds became a rite of passage into adulthood. We split one of the three families away from another—we took the nuclear family away from the extended family. Grandparents rarely saw grandchildren. Neighbors rarely saw each other. We decided mom and dad would be enough to raise a child— with some help from the government. We put more pressure on mom and dad than they'd ever had, and we gave up most of our second- and third-family responsibilities to institutions like schools and welfare programs.

The idealism with which we created the nuclear-family model lasted into the sixties. In the sixties, our culture split again. The nuclear family split into an even smaller atom—the single parent family. Meanwhile, the third family—culture and community—split off completely, forming its own separate culture, so much so that we complain now as parents about how "media stereotypes" act in significant ways *contrary* to the desires and wishes of ourselves as nuclear or single parents. Television, radio, books, videogames, movies—so many of the masks worn by and created by our own popular culture confuse and frighten us. How strange this would seem to my Aiya, in India, when

I was a boy: how strange that parents and caregivers would give up their power to media institutions they believed would hurt their children.

The flaws in the nuclear family have become clear to any of us who have been in therapy, recovered from dysfunctional families, been alcohol or substance abusers, or known how it feels to have been abused, neglected, or underparented by overwhelmed parents. Mom and dad did their best, as every parent does, but their best was often just not enough.

Concomitant with the nuclear family experiment was the increased popularity of divorce, which created single parent systems. Couples who had children began to divorce at higher and higher rates until, now, the rate is 1 in 2. The primary caregiver to one third of American boys in the 1990s is a single mother.

For about two decades, studies appeared that argued divorce was good for kids or at least not bad for them. Those have now been debunked. Divorce, except in extreme circumstances, is more dangerous to children than helpful. The vast majority of studies coming out over the last few years indicate that divorce and single mothering are at least correlates to crime among males. As one juvenile detention officer put it to me: "I don't even read the profiles anymore—in ninety percent of my cases, the male delinquent comes from a single parent home." At least two thirds of violent crime is committed by sons of divorce. The majority of those boys and men have been brought up, primarily, by single mothers.

These statistics are not meant to condemn anyone who has been divorced or any single mother. In many ways, people who have ended unhappy marriages have shown more courage than people who stayed in them. Nonetheless, wherever I travel and speak I meet single mothers of sons who do not feel dishonored or defensive in saying, "I wish my situation could be otherwise. I know my sons, especially as they get older, need more than I can give." In a nuclear-family vision of the world, these single mothers are at a disadvantage because, statistically, their sons have a far greater chance of growing up antisocial as we have seen earlier. In a three-family view of the world, single mothers would seem to have the odds stacked against them, which is why they need to make every effort to provide a three-family experience for their sons.

Boys as Tribal Creatures

Boys have been tribal creatures for millions of years. In group dynamics and activities they find a strong container in which to make their journey of individuation and learn their lessons about how to belong, who to be, what to value.

Until 10,000 years ago, boys were raised to be hunters, working in groups. Encoded in their brains are millions of years of this tribal experience. Since the beginning of the agricultural age almost ten millennia ago, boys did not wander as far from home to make a living, but still they farmed in tribal groups. Boys protected their families and nations in tribal groups, groups we later called "armies," "workforces," "clans." Their brains are encoded with this experience. With the coming of Industrial society some two hundred years ago, individual genius became more respected; yet, still, it was the group of males, working together, that built the mechanisms of the society. As we enter the next millennium, the basic need for groups in boys' lives has not changed much—boys still seek groups to grow up in, and men still work together in groups.

What has eroded is the rich tribal quality of the group. Until very recently, groups in which boys were raised and men worked carried a multigenerational texture, and therefore brought into each new generation a tried-and-true structure for spiritually and emotionally rich male development. Over the last few hundred years two distinct changes occurred in the workings of these tribal groups—changes that are the primary catalyst for their erosion: 1) the leaders became less service oriented and more ego-oriented; and 2) the followers became more individualistic and less collaborative.

Social thinker Robert Greenleaf Whittier has distinguished between servant leaders and ego leaders, saying that the servant leader is one who sees himself as a servant of his group—he exists to help everyone become who they need to be. He takes the respect others give him and finds ways to give it back to them. He is a kind of spiritual mirror. The religious kings and "divinely bestowed" kings and queens of Europe are examples of this kind of mirror. People believed these leaders were given to the people by God and thus carried divine energy. When people were mirrored by a King Richard or Queen

Elizabeth or Pope Pius, they felt blessed. Boys used to be brought up to attain this kind of modeled leadership quality and follow it with passion.

The ego leader, on the other hand, manipulates his group to gain something for himself or for his very small family or political faction. By fear or some kind of dishonest manipulation, he often rules everyone who is not like him or with whom he disagrees. Boys are brought up more and more these days to become or follow this kind of leader. If they don't like the leader, they leave his group and find another. Boys have more freedom to shop around for leaders, but don't feel attached to any one spiritually awesome leader or group who carries the boys' own history in its tradition. Boys are, thus, tribeless.

So, over the last few hundred years, both our senses of leadership and followership have gone through major transitions as the traditional value-bases for each have crumbled. The democratization of the world—the modern sense of utilitarianism and egalitarianism—has given us more individual freedom than human beings have ever known, but it has also starved us for values. This megacultural perspective comes into our own homes when we watch our boys and men. They still gravitate even more than girls toward large groups, yet they have terrible trouble figuring out what to do there, what their role is in family, in society, in culture; when to lead, when to follow; whom to believe; how to serve.

The culture in which you parent, mentor, or educate boys exhorts them to be individualistic and group-oriented at once, but does not give them a tribal structure in which to accomplish both in balance. It used to be that the tribe *formed* a boy's character while the peer group existed primarily to test and befriend that character. Nowadays, boys' characters are often formed in the peer group. Mentors and intimate role models rarely exist to show the growing boy in any long-term and consistent way how both to serve a group and flourish as an independent self. Parents spend far too little time with boys. Fathers and male elders in the second decade of the boy's life do not teach the boy the life of the soul. Boys gravitate toward peer groups and group- and hero-identifications in the media—wanting to become sports stars and superheroes—without elders to help them understand how everything they experience is trying to form them into a man.

Furthermore, our boys grow into men who don't have a spiritual ground to stand on when relating to a woman—they tend to try to become the man she wants them to be, resenting her all the while; or keep her at a distance, resisting her attempts to be intimate. Hundreds of self-help books have been written to understand this problem. Most of them end up saying the male style of intimacy is defective because of something mom or dad did. In a culture that sees boys and men through a nuclear lens, that view will be popular. But when we truly understand the biology and culture of boyhood, we see that these men grew up as boys who did not learn from a tribe an intergenerational structure for relationship. Our boys get so little tribal attention they do not develop good intimacy skills yet are expected to marry with those skills in fine form.

In order to learn how to live and how to love, boys need a tribe. If they don't get one from us, they'll make one, and it may be a dangerous one.

BOYS AND GANGS

Boys don't feel they belong in adult society so they form their own little societies. For many boys, these societies are transitional ones; once adolescence is over, the young man joins the workforce, has a family, consciously or unconsciously mourns never having had an ongoing, intergenerational tribe but beyond that learns to cover up his confusion about who he is for as long as possible. For many other boys, however, these little societies do not drift into the vagueness of American manhood. These boys form gangs, which are very tribal (at least in the boys' eyes). Students of gangs are quick to say, "A tribe is a far more complex thing than the Crips (one of the nation's largest gangs)—a tribe involves elders, supervision, intimate life together." These sociologists are right, yet for these boys the gang becomes family, tribe and, often, a group to follow into death.

One of the questions readers of my newspaper column write me quite often is, "Why do boys create gangs?" For me, the better question is, "Why have we created gangs for our boys?" The gangs that claim so many of our sons, so much of our property, and pose such a challenge to us are simply acting out the hidden distress of our ignorance, racial prejudices, love of violence, indifference to family, and inability to give boys a better tribe. The gangs are a dark, shadowy part of ourselves come alive.

Boys who cannot earn enough money or respect from "socially accepted work" will create gangs in which to earn worth, empowerment, and "juice" from antisocial work. If a tribe does not channel their aggression into work, service, and healthy followership, it will find other outlets. Nearly half of urban African-American boys will go to jail in their lifetimes. The majority will grow up without fathers. For committing the same crimes as whites, they will be given far harsher sentences. They know this. As the mafia did for generations of Italian-Americans before them, these boys know that to protect themselves they may have to join a gang.

Nearly every gang member I've dealt with had inadequate or no fathering and little or no elder male mentoring. Unless the tribe provides a boy with these models, he will find a new tribe of his own and model after peers. The boy is programmed, especially in adolescence, to prove to the adult world, especially the adult *male* world, that he has the stuff of manhood. The less he is loved as a child—usually needing love from more than an overworked mom—the more desperate he becomes to prove himself as a man. Boys seek from the adult male world and its male kinship systems the love which says, "Your young gifts, visions, strengths, and vulnerabilities are acceptable and worthy." If they are not taught otherwise, boys will destroy in order to prove they are men.

Boys do not feel the kind of biological certainty about life-purpose and birthright that girls feel. Tribes have always compensated for this void by teaching boys that though they don't bear the children, their role is just as crucial, once taught by the tribe, and once the boy has proven, through years of tribal intimacy and initiation, that he is capable of achieving it. Boys who do not learn what their birthright and role is from their tribe will often create a gang in which to manufacture them.

A birthright is our psycho-spiritual container of memories, ancestral legends, family stories, genetic material, and social status which generation upon generation of our family and ethnic group have passed onto us. Boys who have little or no positive sense of what birthright they carry in the world of adult society will have lower self-image than other boys, less pride, and far less motivation to contribute to the society. If a gang is available, it gives the boy a sense of mission, birthright, and purpose. The boy will defend that new birthright, however misguided, with his life.

What are the answers to the problem of gangs? The answers are, on the one hand, socioeconomic: better employment, better opportunity, better education, less racism, less sexism. But the answers are family answers too: more first family, more second family, more third family: more tribe.

The First Family

The challenge that faces us as we redefine the "family" in the 1990s and beyond is to include three families again, and make sure the first family is a strong one. The key components of the first family are primary caregivers and role models. Traditionally this has been a mom and dad. In Chapters 4 and 5 we'll explore specifically what a boy needs from mom and from dad, but we won't necessarily extoll a return to the "traditional American family"—mom, dad, kids, and a dog. Those days are, for the most part, gone. Less than half of American families are shaped that way. Single mothers, single fathers, grandparents raising kids, gay and lesbian couples raising kids—these are all first families.

Where single parents, step-families, and gay and lesbian parents have often dropped the ball as caregivers is not, in my view, in "being the wrong kind of family." They have dropped the ball, and community has dropped the ball too, in not supporting them with more second and third family than a close father/mother/kids family may need.

In looking at "alternative" forms of first families, we gain by realizing how previous cultures have supported them as such. When a first family has been wracked by the loss of a spouse—father or mother died, for instance—the extended family and the community have supported the remaining parent. In an Old Testament tradition, for example, when a man dies his brother is supposed to marry his wife if she were childless. Alternative first families have always existed.

The "traditional 1950s nuclear family" is, for many, an economic and emotional impossibility. Despite this, there is presently in our culture a political movement to crush gay rights, shame single women, and revitalize the "traditional" family. I am suspicious of this movement. Building an effective family system for the next millennium does not begin in going back to Ozzie and Harriet but in going further back, into our ancestral past, for structural wisdom about how boy-friendly families can look, then moving forward into a future whose content—the stuff we put inside the structure—is constantly evolving. This future accepts the necessity that blood-ties and marriage vows are no longer necessarily the best definition of family.

The Second Family

The visionary thinker and writer Kurt Vonnegut, Jr., once had this to say:

"Until recent times, human beings usually had a permanent community of relatives. They had dozens of homes to go to. So when a married couple had a fight, one or the other could go to a house three doors down and stay with a close relative until he or she was feeling tender again. Or if the kids got so fed up with their parents that they couldn't stand it, they could march over to their uncle's for a while.

"Now this is rarely possible. Each family is locked into its little box. The neighbors aren't relatives. There aren't other houses where people can go and be cared for. When we ponder what's happening to America—"Where have all the values gone?" and all that—the answer is perfectly simple. We're lonesome. We don't have enough friends or relatives any more. And we would if we lived in real communities."

Almost half a century ago we redefined the family. Now, as we enter the next millennium, we're ready to redefine it again. Boys are teaching us that if we let kids be as lonely as they are these days, we'll suffer dire consequences. Most of us can't go back to having a lot of relatives around us—we live too far from them. But that doesn't mean we can't have extended family, community, tribe.

SHOULD OTHER PEOPLE RAISE MY KIDS?

I sat in the sauna in the men's locker room at my gym. Dan, forty-six, a father of two boys and a girl, told me about a job change he was pursuing—a half-time position so he could spend more time with his children. He had been wracked by guilt for years, he said, because his job—he was a counselor who worked for a nonprofit agency—didn't give him enough money to allow his wife to stay home with the kids.

His wife, an RN, had to work, so the kids had been in daycare and with relatives about twenty hours a week. His Catholic and family upbringing, he said, told him he was a bad parent for letting his kids be in daycare. I'll never forget his words: "God didn't give me kids to let other people raise them."

Dan was adamant and I didn't argue. But once again I was hit with an opinion that has made child-rearing in America very difficult, an opinion that some people feel religiously certain about, others traditionally certain about, others unable to pinpoint how they gained the idea. The emotion that attaches to the idea is usually guilt, a terrible, gut-wrenching parental guilt.

Other cultures—in fact, most other cultures—don't hold Dan's opinion so vehemently, and feel less guilt.

In Israel I had the opportunity to observe life on *kibbutzim*. Each kibbutz is different, but a general view, as regards child-raising, looks like this. A child is born to a couple. If the mother can, she'll take a few months off work, keeping the child close to her constantly. If she must work, her hours are cut and she gives the child to the "nursery parents"—individuals in the kibbutz who run the nursery—for her working hours, coming there at feeding times. Whether the child is with mom most of the day or with the nursery mother, the child is held a great deal. The mothers know that in the first few months of life the child needs to be close to the bodies of one or two consistent caregivers as much as possible.

From very early on, the child is raised not only by mom and dad but by nursery mothers and parents of other children. Kibbutz culture knows that the essential element in early childhood care is consistent and tactile closeness with one or, at most, two primary caregivers. It is not essential that the "child be with mom or dad every moment of the day." Mom will most likely *want* to be with the child as much as possible, but she will feel less guilty than the guilt-taught American parent if she doesn't stay with her child all the time. But she (and dad too) will feel very guilty if the child, at say three months old, is not being held and cuddled and cooed at by a consistently available nursery mother.

There are many reasons—cultural and social—that the kibbutz parent feels less guilt than the American parent. A primary one comes down to a different vision of the family. The kibbutz parent assumes the sacredness and importance of the nursery parents' relationship to the child. This assumption is built into the kibbutz system by the very nature of their close-knit, interdependent society. It is also built into the system by the long history of coparenting and extended family structures that are the main base for raising children all through the Middle East and, indeed, in most of the world.

Work and family hours on the kibbutz are managed in a way that gives parents one-on-one time with kids, without distractions. Whereas in our American household work often spills into family time—parents working at home on the phone, catching up, etc.— kibbutz life is set up so that when parents work they work and the children are in nursery, school, or care-areas; then, after three or four in the afternoon, when the parents have finished working, the children come back and spend a few hours of parent-child time uninterrupted by work. After this time—on many kibbutzim, and depending on how old the child is—the child may go back to the care-area or "dorm" or childrens' house to sleep with his peers.

This system is not for everyone, nor does it always work out ideally, but there are useful things about it for us. With many voices teaching the child, the child hears echoes of values, wisdom, self-worth. The child has more than one or two caregivers whom he can trust when he is feeling hurt, confused, or lost. Parents have back-up systems, babysitters, respected partners in child-raising. Children are being raised by a community so they feel inherently comfortable, as they grow in their community. They do not have to be taught, by external forces, to belong to their community. When children make their inevitable moves toward independence from mom and dad and other primary caregivers, there are other community members with whom they've bonded and to whom they can turn for advice, help, or embrace.

Can the kibbutz system be used in America? Probably not on any big scale, because our geography, cultural experience, and family etiologies are so different. But can the tribal aspect of the kibbutz system be transferred to American life? Absolutely. American communes have, for decades, experimented with the kibbutz system, and had some real successes. Those successes have often been based on the communal group remaining insular, even isolated, from the mainstream of American society. Most of us don't want to do that, but we have, without realizing it, some wonderful ways of imitating the best of the kibbutz system, and thus the best of our tribal past. Daycare is one of them.

DAYCARE AND CHILD CARE

When my wife and I went looking for child care and preschool for our first child, Gabrielle, we read everything we could, consulted everyone we knew, and ended up choosing a place recommended by some friends, "Gram's Happy Face Too." We signed up to start Gabrielle there, part time, after Gail returned to work following a maternity leave. Gail and I are both therapists, we both worked, we were both ready to cut our schedules to be with Gabrielle as much as possible, but still we needed five hours of child care per day.

We were filled with anxiety during our search. "What if our infant isn't held enough?" we worried. "What if something terrible happens to her?" "What if she hates us later?" We started joking that we'd start two funds for her, a college fund and a therapy fund. This joke did little to dissipate our anxiety.

When she finally began her time at "Gram's," our anxiety had not lessened at all. When Gail dropped her off in the mornings, Gabrielle would often cry for her mommy as Gail walked out the door and away from the daycare. Gail would get to work and call me in tears. Had we been able to afford to take Gabrielle out of daycare, we would have.

Over the months, however, Gabrielle came to like it at Gram's. A "nursery mother" named Kathy held her constantly, giving her more than adequate attention. When Kathy had to quit for health reasons, two other daycare providers, Maria and Penny, took a special liking to her, such a liking that even now, years later, they baby-sit our kids.

Then, after about a year at Gram's, all personnel started changing; these women to whom Gabrielle had become attached quit, for various reasons. Gabrielle was not getting consistent loving attention. We were about to have another child. We began our search again and found another daycare—the Paulish Playhouse—that was just beginning as a licensed preschool. We got to know Marianne and Kelly, saw their gifts with children, and settled our kids part-time there. There they ended up for many years. There they found a community that felt like home in the amount of attention they got but was different enough from home to give them new worlds, new horizons. We got to know Marianne and Kelly, so our kids saw us interacting socially with them, and thus saw family bonds form between care-giving adults. This strengthened our kids' sense of security.

Every parents' story with daycare is different. Some swear by daycare, some hate it. Studies themselves are divided. My comments are based as much as research as on my own sometimes negative but basically positive experiences. The thread that runs through my observations is this: when parents and daycare providers work together to form relationships among themselves, they create a community spirit in which their children feel like they are moving between first and second families in a blend of loving attention. With preschool age kids this is as important a thread as it is with infants and toddlers.

When, years ago, blood relatives—mainly grandmothers and aunts—watched over a couple's children, the couple felt normal parental anxiety, but did not tend to feel the gut-wrenching fear we feel when we give our kids to the care of strangers. Thus it is essential we pick daycares where we do not have to remain strangers. It is essential we pick daycare centers where we are allowed to observe, visit for an hour every other day or so should we wish, hear about curriculum, get answers to our questions about what our child did that day. If we search out these sorts of daycares, we are helping create a second family for our child.

In order for more and better daycare centers to be available, we will have to upgrade the status of child-care providers in general. Right now, child care outside the home is considered by many people, especially policy-makers, to be a necessary evil. This attitude will have to change. We will have to come to see daycare centers as second family. We will have to be willing to pay providers more and become more involved, more bonded, with the provider's world; the providers, too, will have to be more accepting of our input.

Corporations, too, will have to get involved. They'll not only help families and kids if they do, but they'll cost themselves less money in the long run. Some enlightened corporations—like IBM, AT&T, Time Warner, Exxon, Eastman Kodak, Johnson & Johnson, and Traveler's Group—have formed the American Business Collaboration for Quality Dependent Care. Elliot Lehman, an executive at Fel-Pro Inc, an automotive and industrial manufacturer in Illinois, and board member of the Child Care Action Campaign, reports: "In Phoenix, they financed projects to help child-care centers recruit and train caregivers; in Los Angeles, they helped provide child-care vans; in Stamford, Conn. they financed a school child-care center."

Businesses are all the more competitive and productive when they care for their workforce. As our culture changes, businesses will have to change to keep up. Child care is an area every business should study.

Over five million kids go to daycare or preschool. Among employed mothers with kids five years old or under, 33 percent use family daycare—a daycare run out of someone's home—28 percent use daycare centers, 28 percent juggle schedules so they don't use any nonparental child care, and 10 percent use nannies or relatives. It is nearly impossible for most working parents to not use at least part-time child care. Why not, then, blend the parental and child-care worlds so that they work together for the kids?

A two-and-a-half-year study done by researchers at the University of Colorado at Denver, UCLA, The University of North Carolina, and Yale, entitled "Cost, Quality and Child Outcomes in Child Care Centers," found the majority of daycare centers to be substandard. This study follows another one, done by the New York-based Families and Work Institute, which also came to similar findings. These studies found that we, as parents, tend to overestimate how good the child care is. We tend to say, "My son's getting great care," when a trained observer finds the child care center to be substandard.

Our childrens' child care can be more like a kibbutz environment if we help it to be. Using smaller daycares usually allows more intimacy. Caregivers come and go more in the large centers. When you are looking for a daycare for your children, look at whether the center provides high staff-child ratios; high-end teacher wages; high-level staff education; low staff turnover; good management. The NAEYC suggests these numbers for staffing ratios: one adult for every three to four infants; one adult for four or five 2-year-olds; one adult for eight to ten 4-year-olds.

Boys specifically need:

▼ a variety of movable objects, like blocks, toy trucks and so on
▼ lots of space
▼ carefully monitored—and scant—time in front of the TV

▼   an environment that will not stereotype boys as "too aggressive" but will allow them to take healthy risks

▼   caregivers trained in raising boys

T. Berry Brazelton, whose books are some of the best available on raising infants and toddlers, says this about preschool: "The studies show that children who have been in preschool programs are better prepared for learning and are better able to handle relationships with their peers." He would also be first to admit that studies can show many things—every parent makes the ultimate decisions based on family needs.

In the end the standard to use, I believe, is this: "Am I sending them to a second family, or to a children's storage area?" If we send our kids to second families, they will feel loved.

CREATING EXTENDED FAMILIES OF YOUR OWN

The most obvious way to create an extended family or tribe for your kids is to rely on blood-kin to help you raise and guide them. If you have a large number of blood relations available to you, you have a built-in tribe for your kids. As boys in particular grow up in the warmth of all these relatives, studies show they will be less likely to become antisocial later. Studies are just confirming common sense. If kids have a lot of generations of family around them when they're growing up, they're getting more of their emotional and psychological needs met, and they'll grow up healthier.

Unfortunately, few people grow up in "clans" anymore. Most of our relatives live far away. So are the majority of us starting with the deck stacked against us? Not necessarily.

Nonblood family interdependence has been a tribal way of raising kids for hundreds of thousands of years. Among the Hawaiians, for instance, family systems included *ho-okama*. These are godparents, "foster parents," nonblood aunts and uncles who are "adopted" by a child's family because of love and friendship. Among Mexican Americans, *padrinos* and *madrinos,* godfathers and godmothers, are often chosen by parents of children, either when the child is newborn, or sometime after. These godparents, among some Mexican-Americans, used to be said to carry the personality of the child. A parent might say, "Young José got his looks from me, but he got his personality from you, *padrino,*" even though the padrino and the parent had no blood in common. Among the ancient Navaho, it was traditional to call someone else "brother" or "sister" and having done so treat him or her as a blood relation, giving him or her, quite often, some of your child-care responsibilities.

In most cultures some kind of nonblood kin system is built into tribal life. The nonblood kin provide a second family for a boy, giving him a place to go when he is in tension with his first family, and providing him with echoes, new voices, and alternative visions.

This kind of extended family can, with effort, be built into anyone's family system in the U.S. What it takes, most of all, is an openness to nonblood "relations." Though we Americans are trained to do everything individualistically, we must come to realize that once we have kids, individualism is impractical and self-defeating. The myth that "all my boy needs is me," is just that—a myth. Even before we're pregnant, we need to ask best friends if they'll play a role in our child's life. While we're pregnant, we need to keep these friends in tune with what's happening with the baby. We need to invite these people to the birth, or at least to be nearby in waiting rooms so they'll bond. We need to ask one or two people to become godparents. And most of all, we need to feel comfortable relying on these people throughout our boy's life. We are giving them as much of a gift as they are giving us—we are giving them the beautiful responsibility over our child.

When I was a boy my parents did this with me. They had me call their very good friends "auntie" and "uncle," which was what we called elder caregivers and friends in India. Sometimes I recall resenting calling people I barely knew—people who were my parents' friends but not mine—"auntie" and "uncle," and perhaps my parents imposed more name rigidity than they needed to. But they also gave me a lot of aunties and uncles. As I've renamed these friends, giving them a family name, we brought them further into our family.

When we parents bring others into our family system, we often find we're providing single people, divorced people, and elderly people with children to care for. Many elderly people live far away from their own grandchildren and would love to be grandma and grandpa to ours. Many single people have decided not to have children but love helping to raise "someone else's kids." Many divorced people are separated from their kids and love being with ours.

A second family can't be imposed on a boy; it must grow organically. Forcing someone onto a ten-year-old is difficult. At that age, the boy needs, usually, to find his own mentors. The time to start building a system of madrinos and ho-okama is as early as possible.

Sometimes we choose kin for our kids but sometimes they make their own choices. Often nonblood second family members appear in a child's life through his friendship with another boy. When our kids pick friends and begin to bond with the friends' parents, it's important to talk to those parents about what's happening. It's important to learn something about the other parents' values, parenting styles. It's important to ask our kids—though not incessantly—what they like about that other parent and help our children model off the other parent. It's even useful sometimes to say, "Yes, Mr. Jameson can do such-and-such. He's better at that than I am. I'm glad you found him."

As we learn the values, morals, and parenting styles of both kinds of nonblood kin—those with kids themselves and those without—it's also important that we don't try to be perfectionists. Neither our blood kin nor our nonblood kin are perfect. A boy might become best friends with a boy whose father is into videogames. We might despise videogames, especially the highly aggressive ones. In our perfectionism we might want to manipulate an end to our child's bond with that father. But before we do that, let's look closely at everything the boy is gaining. Maybe we need to change our standard a little.

This whole world of nonblood kinship systems is best navigated when we trust a few others and build a family to include them. We don't need ten or twenty in our second family—we just need a few people, and a willingness to let our child bond with these people and change his bonds as he grows.

The Third Family

In school, in the media, on the streets, our boys find their third family. This third family is the hardest for us to manage. Often, the values of this third family run counter to the values of the boy's first family—
our values. Community figures are telling the boys to rebel against us. Media action stars are teaching the boys to act in ways that run

counter to the nonviolence we've taught our boys. Large peer groups at school and elsewhere pull the boys into activities that, in some cases, can get the boys killed.

Many of the chapters in the rest of this book will deal with aspects of the third family. I will make suggestions about cutting down media input, teaching values and morals in different ways, and giving boys spiritual growth and initiation so they'll find in the third family the same sort of energy they found in healthy first and second families. For now let's talk about two key third-family components: the educational system and community programs.

BOYS AND THE EDUCATIONAL SYSTEM

I sat with a group of administrators of a school district that serves most of a mid-size American city. We discussed the district's Human Growth and Development program. That program provides curriculum for health classes, family education, sex education. All of us sat there with good intentions, trying to evaluate the possibility of doing some curriculum that educated young males on personal responsibility, goal-setting, decision-making, and emotional growth. When we discussed whether the Human Growth and Development program was a success, the administration's unequivocal answer was, "Yes." They pointed out the many wonderful things it did, and how many different educational modules they had been able to get into the program, especially given the political problems any such program faces.

When I asked, "Who takes the Human Growth and Development classes?" the answer was, "Well, mainly girls." In fact, there had been only one boy in one of the classes in the last two years. There had been hundreds of girls. Taking nothing away from the successes, I said, "But is this a 'success'? No males come."

This discussion is indicative of what often happens in school systems. The boys and young men don't take the elective classes that would teach responsibility because these classes are taught mainly by women about concerns that seem to grow from female culture. It is a given, of course, that many of the concerns are important to male culture, but boys don't see it this way. Schools know this, but give up. They hope the boys will learn about human growth and development somewhere.

In the public sector this kind of gap in male education often goes unnoticed. I served on a panel for a television forum on teen issues. The moderators of the program were female, most of the community guests were female, even many of the male expert guests focused on female teen issues. Of the twelve experts, I was the only one asked to focus completely on "boys' " issues. When my turn came on the panel, the first question I was asked was, "There are so many single mothers out there. What can you tell them?"

The point here is not to say the program did no good. It did a lot of good. I was proud to serve on it. However, I was not surprised when, after the program was over, a man came up to me, a father of two sons, and said, "This was all soft stuff. Who's this gonna reach? Not my boys." This man, black, about forty, knows that his sons need education in their language, with a certain frankness and toughness, and with the backing of public priority. Forums like the one that evening don't reach males.

Our private, public, and media education programs are doing a great deal, and need much more support than we give them. They are a huge part of the boy's third family. Each of us must scrutinize our schools and public programming for equal priority in male education. One reason we don't scrutinize it enough, I think, is that we live under a misconception, borne of gender politics, that we need to look at.

WHAT ITS *REALLY* LIKE FOR BOYS IN THE EDUCATIONAL SYSTEM

We are often told that girls have it much tougher than boys in the educational system. Important books like *Failing at Fairness,* by Sadler and Sadler, have pointed out that teachers call on boys more. Girls often hide more in the shadows to let the boys show their prowess. Teachers unwittingly support this behavior, to the detriment of girls' self-image.

While the Sadler research is compelling and valid, the general conclusion that many have used it for, namely to show that girls have it worse than boys overall, is dangerous and untrue. Boys and girls each have problems. Trying to paint girls as victims and boys as victors just sets social policy back, and in the end hurts our kids.

The U.S. Department of Education surveyed both males and females and asked independent researchers to conduct their own surveys. All the researchers found that not female but male students have lower educational aspirations. Eighth-grade girls, for instance, are twice as likely as eighth-grade boys to aspire to a professional career. They also found that claims of generally lower self-esteem among female students compared to male was unfounded. In many cases, just the opposite. Researchers found that many of the girls who "held back," letting the boys talk, had higher self-esteem than the attention-seeking boys.

Not girls but boys are more likely to drop out of high school. High-school boys commit suicide at a rate of 4 to 1 in comparison to high-school girls. In early school years, boys have much more difficulty than girls in reading, writing, and other verbal skills. Many boys are held back because the way these skills are taught does not match the way the male brain, slower in learning these skills, can grasp them. Eighth-grade boys are, according to Diane Ravitch, an NYU researcher, "50 percent more likely to be held back a grade than girls, and in high school, two-thirds of special education students are boys." In high school, boys are more often victims of physical violence (this statistic *includes* statistics on rape, date rape, and sexual abuse) than girls, and three times as likely to die of homicide in and around school.

Many social thinkers who seek to insist girls have it worse than boys are locked politically in the past when, for instance in the 1970s, males did outnumber females in American education. Now, however, as Ravitch puts it, "Those who claim gender bias in the school purposefully ignore the remarkable changes that have occurred over the past generation." Now, females outnumber males both in college and in graduate school. Women are 55 percent of all undergraduates and they are 59 percent of all master's degree candidates. Women are nearly 50 percent of the enrollment in American law and medical schools. In fact, women now constitute the majority of all graduate and professional students in American higher education.

I have found in my consulting with school systems a trend toward accepting the false premise of male superiority in the educational system. All of us in community must work together to stop this trend and return the educational culture to common sense. Neither gender's suffering is superior; both need our aid.

As our educational system advances to accommodate boys' needs, I hope we will find educators more willing to adapt educational styles, especially in the first school years, to accommodate different brain systems. For instance, because boys have so much more trouble than girls in learning to read, educators might follow the example of a Dade County school district which is using more spatial strategies to teach boys reading. Human growth and development also need to be taught to boys in classes boys are required to take, like gym and other athletics programs, making them not electives but requirements for participation. Mentoring programs should be mandatory for at least a year of junior high and a year of high school in which parents and a teacher, coach, or counselor mentor the boy on delicate issues, like sex education. In addition, we need to study and stem the tide of male dropout rates with as much money and energy as we have studied female self-esteem in high school. All educators should also be trained in brain and biochemical sex differences so that the educational community will understand how to stem the tide of "special-ed" boys, many of whom are simply "difficult" because educators—themselves untrained in male brain chemistry and the stimulation, discipline and structure it needs—aren't sure what else to call them.

It would be very beneficial to link schools with other community agencies to build co-curricula for boys. If schools can link up with churches (this is very doable in private schools) and neighborhood action committees to provide programs *for boys,* foundation will be set for the boy to feel that his third family is providing a place for him to learn who to be. This is better than the present situation, in which schools, churches, youth centers, and so on rarely link up to help boys. Boys may gain fragments of third-family teaching through each, but not an integrated, safe network or "tribe" through which to hear holistic role-training.

Parents and extended-family members can become involved in school classrooms. Some programs, like a program in Washington State called Apple, make parents commit to ninety hours a year of service to the school. This is a good model for parent involvement. In order for parent involvement to work, parents will have to take more time off their jobs. Extended family can help both the parents and the school by giving their time in classrooms, gym classes, and community centers. If, say, the parents are committed to ninety hours, they can give ten or twenty to a godparent, family friend, grandmother, or grandfather. Link-ups between parents, mentors, and educators are all possible if we want them to be.

A small minority of parents will cry, "I don't want anyone else in the classroom with my child except the teacher even for an hour. And I'm not sure I even trust the teacher . . ." This may be the same minority that wants unreasonable censorship of books. The majority of parents will have to unite against this tiny group, giving legislators and educators more room to involve more parents and community members in public and private education.

More voluntary spirituality in school should also be permitted. *Voluntary* school prayer does little harm to anyone, and will help everyone see the gentle mystery of spirit. As schools become more spirit-friendly, inviting church/synagogue/temple professionals to speak on spiritual topics, boys will get yet another echo of spiritual grounding.

But in order to include more spiritual education in schools, we will have to join together as communities to make spiritual education valuable and promote it to legislators and administrators; and make sure our kids receive the *whole* variety of spiritual teaching, not just one religion.

When they ask, school administrators discover that pastoral professionals from the community are glad to form advisory committees to help schools develop programming that curtails no one's rights to freedom of religion—programming that is inclusive of all religions except hate-based cults and philosophies. For this to occur, the majority of us would have to recognize how bereft our males are of spiritual education, how dangerous that is, how artificial a complete separation of public education and spiritual education is, and how beneficial a respectful melding of the two would be (we will get into this in more depth in both Chapters 8 and 10).

And, finally, school and the workplace should be linked whenever possible, giving boys a day off, for instance, as girls have, for "Take your son to work day," and creating more and more programs to inspire boys to enjoy "learning to work."

Many boys drop out of high school to get jobs that later bore them because they feel school is boring them with "silly classes" and "useless information" that don't fit their young vision of "the workplace." If workplace and school were better linked, students and educators would know much better what information is essential. One career day a year is not enough. Again, gym and other boy-populated classes and activities are a good place to reach boys by having professionals come in to speak to and inspire them about educational links to the workplace.

ENERGIZING COMMUNITY PROGRAMS

At a lecture I gave for a school district, a mother named Kathy raised her hand. "America is a country based in the ideals of individualism," she said, "so all this stuff about 'it takes a whole village to raise a child' and what you've been saying about boys needing a tribe, it all sounds good but how do you *do* it? It would take a megashift in American life. It would take a megashift in *my* life. I'm a single parent of three boys, a widow. None of my relatives are around. I make enough money not to have to turn to the government for help. Our church doesn't really do a lot for my boys. Sports does some but not enough. Big Brothers has got a long waiting list. I'm on my own. How am I supposed to find a 'tribe' for my sons?"

One of the things I do when I go into a city for workshops is hold community councils. An hour or two is set aside for the people at the workshop to build "three families" in their church, school, community, neighborhood. Many of these venues already have related programs in place, so the community council is often a way of advertising what's out there. It is a place to begin, even though most of the people at the workshop don't know each other.

One man will say, "Yes, I have time to volunteer." He and a single mother will agree that she needs to talk to him more fully, even check to see if he has a criminal record, and so on. But still a connection is being made. People are coming together to talk in the council about how to build more tribal life into their childrens' upbringings.

Taking the "Boys Need a Tribe" *theory* into *practice* does, as Kathy expressed, seem to need a megashift in our culture's way of doing things. And yet, not only can we make that shift happen, it is already happening.

In Kellogg, Idaho, inside a classroom at the Elk Creek schoolhouse, a makeshift boxing gym has been set up. Boys meet three nights a week at the school to work out on heavy bags, do calisthenics, and spar in a ring whose ropes are garden hoses. John Hill, forty-two, mentors the boys. "You've got to coach them, raise money, and act as a surrogate father. A lot of these kids are from broken homes."

Big Brothers and Sisters of America serves 125,000 children and families each year. They have a waiting list that grows and grows every day. Wherever you are, there is probably a BBSA agency. It focuses mainly on kids of single parents. In my years of doing consulting with BBSA, I've never known an agency head who said, "Hey, we don't need more volunteers." BBSA is always looking for ways to bring more people into the community loop. By spending four hours a week with a youngster, the Big Brother becomes a part of the boy's third family. Sometimes, over a period of years, the Big Brother and Little Brother get so close, the Big Brother has become an important part of the boy's second family. BBSA has recently begun a Teen program so that teenage youths can become Big Brothers and Sisters to younger kids.

Waiting lists for Big Brothers are usually longer than for Big Sisters. More women volunteer per capita than men. There are many reasons for this. Men are less likely to reach out into community support networks than women. Men are per capita working longer workplace hours than women, so they have less time. Boys, especially sons of single mothers, are seen as harder to handle than girls. Many men don't feel emotionally capable of taking on an intimate mentorial relationship. No matter what the reasons, the boys are out there, seeking nonblood kin, and BBSA is one of the best venues for them to find it.

Some states are turning to communities to work with their juvenile delinquents, most of whom are boys. Giving some of the less chronic and dangerous boys "Diverted JD" status, the criminal justice systems are focusing not on incarceration, which tribalizes boys into antisocial groups, but on three alternative components—community service, education, and restitution—which show the boy how to belong to his larger community. These diverted JDs take courses in personal goal-setting, refusal skills, substance abuse, victim awareness, and anger management. They work as volunteers and pay off debts from their crimes. Recidivism rates for these boys are lower than comparable boys who go through the incarceration system.

Throughout the country, Neighborhood Accountability Boards are being set up to bring community members together to help first-time juvenile offenders in a special way. Board members—people like you and me—are volunteers who work as a team, meet with parents of first-time juvenile offenders, meet with the offenders themselves, and develop ways of giving the offenders community service work. Through this third-family structure, these first-time offenders see themselves and their "punishment"/"service work" in community terms.

In both the Bush and Clinton presidencies, Youth Service has become a national priority. Consultants like David Sawyer, whose Students for Appalachia at Berea college won the Presidential Points of Light award in 1992, travel around the country helping build youth service programs in schools, campuses, businesses, and institutions.

These are just a fraction of the community programs burgeoning everywhere. The feeling that "we must work together" is beginning to take hold, and positive results are showing up everywhere. Part of our third-family life is voting and watching that our legislators create policies that help, not limit, the development of a tribe for our boys. The more our lawmakers cut away funding for programs that build community spirit, the more our country languishes in the myth that individuals can do everything, that tribalism is really dangerous socialism, and that families all have to look one way to be right.

If we give boys three families—that is, a tribe in which to grow and flourish—we are better able to:

1. Help boys express *their* needs rather than guiltily believing we should, because we're parents, *know* what they need.

2. Support boys in working hard for everything they get so that every prize they get they earn.

3. Teach boys to turn their failures into opportunities, especially opportunities to take stock of themselves and grow.

4. Teach boys who they are, especially the demands of their biology, and enable them to appreciate and respect their gender.

5. Give boys more of the discipline and structure they need in order to know how to live and how to love.

6. Give them more elders to model after, learn from, and believe in, thus teaching them more about honor, respect, and integrity.

7. Cut out as much as possible influences in their lives that desensitize them and dehumanize them. Some of the seven hours a day they

spend in front of the television could be spent with a member of their "tribe."

8. Give them increased opportunities to develop their skills and talents through increased mentoring and availability.

9. Give them more adult time, more consistent but flexible authority.

10. Give them more of an incentive to serve, thus more contentment in themselves.

If we are to provide boys with a tribe we will probably have to make that provision a high priority; thus we'll have to take time and value away from other things. We may have to work less at things that are not essential to the lives of our boys. This may require us to lower our standards of how much money we need to make, and to buy fewer *things* for our boys but give them more love. We will have to spend more undistracted time with our kids when they're with us and project less guilt and worry when they're not. Most of all, we'll have to build family systems that do not necessarily include our faraway or otherwise problematic blood relations.

Can we do this? Indeed we can. It is already happening around us everywhere. Other people are doing it in South Carolina, in New York, or just down the street from us. The key now is for each one of us to see ourselves as that "other person." If each one of us seeks out one other person to bring into our child's family; if each one of us moves, where welcomed, to the forefront of a family and community—we will do our part to create the tribal world a boy's biology and culture compels him to seek.

With all this said, still we know that creating a tribe for a boy is an amorphous idea without a strong first-family foundation. So let's turn now to the mother-son and father-son relationships that most often comprise a boy's first family. When we say "mother" or "father," let us be clear that someone other than the blood-parent can fill that role, especially in the case of adoption. But whatever the family profile, there is a special sanctity to the mother-son and father-son bonds.

c h a p t e r   4

Love You Forever: What Boys Need From Their Mothers

*The mother-son relationship is usually a
subtle interaction between letting go and
grasping—and that is what makes the
process and the understanding of it so
infinitely complex.*

—*Paul Olson*

There is an old Italian saying, "Every woman is a whore except my mother who is a saint." When my grandfather—my mother's Italian father, a first-generation immigrant—first told me this saying in my early twenties I had come to him with deep anger at his daughter, my mother. Throughout my boyhood, she and I had fought, I had run away, I had come back, we had fought some more. When I left home for good we had both said, "Good riddance!" By the time I was talking to Grandpa Mike, the man after whom I was named, I still felt a lot of unresolved rage toward her.

Grandpa Mike's advice was old world, simple and, at the time, unsatisfying: "Respect your mother. She brought you into the world. There's a saying in the old country: 'Every woman is a whore except my mother who is a saint.' Remember that and be done with all your petty angers." Never one to hold back a response, I said, "So, every woman gets dumped on so we can hold mom in awe. That's not for me." My mother, whose parents divorced when she was a newborn, didn't meet her father until she was twenty-one. Their relationship was not terribly close and neither was mine with him. We went no deeper into the subject of mothers and sons than that Italian saying.

Now, years later, it still sticks in my memory. My mother and I have made peace, and yet I cannot consider my mother a saint. In fact, I think that the saying implies a kind of overprotectiveness toward moms (to say nothing of its destructiveness toward other women!) that I find all over North America when I ask audiences to tackle the subject of the mother-son relationship. Because in most cases the boy attaches to his mother first and in most cases is brought up by his mother foremost, their relationship is perhaps the most subtly complex relationship a boy will experience.

Yet I have found, especially since the publication of my book *Mothers, Sons and Lovers,* a protective response from mothers, sons, fathers, and others in society to a wholistic and sometimes painful analysis of the mother-son relationship. Because of this reaction, important things don't get said. Sometimes moms get honored, even deified—like "mothers and apple pie"—for things they don't really do but are never acknowledged for what they really do accomplish.

In order to improve the lives of boys, we have to be acutely honest. Bashing moms is not my intention, yet, as one mom said to me after a lecture I gave, "Don't be so careful around us moms. We can take some criticism. We're pretty strong."

She was right. So let's dig into this material and work hard to say, "Mom is most often the most influential person in a boy's life. Let's study that influence and help boys thrive in it." Because specific topics germane to the many issues in the mother-son relationship—like "boys and discipline," "how to teach boys about sex and love," "how to teach boys values"—are covered in other chapters, we won't focus on every aspect of them here. Instead, we'll focus on key issues and stages in the mother-son relationship—early life, then puberty and adolescence—that mothers ask me most about.

The Right Conditions for "Good" Mother-Son Relationships

In the last three generations, a mother has increasingly raised her children with little hands-on support. Her extended family is frequently nonexistent. Her husband may work away from the home most of the time, or may be, in divorce, pushed away by his ex-spouse and the courts or opts away on his own. More and more moms are working themselves. Thirty percent of American children are born to unmarried women. More than half of American children spend part of their childhood in a home run by a single mother.

Many single mothers have done incredible jobs to balance their lives and raise healthy sons. The jobs they've done are heroic, especially given how little support they've had. Nonetheless, the fact that most juvenile delinquent males are being brought up by single mothers indicates that as much as a boy needs a tribe, so does a mother.

Working outward in concentric circles from the single mother's situation, we can easily draw a picture of what a "good" mother-son relationship needs in order to flourish. In its ideal form, mom would be experiencing physical, material, social, and emotional support from four interdependent sources: an intimate partner who is also attached to the child; a select group of close friends and family; a wider community that supports mom's values and goals; and a maternity-flexible workplace.

Mom should receive this support throughout the stages of her son's life. When the mother-son relationship is viewed with a wide lens, that support is the key to a positive relationship. With that support a mother is able to bond and attach well with a boy so that the boy grows up feeling he is loved and always deserves to be loved; allow the boy to separate from her as needed so he can develop his own identity from a secure base; work out her own issues with the help of family and community members, so she doesn't exploit the boy as the object of any psychological baggage; receive hands-on education from multi-generational sources about boy biology and culture so she knows how to best raise a boy; model good teamwork with others, i.e., school figures, other family members, community and neighborhood alliances so the boy learns how to contribute to an interpersonal community; live with strong self-esteem so the boy can do so as well; provide empowered female guidance so that the boy learns respect for the feminine; provide discipline, rules, and structure so that the boy learns his limits; engage, when the boy needs her to, in his activities, whether sports, school or other; get help in selecting the proper stimulations for her boy, and get help in steering him away from obsessive stimulations like excessive TV and video games; be available as he needs her and open to topics, like sexual and aggression-oriented questions, that might startle her; have trusted allies who help her critique and alter her own mothering techniques when necessary; and be able to love him unconditionally.

What Boys Need From Mom in the First Decade of Life

Pediatrician and parent-infant specialist T. Berry Brazelton has long argued that a mother should stay home with the child for the first year of his life. Interviewed again only a few months ago he was asked by journalist Bill Moyers, "Do you still believe that?" His answer was: "Absolutely." His reasoning is, of course, common sense.

When a child in any primate species is born, it needs to bond with a primary caregiver in order to physically survive. If the natural mother dies so that 1) the feeding breast and/or 2) protection from the dangerous, unyielding natural environment are not available, the infant needs to bond with a new wet nurse/bottle holder and protector. Whether we look at bears, ducks, or bees, nature is nature. These infants need not only to *bond*—which is the initial feeling of "I love this other person"—but they also need to *attach*. Bonding happens for most parents at the moment of conception, then through gestation, then again, monumentally, at birth. Attachment is the long-term commitment of child and parent and continues to varying degrees throughout our life.

Because of our human brain, we need intimate attachment more than most other animals. The human brain is about the most sophisticated we know of. The trade-off nature has worked out for this sophistication is to make it begin life as one of the most impressionable and therefore emotionally fragile brains in the natural universe. If that little brain does not get attached to primary caregivers, it will probably grow up twisted, confused, and dangerous to itself and to others.

Mom is often best suited to be the primary caregiver to an infant. Her hormones—like progesterone, the bonding hormone, which increases up to ten times in a pregnant woman; her mammary glands should she choose to breast-feed; her female brain structure, developed over millions of years to include, as one of its primary functions, intimate, moment-by-moment infant care; and her socialization tend to suit her for the job of being the primary attachment object for the newborn. Saying this does not mean a man can't do the job; nor does it mean every mother of a newborn "has all the right instincts." It simply means what we've all always known. Moms, for the most part, make the first and most profound bond with the newborn and also the first primary attachment. Even most dads are willing to admit mom's unique experience. So often we hear fathers say: "I just didn't have as complete an experience as my wife did. It's when my kid got a little older that I really began to feel like a father."

As the infant grows up with his mother's (or another *primary* caregiver's) profound activity of attachment, he feels safe in the world. He is physically and emotionally fed, and his body and brain develop normally (given no abnormal genetic influences or traumatic environmental events). In his first months of life, too much detachment from a primary caregiver—too little feeding, holding, cuddling, cooing, playing—will make him feel unsafe, unloved, and he will spend a great deal of his neural energy confused by the lack of safety rather than devoted to normal emotional growth. Among boys, says some research, there is an even greater need for mom to be around early on because boys' brain development is, in some areas, slower than girls'.

Thus experts like Brazelton suggest a year at home. If the mother can extend that year to two years, all the better. If a mother is going to make (or is forced to make) another choice, the infant boy needs her to place him with a caregiver *who will remain consistent* during the hours the mother is not present, and who will hold, cuddle, coo at, and talk to the infant to much the same degree as an emotionally healthy mother would.

This is an ideal picture. The reality of infant-mother relationships today is more complicated.

WORKING MOTHERS

It takes, on average, two incomes to fund a family in 1996 at the same level as one income funded it in 1976. Many mothers of newborns work. As we've seen above, with a divorce rate at one out of two marriages, one third of America's boys are raised by single mothers who either work or are on welfare. So, in total, the majority of American mothers are working or experiencing conditions near or below the poverty line as they raise their kids. Neither circumstance is optimal. The working mother does not often have the freedom to take a year off. The impoverished mother does not have the ability to attach to a child with a sense of personal economic safety in her life.

For this situation to change, for mothers to be in a better position to attach to their children completely during their infancies, our culture will have to become more communal, more supportive of parents, more personally responsible, less inclined to seek immediate gratification, less obsessed with perfect romantic partnerships, more child-focused.

Therapists can often tell how a child's relationship with mom will go by how the attachment goes in the first few months of the child's life.

Working mothers often talk about how guilty they feel leaving their children at daycare. Their guilt is like a mist that surrounds them as they pick up their children. Sometimes they clutch their child, even overmother him when they come home from daycare, buy him too many toys, avoid disciplining. The child acts out, often growing up with hurtful behavior patterns during transitions between caregivers—yelling "Go away" to mom when she comes to pick up the child, "I don't like you." The mother's guilt has the opposite effect of what mom wants. The child picks up on it and pushes further away at just the moments that will hurt mom the most. If we send signals to our children that we want them to punish us, they'll do so—they will, quite rightfully in their minds, be doing exactly what we want them to. For a mother's guilt, sensed by a child, deletes her authority, complicates her attachment, and debilitates her own self-image.

There's no simple solution to this guilt working moms carry with them. Hopefully, as three families work together, it will dissipate a great deal. Moms won't feel, in a gut-wrenching way, that their absence is hurting their child.

WHEN A DIVORCED OR SINGLE MOTHER BRINGS HOME
A BOYFRIEND

Often divorced or single mothers have spoken to me about the rivalry that occurs between their son and their new boyfriend or husband. One divorced mother put it to me this way: "I know that too many casual men in my life will hurt my son. I also know that whatever I do with men is going to shape how he treats women. I also know I have a God-given right to be loved; my son shouldn't control my destiny, and, dammit, if I don't find love I'll be a wreck and that will damage my son too! But all in all what I'm facing is: if I take care of myself and find a lover, he'll be hurt. If I don't take care of myself and try to go it alone, he'll be hurt." Isn't that it, in a nutshell?

A friend of mine, the mother of a nine-year-old son, told me about her experience with Lane. Earlier in his life, before his parents' divorce, his mother knew him as a tender, caring boy. Now, after the divorce, he was angry and demanding. Enough time had passed since the divorce that Marcia wanted to date. When she did bring a new man home to meet Lane, he became very disagreeable. Even when the man tried to be his friend, get to know him, show him respect, he rejected him rudely, sometimes abusively. And he treated his mother more and more abusively.

Lane's behavior is like the behavior of many sons of divorce who live with mom and eye a new man in the house. For many reasons, boys will not attach with the new man at all or, if ever, very late down the line. Here are some of those reasons.

Boys are jealous, pure and simple. They have a sexual and emotional rivalry with any man who loves mom. This competition is pretty well worked through if the man who loves mom is also dad since other psychological instincts between father and son, instincts to love and care for each other, take a front seat in the father-mother-son triangle. But if the man trying to love mom is not dad, there is no other substantial psychological instinct to stand within the boy against his jealous love of mom.

The boy's initial male alliance is with dad, no matter how much mom doesn't like dad or how dad behaves. Unless dad has outrightly tried to take the boy's life—and even in that case, some boys do not detach from him—dad will be his instinctive male attachment. He will resent anyone else trying to be.

Boys are profoundly angry at mom for pushing dad away. They will find as many ways as possible to punish mom for what she has done. Whether she perceives that she did not push dad away, the children will feel she has. Often they will see more clearly than she can the things she has done over the years to play her part in the destruction of the marriage.

Boys often idealize divorced, even distant fathers, as much as they feel anger and pain about the father's physical, geographical, or emotional separation. Boys will rarely see a new man as capable of being the ideal father they have in their minds, and thus will most often be unable to risk attachment to a new man. Their attachment to dad led to profound trauma when he left or was forced away from them.

The new male elder will probably have a different style of interaction and discipline than dad. The boy will find it lacking and resist it as much as possible, often out of loyalty to dad's way of doing things.

The boy will hope, for years and years, that his parents will reconcile. He won't invest in a new man when he feels he should be working toward getting his mom and dad back together.

The boy will feel a profound responsibility to "be the man of the house" when dad is gone. He will not want a new man to take his place.

The boy will try to protect mom at all costs, fearing for her very safety with a new man. He will resist, spar with, be rude to, ignore, even fight with the new man in hopes of getting him to leave so that the new man will not get an opportunity to hurt mom.

The boy will want mom to put him first above everyone else. Anyone who gets in the way of his basic need for attention—a need amplified by divorce and single parenting—will be scorned.

Many single parent families do navigate their way into blended families. Many sons do form bonds with "new men," "boyfriends," and "stepfathers." Here are some ways they do it.

The mother does not expose the son to myriad male influences. If she dates, she does so when the son is staying with dad. She brings a man into the boy's life when she's really ready to invest a long-term attachment in him herself.

The new man is never seen as a substitute for dad. He is given a *different role.* This is consciously verbalized between mother, father, stepfather, boyfriend, and son.

Discipline structures and household routines that are imposed by the stepfather are explained clearly to the son and imposed as augmentations, not substitutes, for a father's and mother's structures.

The new man lets the son be angry at him more than he normally would because he knows the son needs to work out his anger at his father for leaving him.

The mother becomes increasingly aware of how she has played her part in distancing the father from his son. With the ego-ballast of a new relationship with a man, she now gathers the strength to confront her part, mend fences with the father, bring him back into the loop. Even if there are angry, hurtful times between them, she goes through them (and the father must too) for the good of the boy. Exceptions to this exist again in the minority of cases where true danger occurs.

The new man forms as much of an alliance with the father as possible so he and the father can compare notes about how to bring the boy into male culture.

The mother gives the birth-father more custody time than she wanted to give before—the entrance in her life of a new man will go more smoothly if the boy spends more time with his own father. Exceptions to this exist in a minority of cases, in which the birth-father is dangerous or wants absolutely nothing to do with the son. The mother, when the son asks for it, lets the son go live with dad. As the boy moves toward puberty, she may need to offer it so the son will feel okay about asking. He may not ask on his own—until he really feels imprisoned and desperate—out of his loyalty to her.

If the father refuses to have anything to do with the son, then the mother, stepfather, and son get outside help to create a new attachment between the son and the stepfather. In some cases, the son will have already attached to another male, an elder brother, an uncle, or grandfather. In that case, the stepfather again steps out of the way.

The mother reassures the son whenever possible—not through material objects but other emotional channels that exist between her and her son—that he is irreplaceable in her life.

New bonds can form between boys and other men, but they will happen more slowly than mothers (and the men) often want. The adults' responsibility is to have few projected expectations on the boy.

If mothers expect sons to go along with what they want in their life with men, moms will, in the end, be worse off.

The divorced and single mothers and sons who are best able to navigate these waters are those women and boys who keep communicating, keep talking, keep family rituals strong, keep having dinner together, family time together, reading time together. For the boy who is living with mom and not with mom and dad together—whether because she was unwed from the beginning or because she and his father divorced—stability is diminished, and often feels lost altogether. The greatest gift his mom can give him is *her* stability.

For many boys raised by single moms, she is the only anchor. There is no father, there is no tribe. As the son reaches out to male culture through peer groups and other men, she can roll up her anchor a notch, then another, then another. As *he* pulls away, then she lets him go. But especially in the first months, even years, after a divorce, he'll be caught between clinging to her and being angry at her, whether he hides that anger or not. The more stable she is, the more he can learn to feel comfortable again and secure again in finding himself.

MOTHER-SON WOUNDS

Boys are more likely than girls to be physically abused by a parent. The parent most likely to physically abuse a boy is a mother. From government statistics to private studies, these two statements have been verified over and over again. Our culture has tended to avoid them, yet they make sense. A mother is home with the kids more, thus she's got more opportunity to abuse. Many single mothers, getting little support and faced with unruly boys, end up abusing out of sheer frustration.

Physical abuse is a clear statement of a "mother-son wound." By wound we mean an overwhelming negation of the boy's core self. Children are born to be loved for who they are. When a parent's discipline is not discipline of a boy's core self (who he is) but, rather, a parent's way of acting out—with the boy as object—the parents' own distress, the boy's core self is wounded. The boy comes to feel that he is an object of the parent's distress. He is not, intrinsically, a worthy and separate self.

This kind of wounding happens most often in the first decade of a boy's life, especially the first few years of life. The less a boy feels loved during his most formative years, the more that self is abused and learns to hide or is, in extreme cases, obliterated, the more he will act out in adolescence and adulthood.

While overt abuse and neglect in the mother-son relationship are statistically increasing each decade, a hidden wounding process can be equally dangerous. We need to be honest about it. In fact, I am finding more and more mothers acknowledging it in workshops and seminars. It has to do with boundaries between mothers and sons.

The clinical term for "boundary problems" is *impingement*. It occurs especially between mothers and sons because mothers are generally a boy's primary caregiver—there's more likelihood of emotional violation there. Impingement is the process by which a boy learns that without his attentions—and a specific *kind* of attention a mother indicates she wants—the mother's self-image will not flourish. Thus, a boy may learn to put aside the development of his core self and instead focus a lion's share of his emotional energy on taking care of mom. He learns not to be himself when it will get in the way of what mom needs him to be. Often, mom is married to someone (or divorced from someone) who does not meet her needs or expectations; the son becomes her surrogate male companion, developing an emotional structure—a false self—that she seems to need. Common sense tells us that children are put on this earth to be taken care of by parents and not vice versa—at least until the children are adults. But many of us force our children to take care of our emotional needs and thus wound them terribly.

The son of this kind of mother-son relationship will later take a false self into adult relationships with women. The women will complain that he isn't truthful with them, honest, fully capable of loving them. What often happens is that a man is loving a partner through a false self. He doesn't really know who he is and certainly can't devote his core self to a partner in that ignorance. Many women have also been forced to create false selves to please and take care of dad. So many women and men marry in our culture with these false selves at the altar.

It's important that mothers pay close attention to impingement. A family system that puts the majority of the child-rearing responsibilities on a mother puts her at increased risk. When you add in the epidemic of absent fathers and broken mother-mate love relationships, and the fact that mothers often do not feel valued as women and therefore turn to sons to find self-value, the risks of impingement increase again. Mothers are generally unmalicious and unconscious of doing it, but more and more boys are wounded.

Wounds of abuse, neglect, emotional abandonment, and impingement often begin in infancy, with a lack of adequate mother-son attachment and continue through the first decade of life. Physical abuse of boys tends to end as more independence comes at around puberty. Boys become bigger, stronger, more free, more able to fight back or turn away from an alcoholic, abusive, abandoning mom. Boys tend to have enough ego-strength to find peer groups and other parental figures. Dads often get custody of boys as they get older, releasing the boy, physically speaking, from the wounding mother.

Unlike overt abuse, however, impingement often becomes more subtle and ingrained as the boy becomes an adolescent, in the second decade of life. Instead of calling it impingement, it might get called other things, like "enmeshment" or "entanglement."

What Boys Need From Mom in the Second Decade of Life

The boy who shared this dream with me was going to be twelve in four days. He and his parents had been consciously discussing the process of manhood because the boy, Jared, was in bar mitzvah classes. His mother is not Jewish but his father is, and before the couple had children they had decided to raise the kids as Jews. The boy was being tutored by a conservative rabbi. His father said, "In many ways my bar mitzvah was the most significant event in my life. The four years I spent preparing to lead my bar mitzvah service gave me a spiritual base for the rest of my life. I wanted my son to have that too." Jared and his parents live in a small town fifty-eight miles from the nearest synagogue. For Jared to go through the bar mitzvah process, one of his parents had to drive him to the synagogue two nights a week and once on the weekend, sometimes in dangerous winter conditions, for years. This huge family effort gave Jared an even greater sense of the importance of his conscious, community-supported journey to manhood than perhaps other boys would receive. In the midst of this family effort he dreamt this:

I was in London and I got thrown into a dungeon jail there like the one at the Tower of London [the family had visited England the summer before]. *Mom was the guard of my jail. She looked like mom except that she had short hair. It was boring and I felt stuck being in the cell. Every night, all my life, I would try to get out of my cell and get the key to the big outside door and run away, but I never could get through the bars of my cell to get to the key that hung on the wall. Mom marched back and forth and just watched and kept an eye on the people in jail.*

Then I grew into an old man and I died in that cell, and after I died nobody put me or anybody in my old cell because I was a legend because I tried to get out every day of my life. Because I was dead, I could just walk through the bars easily because I was a ghost and then I'd go to the key and take it. Then my mom, the guard, would see the key was missing and that I had it. Then I would run down the hall a while and up a flight of stairs, and then I would always get to the door leaving the jail, and I would know it because it would be all light at the end of the stairs even though it was at night.

There would still be daylight right out the door but no matter what, every night, I would get caught by mom. I'd sometimes be really far ahead of her and sometimes I'd be right next to her and she'd be right at my back, but she would catch me at the door every time.

One night I was running and I got up to the door and I couldn't even see her because I was so far ahead and she had tripped, and I dashed ahead of her, and I got to the door and she wasn't anywhere near me. I felt scared that mom was hurt but happy that I got out.

I heard her yelling, "Stop, Stop, Stop!" She had never said that before on any of the other chases, and I heard her yelling Stop and it was echoing through the halls. When I got out of the door I went two steps out and I waited because I guess I was worried about her because I felt scared that mom was hurt and I watched for her and she kept yelling, "Stop. Stop."

Then I decided that I wanted to wake up. I woke up and I was half asleep and half awake, and I kept hearing the "Stop. Stop" with mom and then I realized that after waking up it was really Josh [his younger brother] *breathing and his breathing just sounded like mom yelling Stop.*

Dreams of this sort are common among prepubescent and pubescent girls and boys, for both sense that their parents imprison them somewhat. In the early years of their life's second decade, they realize they must get out of the prison if they are to find themselves. The need for a boy to separate psychologically from mom is acute and shows up, by developmental instinct, at somewhere near the end of the first decade of a boy's life and around the beginning of the second. It has been this way all over the world for millennia. To become a man, the boy must rely on himself, must model more after male models now than mom, and must prove himself to belong in the world of men.

When a boy separates psychologically from mom he is moving from *dependence* on mother in his early years to emotional *independence* during adolescence and early adulthood to emotional *interdependence* when and if he couples with a mate. If a boy doesn't separate from his mother, he will never achieve the independence necessary to discover his own psychological boundaries. Thus, he will never achieve true interdependence with a mate.

Jenny, forty-six, the mother of two sons, fourteen and sixteen, and a therapist, knew this and described her second son's recent feelings around her:

"He's a chiphead [a computer enthusiast]. His separation-individuation has begun to show up in regards to his computer work. One week he'll be mad that I say, 'Hey, I'm glad you enjoy all that computer stuff, but I don't get it.' I mean, he'll be really mad at me. He wants me to get it. That's one week. Then the next week he's glad I don't get it, glad I don't look over his shoulder, glad I'm not in that very important part of his life. He gets mad when I do try to get it, like I'm an invasion.

"I pointed this out to him, I said, 'You need me but you hate me because you need me.' He said, 'Yeah, Mom, that's it,' like a lightbulb went on for him. He and his older brother and their father and I talk about his feelings, their feelings, as they grow up and away from me. It's very liberating for all of us."

The love a mother and son have for each other must change as the boy becomes a man. That is a commonsense given. The mother must let him go into the world of men. What she may not realize is that she doesn't only do this for him but for herself. If she can't let go of her son, she won't make her own passage into the next stage of her life. She'll continue to live through her child, not herself. And she needs profound help from the men in the boy's life. If they don't help, it is most likely she will hang onto her son in myriad ways, and her son will grow into adulthood feeling, as does the son in the Grimm's fairy tale, "The Shroud," feeling trapped in a world not his own.

In "The Shroud," as in many tales of world mythology, separation-individuation of a loved one from another is symbolized by the death of the loved one. In "The Shroud," the boy's separation from the mother is represented by the boy's death. The story goes like this.

Once upon a time there was a boy and a mother (no father is ever mentioned) who were incredibly close. In fact, the story says, the mother worshipped the boy above everything else in the world. The boy died and the mother wept and wept. Her grief became a terrible and ongoing depression. No one could console her. One night, long after the mother had buried the boy, the boy began to appear in places where the mother and boy had played and spent time together. As the mother wept, the boy mirrored her tears, weeping. When morning came, he always disappeared.

This went on for some time. The mother's depression continued. One night, dressed in a white shroud and wearing a wreath of flowers around his head, the boy stood at the foot of his mother's bed.

He said, "Oh mother, please stop crying, or I shall never fall asleep in my coffin, for my shroud will not dry because of all your tears which fall upon it."

The mother had been able to figure the boy's many appearances as her own delusions. But when the boy actually talked, she was shocked. And when she realized she was preventing the boy's journey to heaven, her depression lifted. Her tears dried up.

The next night the boy appeared again. "Look," he said to her, "look how my shroud is nearly dry now. I can continue my journey."

And the mother said goodbye to her son. And the son made his way onward.

The lack of elder male presence in the story is painfully telling. This mother is not supported by the men around her. She has no one else but this boy to give her sustenance, no one else to help her work through her grief and let go of the boy. Her courage in letting go of him alone, without help, has to be honored. It is very difficult for a mother to let go of a son, work through her grief at his passage, lose the only male who may be emotionally fulfilling and for whom she may be living—and do all this without help.

SUPPORTING MOTHER-SON SEPARATION

Sometimes male culture can try to yank sons away from moms so far the sons forget to respect mom and women. Or sometimes moms try to keep sons from separating, and make the rest of the boy's life a kind of emotional spider's web in which he feels as if he is always emotional prey, and cannot find his way out of her world and into his own. Sometimes there is so little supportive male culture around a mom, especially a single mom, there's nowhere healthy for the boy to go. Sometimes sons, as they separate from mom, do it by abusing her, physically or, more commonly, with words.

I witnessed this first-hand one Saturday during my family's ritual grocery shopping. In public, and seemingly without shame, a young teen male yelled at his mom: "You're a bitch, you're a waste. I wish you were dead!" The mother asked him to apologize. He retreated into silence. They moved on. Indeed, their situation is very common. One of the most frequent comments I hear when I do radio talk shows is from moms: "My sons are getting to an age where they've decided I'm the root of all evil. They abuse me. They degrade me. I can't seem to do anything about it."

The boy's need to pull away from mom, to escape his attraction and servitude to her, gets acted out too often in our culture by uncontrolled boys in rude, even violent ways.

Moms often tell me it helps them, during the separation process, to focus on their specific feelings, especially the deeply hidden ones—to bring them to the surface and talk to others about them, and have others help them deal with the feelings. Three of these are guilt, fear, and abandonment.

1. Guilt. A mother often thinks, quite subconsciously, that she must keep doing more and more for her son. She thinks if she doesn't, she's a bad mother.

2. Fear. Mothers often want to protect their sons from the sufferings of the world in general, and especially manhood in particular.

3. Abandonment. In many ways, without either mother or son realizing it, they have become an intimate couple. Many mothers, especially wives of emotionally distant husbands, experience letting go of the son as the destruction of their only love relationship with a giving, loving male.

Just as it helps mothers to be conscious of the hidden feelings and have others to talk with about them, it can also help the son.

1. Guilt. Guilt for pulling away from the woman who has meant more to him than anyone. He knows he's hurting her by leaving. If she uses passive-aggressive behavior or other ways to show him how much he's hurting her, he'll feel even more guilt.

2. Anger (sometimes Rage). Anger at himself because he can't let go of dependence on mom; anger at mom because she can't teach him manhood; anger at mom because she won't let him go easily; anger at fathers and other men who, so often, do less than they can to help boys separate from mom and find manhood.

3. Fear. Fear of leaving the safety of mom's psychological umbilical cord. Who else will he ever be able to trust like he trusted mom? A boy's fear of leaving her safe world often keeps him dependent on her long after she's dead.

All over the world, cultures ritualize a young man's psychological separation from his mother. We'll focus on how we can do this in Chapter 6. How does our culture help mothers move on to the next part of their lives? How do we help sons gracefully mature beyond psychological dependence on mom?

Unfortunately, our society doesn't support a boy's adolescence very well at all. We teach mothers that to let go of sons is to be a bad mom; we teach boys to separate by beating up other boys, doing drugs, joining gangs, becoming addicted to media imagery, or becoming, like the boy in the grocery store, a mom-hater. We assume all teenagers will separate from parents by rebelling, so we just go ahead and toss them toward adulthood as if, when they hit puberty, they didn't need us anymore.

If a mother is having trouble with a son during his second decade of life, it's often because of emotional entanglements and unconscious patterns that have their source in mother-son confusion about how he should separate emotionally. Counseling can be a great help in these cases. Centuries ago, when moms had a tribe, they could turn to grandparents, uncles, aunts, and others in the neighborhood when they needed help or advice. Counselors now fulfill many of these functions. A mother will know she has let go of her son when she sees that he can now become her emotional peer, as emotionally powerful and competent as she is.

MOTHER-SON ENTANGLEMENTS

"My mother and I were always so close," said Jake, a man I saw in therapy. "Throughout my life she was unsure of my father's love for her. I was her favorite son. I remember one time when I was about fourteen she started to cry, and she said, 'How am I ever going to live without you?' I felt so sorry for her, so sad. When I was eighteen I met my first wife, Laurie. My mother immediately liked her, she and mom become great friends. I got married and mom and dad stayed together. When our kids were six and eight, Laurie and I divorced. I've been in three major relationships since. I've learned that I get into relationships with a lot of love for the woman, but then after maybe a year or so I resent the woman, I become distant, she resents that I can't open up, this goes on desperately for a couple years, then we break up.

"I took your suggestion to ask my mother to honestly describe our relationship when I was a boy. She said, 'You were the perfect boy, always there for me, you'd do anything for me.' What about when I was a teenager? I asked. 'Oh you were never one of those kids to rebel and hurt me,' she said. 'You were my little man.'

"To this day, I still don't have the heart to tell her I had become her little man but never became my own."

For the same personal and cultural reasons that impingement is so prevalent between mothers and sons, mother-son entanglement is prevalent among many adolescent boys and mothers, only to be transferred onto lovers and wives by those boys when they become men. In studies done throughout the 1980s, American men reported that their mother and father were in marital distress during crucial times in the man's boyhood. Both fathers and mothers turn to children to fulfill their needs when they don't believe their spouse is doing so. Statistically, it is more likely that a mother and son will become "entangled" or "enmeshed" than a father and son because the father is away from the son's life more, and tends to be the more independent parent. If anything, fathers tend to become more enmeshed with daughters, asking one favorite girl to be a kind of surrogate emotional mate. Some mothers tend to do this with sons. In emotionally unhealthy circumstances mothers form a lover relationship with an adolescent son. Some psychologists call this "emotional incest."

Jake was unable to attach completely to his wives and lovers in large part because when he was growing up he became his mother's emotional lover. His self and his mother's became entangled, like branches from separate trees that grow together and no wind can pull apart. Our culture has set up a family situation in which tribe is pretty much unavailable. Because fathers have to be gone so much, we've set up a situation whereby mothers will enmesh and entangle their sons in inappropriate relationships. Often mothers and sons will align themselves against a father. Often mothers and sons will align themselves against the whole world.

The message mothers need to give their sons as they go through adolescence is, "Every day, you need me less and less, both physically and emotionally, and I need you less and less. And that's okay." Instead, the message moms often give is, "I need you, don't go." Mothers don't realize that this adolescent entanglement will make it so difficult for the boy, once a man, to feel himself as real, whole, empowered, and capable of true commitment to mates. In *Mothers, Sons and Lovers* I estimated that most American men carry some unresolved issues with their mothers to their marriages. I indicated that these issues—in tandem with womens' unresolved issues with their fathers—are predominant factors in the high divorce rate. I've learned nothing in the last few years to negate these statements. In fact, my intensified work with boys has shown me that the mother-son relationship is only getting more and more difficult and more and more dangerous with each generation. Given the isolated, tremulous family systems in which we raise kids, this is unavoidable. Until we build a strong three-family system, I believe we'll see a lot of troublesome mother-son relationships continue through the generations.

Tim's mother and father divorced when he was eighteen, but their marriage began disassembling when he was about ten. Tim came to me during his divorce process from his wife of eight years. Two previous counselors had said, "Your biggest internal work right now should be about your anger, especially at women and your mom."

"I'm not angry," he said, "especially not at mom."

As we worked together we discovered what we so often discover with sons of troubled marriages. Tim had aligned with his mother very early in his life. As her marriage was dissolving, he aligned with her even more. She had controlled this alignment, unconsciously for the most part, asking him to be her companion against father. Tim and his father became increasingly estranged, something for which he would later be enraged at his mother. Again unconsciously, Tim's mother taught him to repress his anger. She did this perhaps because she was afraid of his anger, as many mothers are (see Chapter 7), but she did it for another reason, too: she did not want her son being angry at *her*.

Tim did not learn until well into his forties that he carried an incredible rage toward women that was based in anger at his own mother for turning him against his father, and therefore against manhood, masculinity and, in the end, Tim's own manhood. This was not the only reason he had marital troubles, but it was a major factor. As Tim worked with this information, he changed his life and the way he related to women. He demystified his mother, got closer to his father, was angry at his mother for a while but then forgave her, and learned to see that he could be whole without getting in push-pull relationships with women.

Does Motherhood Ever End?

M. S., a mother of an especially difficult teenage son, wrote a long and moving letter to my newspaper column about the efforts she, her husband, her family, and counselors had made on his behalf. In describing her efforts, she speaks for so many mothers:

"I gave my son freedom to make his own choices. I encouraged him to be accepting of all people—both my sons can cook and know how to do laundry. I've tried to teach all my kids to be independent—I wasn't the kind of mom that did everything for my kids. I feel I've been a good mom, much better than I ever knew. My son has problems, but I did the best job I knew how."

There is so much wisdom in being able to say, even in the presence of a difficult or dangerous son, "I did my best." One mother, E. B., asked at a workshop: "When do you know you can let go? I made a lot of mistakes as a mother. My son is in his forties and I still blame myself for his troubles. I've tried everything to reach him."

Mothers need more honoring than we often give them. Hopefully, all of us can join them more than we have in raising their sons so that E. B. and every mother knows that once her son has become an adult male she can say to him, without guilt:

"I did my best for you, son.

"I did many things imperfectly, and you will have to confront their results in yourself throughout your life.

"That is part of your job now, not mine.

"I will always love you though.

"I will always wish you well."

chapter 5

From Daddy to Dad: The Father-Son Relationship

The father must live a vision he himself has searched through and accepted from a position of spiritual freedom so that his son can find that freedom as well.

—Loren Pederson

Richard Louv, author of *FatherLove,* once wrote: "The degree to which fatherhood is valued by our culture depends fundamentally on the stories men tell each other about fathering, and on the stories we tell our children." One of the most beautiful reflections of this philosophy is the classic American novel of a father and son, *The Day No Pigs Would Die,* by Robert Peck. In it, young Rob asks his father about fences:

"Lots of times," says his father, "when you hear that old robin sing, what he's singing about is . . . keep off my tree. That whistle you hear is his fence. Ever see a fox?"

"Sure, lot's of times."

"I mean really watch him. He walks around his land every day and wets on a tree here and on a rock there. That's his fence . . . all living things put up a fence, one way or another. Like a tree do with its roots."

"Then it isn't like war."

"[Our neighbor] Benjamin Franklin Tanner would want a fence to divide his and mine, same as I do. He knows this. A fence sets men together, not apart."

So often boys come to fathers for simple wisdom like this. As I've traveled the country working with fathers and sons, I've seen the hunger on the faces of the boys and the men to find a father-son relationship in which love and wisdom can be imparted and received in a way that Peck lays out in his novel. Sometimes I think of the simplicity in Peck's novel as a kind of eulogy for the close father-son relationship. The father-son relationship has changed so drastically in a few decades.

In Part III of this book, we'll focus on issues of how to discipline boys, teach them values, talk to them about sex, love and commitment, help them find an important role, give them a spiritual journey. In this chapter, these practicalities will come to play, but let's focus here on defining not the behavioral practicalities of the father-son relationship but the redefinition of that relationship.

Among all his other ways of nurturing a son, a father raises his son in the father's shadow, a shadow both dark and beautiful, in which the son will learn essential lessons about how to live, first as a boy, then as a man. Whether he is teaching a son commandments for living, or why fences must be built, or what it means to have a sacred mission, the father blesses the son with a man's power to shape both his inner and outer world as a male.

Fathers have done this for millennia and even though men's roles are changing in many ways at the end of this century, a father's responsibility to mold and shape his son has not changed. There are many reasons so many fathers are not fulfilling this responsibility in late-twentieth-century America: their own confusion about roles, some women's antagonism toward them as fathers, their own lack of training as fathers—reasons that are reported, daily, throughout our media. In a way, our cultural confusion about fathering is not without history.

Throughout human history—in fact, throughout the history of most species on earth—one of the great impulses of socialization is to teach males to remain constantly and intensely active in their children's lives. Whether four million years ago, when our ancestors were first learning to stand upright, or four days ago when yet a man down the street left his kids and never looked back, fathers have often been absent from their childrens' lives.

Frequently I go to conferences and listen to speakers decry the absent father as somehow a new phenomenon. Though their recriminations against absent or emotionally distant fathers are generally meant to help society, at the same time they are built on a lie that evolution disproves generation after generation. Fathers have often gone to war, or the long hunt on the savannah, or to work in another village or city. But only in the last decade or so have manhood and fathering been trashed completely. This kind of blaming, that isolates one parent, is a convenient way of denying systemic social responsibility. One way we've done this in the popular media is to call fathers who don't pay child support "deadbeats," and pretend we can solve this problem through government intervention. We neglect to look at why the men aren't paying. Many aren't paying because they are irresponsible. Others aren't paying, however, because they've been refused joint custody by the courts and by ex-wives who, in anger at ex-husbands, turn children against them. They are being asked to gut their financial resources in order to take care of children that some of them didn't want, some of them didn't know they even had, some of them have little access to, some of them don't know, and some of them won't be allowed to know. As with all things regarding the family these days, everyone's got a simplistic political solution to a problem that can't be solved through policies that emerge from parent bashing.

Of Princes and Kings

In my book *The Prince and the King: Healing the Father-Son Wound,* I traced throughout mythological history the metaphor of the father who is king to his son, the son who is prince to his father. That metaphor is beautifully played out in the mythology of the 1990s by the Walt Disney movie *The Lion King,* in which Mufasa, the lion king, is responsible for the spiritual and social nurturance of his whole domain. As sacred king he is beloved not because he is an ego leader but because he is a servant of the people, a spiritual mirror of their ambitions and needs. When he has a son, Simba, he tells Simba that it will become Simba's job to be the lion king one day. "All that you see is in the great circle of life. One day you will be its king. One day you will be responsible for that circle." He gives his son a sacred mission. Simba goes through many trials, including the belief that he has killed his own father, but one day does become king.

In this metaphor of princes and kings every father and son can find an emblem of their efforts with each other, for every son wants from his father to gain a sense of mission in life and receive permission from an elder male to pursue the mission; to feel a strong, loving masculine ground beneath his feet so that he will not, once he's an adult, have to say to his wife, his children, or to strangers, "I don't know what a man is, please teach me"; to be challenged toward a vision of faraway stars—impractical dreams and ambitions, that he may make, one day, possible; to learn what part of the sacred circle of human and spiritual life he will be responsible for; and to be mirrored by an intimate elder male and found, in that mirroring, to be a loving, wise, and powerful man.

When fathers were inevitably gone in the past, male mentors from the tribe—grandfathers, uncles, elder brothers, nonblood uncles, other teachers—filled in. They were the king, or the magicians and mentors who supported the king. In the story of Mufasa and Simba, the shamanic monkey plays this role, redirecting Simba back toward his destiny as lion king after his father is long dead.

In the mythology of princes and kings, which we find in cultures all over the world, the king is always part of a male kinship system that sustains him, his family, his sacred duty, and his children. One well-known version of that system comes to us from warrior-based cultures, in which that system's prime directives were to protect families and communities against enemies, and train sons in how to do battle toward that end. This warrior culture is merely an extension of masculine culture, not vice versa, as some people like to argue. Warriors and soldiers grew out of male kinship hunt systems when population began to grow to such an extent that resources got scarce and males were required to fight each other in protection of those resources.

An evolutionary view of the father-son relationship reveals that the key problem in our age is *not* that once upon a time individual fathers were deeply intimate with sons and now they are not. It is better summed up: once upon a time men in general were intimate with boys through male kinship systems involving fathers, uncles, grandfathers, and mentors; now those systems are pretty much broken down, leaving dad to be the only king a son has, but forced to work most of the time, often at a job that makes him feel more like a mule than a king. So, without a proud, nurturing male kinship system to help him raise his son, his son may never get fully raised.

So a first precept for me in working with families and fathers is to see in what kind of male kinship system the father has been trained. What did his dad, his male relatives, his other mentors teach him? I try to help him discover the best principles of that system and release the worst so he can absorb from the old and painstakingly create a new male kinship system when he has kids. In helping with this I am not absolving him of any individual responsibility for his children. Quite the contrary. I am asking him to become better for his wife and kids by gaining support for himself as a man. This is even more important now than ever before because, given the breakdown of extended family and male kinship systems, fathers have the primary male responsibility for raising children. If they are not well supported, they're pretty much sunk.

The mother and wife's role in a man's search for his own support system is crucial. As he seeks time away from her to bond with other males, her jealousies can kill a marriage and damage the children. When the tables are turned, his jealousies can do the same. Yet both mothers and fathers must seek their own support systems, and both must let the other go. When they were first married, perhaps their romance was enough to sustain them in an almost myopic love of each other. But once the kids come, the good of the children must replace much of that ecstatic myopia. That usually means the parents remain loving with each other and work together, but also find more detachment from each other and more attachment to their own same-sex communities and communal systems.

Women are often surprised to hear that most men do not feel supported as men and that this lack of support is one reason they so often don't measure up as fathers. Often it seems to women that male-kinship systems—"old boy networks"—are working quite well these days, thank you. Often women will say, "What do the men have to worry about—we women are the ones in trouble!"

These statements, politically charged, are one-sided, jingoistic, and not, in their polarity, supported by facts. For most men, struggling to make a living, satisfy wives and children, and reach their dreams, there is very little support. The old boy networks do some good for a few men but not most. Charities and government agencies serve mainly the needs of women—85 percent of the homeless, for instance, are male, not female; women are cared for by social services far more readily than men. Even the health-care system—despite some instances where more research is done on men than women—serves women at two times the rate it serves men. Most of the drug addicted are male. Most criminals are male. These princes and would-be kings have had little male support during their lifetimes. If we want fathers to be better fathers, we will certainly have to learn the real pressures and pains that fathers face daily.

The Father a Boy Needs

A recent *Newsweek* carried the face of a black boy about seven and the headline "A World Without Fathers." More than half our black males are raised without fathers. A large percentage of these males become at risk in adolescence. More and more white males are being raised similarly, without fathers and thus at risk of undisciplined behavior, unclear responsibilities, antisocial behavior, and an inability to attach completely to adult women, thus continuing the cycle of divorce.

Pete du Pont, former governor of Delaware, now policy chairman of the National Center for Policy Analysis, reported this in a recent editorial: "Four out of every ten children in America will go to bed tonight in a home where their father doesn't live. By the end of the decade it may be six out of ten. . . . Sixty percent of rapists, seventy-two percent of adolescent murderers, and seventy percent of all long-term prison inmates are boys who grew up without their fathers in the home."

Crime statistics are only a very dramatic way of pointing out the commonsense idea that if dad's not around, the son has a greater chance of acting out against society. Society's values need to be carried to the son, like a torch between runners, from dad. Mom is often just not enough. Yet more and more fathers, feeling betrayed by women who have left them, feeling confused by unspoken expectations of them as men, feeling incapacitated by court-mandated agreements, feeling like failures as fathers and men—are physically, emotionally, and spiritually abandoning their sons. When a man feels that he has failed, he is very likely to try to cut himself off from his past and start again.

WHY FATHERS DISAPPEAR

Two social phenomena—illegitimate births and divorce—have increased our chances of men leaving children behind. In 1960 only 15
percent of teen births occurred out of wedlock. In 1991 69 percent did.
According to the National Fatherhood Initiative 30 percent of general
population births occur out of wedlock. There is no simple solution to
out-of-wedlock births, but if we sanction them as societies and communities, we must be ready for the fathers, many of whom don't want
the partner to have the children and many of whom don't know till
years later they're fathers, to walk away. From the father's point of
view, society values the needs of the mother more than the needs of
the father. He has little incentive, outside of some profound social
contract like marriage, to acquiesce to what, from his point of view,
are unbalanced priorities. One eighteen-year-old father put it to me
this way: "I wanted an abortion. She didn't. Now I have to pay the
rest of my life because what she wants is more important. Why should
I pay? Let *her* pay."

My counseling with this man was to try to bring him closer to his
child. Yet it's hard to argue with his point of view. In most states, his
former girlfriend is legally in control of her body and the fetus, but
the byproduct is that she is legally in control of her former boyfriend's
future too. As long as this is the system men face, there will be billions
in child support still owed. No amount of wage-garnishing and
"tracking deadbeat dads" will solve the problem. Many of the fathers
vilified for not taking care of their children have not considered themselves fathers. Society has told them they are.

Divorce is the second social phenomenon that increases the chances
of men not taking care of their children. Most research, like Judith
Wallenstein's twenty-four-year study, indicate the destructive effects
on children of divorce. "[In our study of children of divorce] we didn't
see a single child who was well adjusted," says Wallenstein. "And we
didn't see a single child to whom divorce was not the central event of
their lives." Despite these studies, the divorce rate is 1 out of 2. When
men are forced by their wife to disengage emotionally from her or
when men choose to do so of their own initiative, their chances of
leaving the children behind increase significantly, especially when the

men have been pegged by themselves or their partners as simply breadwinners, and especially when the men have not bonded and attached to the younger children to the same degree their wives have. To expect otherwise goes against not only the human biology but also common sense. The men have not been around to bond as much with the child. This has been the way it is for millions of years. It is still this way (with, obviously, some notable exceptions). Our profound difference from our ancestors' societies is that now if a man leaves his children, there are not usually other men from the family or community to stand in his place.

As much as we must rebuild male kinship systems into places of spiritual and emotional support, we must also do what every culture has done for millennia: train fathers to raise their kids. As we do this, we will have to change the way we train our young girls too—they'll have to understand that they'll suffer if they bear children too early. And we have to make it harder to divorce.

THE HEALTHY FATHER

What is a father? How can we be better fathers? How can we be "healthy fathers?" Here are my answers to these questions. They are not the end but the beginning of a list of qualities and circumstances.

▼ The father must make a conscious decision to be a father. Women who talk men into having children before they are ready, and men who let themselves get talked into it, may doom their children to terrible distress later. When a man is not ready for kids and his wife is, the two of them need to get into counseling. How can a man be a healthy father if he doesn't want children? How can we expect him to be?

▼ The father must begin fathering during his wife's pregnancy and very early in the child's infancy. In the next section we'll look at that specifically.

▼ The father must be self-aware. We'll also look at that idea in a later section. How can a man raise a son, who is striving toward self-awareness, if he the father is closed-down, unaware, unable to change and grow?

▼ The father must be comfortable with his body, his gender, his sexuality, his sensual apprehension of nature and the world around him. He must know how to flourish in himself physically so that he can help his very physically oriented son to flourish as well. He must talk to the son about sex, nature, biology, gender, and he must listen.

▼   The father must learn how to communicate with the boy he is raising. That boy will be like other boys, but very individual too. The father will have to learn new skills to keep up with his son's growth.

▼   The father must not only let the son find other mentors but must consciously help him do so, as we'll explore more fully in Chapter 6. Throughout human history, fathers have found mentors for their sons, mentors who could train the boys in skills the father did not possess, mentors to whom the son could turn when he needed to learn more about certain aspects of the male mode of feeling the father just didn't have the ability to teach.

▼   The father must let go of the son yet still remain a model. He must live a vision he himself has searched through and accepted from a position of spiritual freedom so that his son can find that freedom as well.

These are some key principles to fatherhood. When the energy of fatherhood does not revolve around them, fathers and sons become isolated, emotionally and often physically, from each other.

Let's explore some of these principles more deeply.

FATHERS AND INFANTS

In a social system in which male kinship systems around child-rearing are basically dead, a father's isolation from his children often begins very early, at their birth. This is not just about our fathers being restricted from birthing rooms in the 1950s. In many tribal cultures fathers are not present at births, yet still they bond and take their son into their kinship system. The lack of bonding between a father and infant these days is more about a whole society's confusion around the father's role. I found a metaphor for this confusion just recently.

As I write this, Christmas is over for another year. Tinsel hangs over the edges of garbage cans. My family's Christmas tree is down, yet I'm struck this year by something that's always missing in the annual retelling of the story of Jesus—something about fathers and infants.

I miss a deep sense of Jesus' mortal father, Joseph. I know from biblical culture a lot about how Mary bonded with her son. I don't know much about how Joseph bonded with his. I know that theologically the writers of the New Testament needed to put Joseph in the background because they wanted us to focus on the story of Jesus as God's Son, not Joseph's son. But for me right now this is feeling a lot like a metaphor of what's happening between fathers and infants. The father feels relegated to the background from very early on. I wonder, how did Joseph feel when he saw that baby being born? What did he, as a man, experience during the first few months of Jesus' life? Does his experience, like so much else in the Jesus story, hold wisdom for us?

"Once he can talk," one young father said to me about his infant son, "I'll be able to relate to him better. Until then, I'm sure my wife doesn't mind me staying out of the way." This is one thing fathers do and wives support without realizing fully what's going on. Studies show that a child recognizes his father's voice consistently after fourteen days. That child knows his father. The child is ready to bond. It is normal for a mother to do more child care than the father, but for the father to "stay out of the way" too much is to risk not fully bonding. If he doesn't fully bond, he will be more likely to abandon the child later in life.

When a father gets shut out, he not only loses his connection with the child. His distance from the child can affect the whole marriage. Studies show that men who do not attach well to their child have greater marital difficulties with their wives. Divorce is one of the most devastating traumas to a child's growth. Many divorces begin at the birth of children.

Fathers often feel surprised by or ashamed of their feelings of resentment at wives as, during pregnancy and in the first months of a child's life, she turns inward, away from her husband. Her behavior is her natural adjustment to the radical changes in her body and life. Men must communicate feelings about this without relying on her to "fix" things. A wife's pregnancy is a good time to call on support networks of other men for compassion and companionship. Men need to find or start support groups for themselves at this time of life. These groups can become like second family.

Many issues about how a man's mother and father treated him will come up as he moves through a wife's pregnancy and the child's birth. It is essential that men get counseling as needed. The counselor can become like a third or second family. If a new father does not use this opportunity to cleanse the painful memories and patterns, destructive behavior from his own family of origin will replay on his kids.

As new fathers, men are often challenged to accept feelings of inadequacy as their infant children want mom more during times of crisis, sickness, or sadness. Studies show that kids rely on dads for play and discipline more than compassion and comfort. As men talk to other men about these feelings, they find out how normal they are and get support for what they're going through. They become better fathers by becoming closer to other men.

New fathers must read everything they can about the interpersonal world of children. From books like *The Earliest Relationship* by T. Berry Brazelton, *Babyhood* by Penelope Leach, and *The Amazing Newborn* by Klaus and Klaus, men who are usually untrained to understand infant children can learn more about children's cues. The vast majority of these books are bought by women. Men need to start buying and reading these books. As adults in general we make a mistake when we assume we'll "naturally know what's best for our child." Caring for a child, especially one between birth and three years old, is something we are probably least trained to do well—especially if we're male.

From books about newborns, fathers learn to "refuel" a child: to give the child an emotional recharge through a hug or pat. As the boy grows up, this concept of refueling will continue to work, with modification. Even a five- or seven- or ten-year-old who appears to be demanding huge amounts of time from a tired father is often just demanding five or ten minutes of a refueled father-son relationship. If the father, tired from work, spends just ten minutes with the boy, or a half hour, both will feel refueled. If, whether in the boy's infancy or later in life, the father doesn't spend the minimal amount of time with his child, he'll actually end up spending more than that amount of energy dealing with his son's anger, rejection, and abandonment throughout an evening, weekend, or lifetime.

By educating themselves in the intricacies of fathering, men learn to look infants in the eye and coo at them, for this is heaven to an infant. Fathers learn that men tend to wind infants up, women tend to calm them down and both styles are okay. An infant needs and wants both kinds of attention. When he gets overstimulated, he'll let dad know by turning his head away or crying. Fathers also learn that until the boy is about eighteen months his brain cannot really understand a parents' demands for rigid discipline. The little boy, until that age, needs to be spoiled with physical touch and pure emotional ardor.

Fathers of infants often work extra hard and worry more about money as a man's way of "attaching" to the newborn. Often fathers will feel that hard work is enough. It isn't. Unless the man has lots of hands-on contact with his child, he risks emotionally abandoning the very child he is overworking to nurture.

Joseph, I think, might envy the kind of closeness we fathers can have with our infants today. He might envy the fact that men can enjoy being more than the breadwinners, family photographers, and baby-sitters our own fathers often were. I think if he were with us today he would tell us to write ourselves into the family story with everything we do.

What Fathers Need

A boy needs a father who is confident as a man, feels that he belongs in the society around him, models male spiritual growth, and brings to the son's life a lot of healthy influences. How do men find communities of men in which to grow spiritually and socially and in which, therefore, to find their own healthy masculinity so that they can pass it on to sons? Some men look to the workplace for these things—a few find all they need there. Some look to church. Some look to bars, good times at sports events or in front of the TV. Some look to old male friends, old buddies.

Many men find some sustenance through these structures and people, yet few men feel comfortable talking about their deep spiritual life among these male friends. Few men in our culture really get to go through the spiritual challenges of exploring and constantly revising their own masculinity. Few men, therefore, make the kinds of emotional connections with other men that will sustain their deep growth and help them teach their kids how to be spiritually responsible adults, capable of sustaining the circle of life, capable of becoming the lion king, the man who respects all others, the confident fence-builder.

Yet men need this kind of friendship and support.

In the last decade or so, men's groups have begun all over North America to help men find male kinship systems. Here are some comments from men in groups.

Larry, thirty-six: "My men's group gives me a place to feel safe. There's nothing like expressing my feelings in the safety of other men who care. I don't know who I am sometimes until I do this."

Clayton, forty-one: "I learned what a man is in my group. My son is growing up knowing all these other men as my brothers and learning how to be a man through all of us."

Hank, forty-six: "My men's group saved me during my divorce."

Ruiz, twenty-nine: "I've tried lots of crazy things over the last few years, and some good ones, like ACOA [Adult Children of Alcoholics]. For me, my men's group is where all these things come together. It has changed me, my marriage, my whole life."

Bradley, fifty-one: "I served in the army and I work with mostly men. I have four brothers. But until I found a men's group that worked for me, I didn't really know how to get down into the guts of my own life as a man."

Some men have bad experiences in men's groups. That happens with anything. Many men have to try more than one group in order to find the place they really belong. Many men don't need groups because they have close families or other deeply spiritual male kinship systems through churches.

But many men, so many, have no place to go and, if they gave it a chance, would find a spiritual home in a men's group. I've led a lot of men's groups over the years—in churches, prisons, counseling agencies, men's homes. Men's groups are our culture's way of bringing men together to experience the depths of male experience. Every culture, including the cultures of our own ancestors, have found ways for men to do this—to find male community that is spiritually focused. Every culture has helped men to find a company of other men where the man can be self-aware.

Often men will say, "This all seems abstract to me." These men will talk about how they come together with men to work, play and watch sports, hunt, fish, and socialize at family occasions. Yet few of these encounters include the emotional safety to discuss a family problem, how it feels to grow old, fears about intimacy, joys about raising kids, doubts or revelations about spirituality, shame from childhood, or wartime wounds. Once a man admits this, he begins to find a group of some kind.

Every day, men get together with women, have sex with them, love them, raise children with them, work with them. Many men feel safe to discuss their emotional lives with women. Yet, still, there's a lot a woman can't understand about being a man. There's a lot a man can't say to a woman.

Often, men cause their own relationship problems by letting women be their only confidants, or, not knowing how to explain themselves to women, they don't look to other men for help. These men live in emotional isolation. Their sons feel that isolation.

Lately, our culture, afraid of male emotionality, has targeted men's groups for sarcastic jingoism. The media has presented them as frivolous exercises in drum beating and tribal imitation. Some women activists have overreacted and backlashed against them, calling them secret men's clubs. Some men, afraid of their own emotions, have laughed at the tears of men in men's groups. Nevertheless, this hasn't stopped men's groups from starting every day all around us.

Boys raised by men in men's groups see a tribe of men available to them. "My son," said one man, "thought I just went to some crazy men's club when he was seven. Now he's ten and he's becoming curious about what I do and where I go for my Monday night meetings. He wants to find out more. I've had the guys over for poker and he's sat with me, watched the men. He's not much of a talker—in that way he's like his dad—but he likes to talk to me about those guys, each of them. He has his opinions about each one. He likes such-and-such about so-and-so, but he doesn't like such-and-such about another guy. He's thinking, discerning, deciding what kind of man to be. If he didn't have these guys, he'd have no older male friends to really get to know. I don't really reach out well, especially to other men. I've been hurt by other men most of my life, starting with dad. So what's happening with Kelly is, he's getting something from the men in my group, an acceptance from older men, that I just never had."

SINGLE FATHERS

"It's incredible. It's painful. It's like being in heaven and hell at the same time."

"There's this perception out there men can't do it, but we're doing it all the time."

"If I hadn't raised my kids alone, I wouldn't have understood the world the way I do. No other thing in my life has changed me as much as raising my kids without their mom."

At a recent conference, the topic was single fatherhood. I listened as the men talked. Toward the end of the discussion, the question was asked, "What helps you the most?" One man seemed to speak for everyone:

"If it weren't for the support I got from family, friends, and my support group, I don't know what I'd have done."

Fifteen percent of single parents are fathers. That percentage is growing every month. Somewhere between 1 and 2 million American children are being raised by single dads at any given time.

Men face particular challenges as parents, especially single parents. Our bodies—lacking massive amounts of the hormone progesterone—don't set us up to bond in quite the same way a woman's body does. Our culture, too, follows this part of our biology in training us to let women do most of the touching, holding, cooing, and cuddling of young children.

As our children grow in our single-dad house, we realize just how untrained we really are. From not knowing how to change diapers to not knowing all the nursery rhymes, to feeling uncomfortable at PTA meetings, we feel ignorant, awkward.

In their desire to hurt or to help men, people around us say things like, "See, now you understand what women go through." Or, "You? A single father? That'll be the day."

If we're lucky, grandma and grandpa are around, or an aunt who can step in and help. If we're not, we find ourselves quickly looking around for a new mate to help us raise these kids. In this, studies show, we tend to be more rushed than women who become single moms—men remarry more quickly.

When the conference group was asked about remarrying, one man said, "I remarried a woman who was wrong for my kids. I divorced her. My biggest priority had to be my kids. We're happier without her." This man admitted to feeling lonely without a woman, but he also learned to redirect his energies toward other friendships in order to fill his need for adult companionship.

Like any parent, single fathers want the best for their kids. They face incredible adversity. They retrain themselves to be parents. They need our support. All of us can help single fathers by believing in them, helping them learn skills they were probably not trained for, treating them with respect. Single fathers are in the trenches of American social change. As they do some of the most important work a man can do, they are learning and teaching all of us new roles for men.

When a Father Gives His Son His Name

In *The Chosen,* Chaim Potok's classic novel of New York Jewish culture, the elder Reb Saunders talks about how he was raised:

"When I was very young, my father, may he rest in peace, began to wake me in the middle of the night, just so I would cry. I was a child, but he would wake me and tell me stories of the destruction of Jerusalem and the sufferings of the people of Israel, and I would cry. For years he did this . . . he never talked to me except when we studied together. He taught me with silence. He taught me to look into myself, to find my own strength, to walk around inside myself in company with my soul. When people would ask him why he was so silent with his son, he would say to them that he did not like to talk, words are cruel, words play tricks, they distort what is in the heart, they conceal the heart, the heart speaks through silence. One learns of the pain of others by suffering one's own pain, he would say, by turning inside oneself, by finding one's own soul. . . . Only slowly, very slowly, did I begin to understand what he was saying."

This father took the risk of deciding his son's destiny. This risk was supported in the Orthodox and Hasidic Jewish community. Once the father took the risk, he became responsible for his son's development of compassion, wisdom, and responsibility. Every father is responsible for these things, yet if a father does not take the risk of naming the son's destiny, he often neglects to nurture the son's development.

Most of us are not Hasidim. We do not name our son's destiny—we do not say, "You are a Gurian, my son, therefore you will go into my business, become like me." We say to our sons, "Find your own way, I wish you well." That is a father-son philosophy that serves our American culture of individualism. Yet we have abused it. In holding to it and not taking the risk of naming our son's destiny, we have neglected his development.

Every father must find a way to do what Reb Saunders's father did—teach the boy compassion, wisdom, and responsibility by perceiving the way the son needs to learn it. In that way each father does name a son's emotional destiny. A father who does not take the risk of naming the son's emotional destiny during the son's years between five and fifteen has neglected his paternal responsibilities.

What do we mean by "emotional destiny?" We mean that the father more than the mother is able to identify with the boy's emotional world because he is male like the boy. He must see—with the mother's help—the emotional challenges this boy faces. For some boys the locus of emotional challenge is a sense of isolation, for others a lack of compassion, for others a fear of community, for others an obsession with taking care of people at his own emotional expense—for all boys, perhaps, a combination of all these and more. The father must recall his boyhood and see what parts of it apply to the boy. He must find structures, disciplines, rituals—whether in martial arts, sports, religious traditions, waking the child up every night, taking him to homeless shelters, taking him hunting—through which to teach the boy the spiritual discipline of his own emotions.

In the recent film *Legends of the Fall,* Isabel says about her young nephew, "He comes from a proud name—I'm sure he'll live up to it." She is saying about the boy, "His father's name, Ludlow, has great value. Inherent in it is a long lineage of honor, responsibility, compassion, wisdom." Assumed in her comment but not spoken aloud, is her belief that Tristan, the boy's father, the one who bestowed the Ludlow name on him, will train him up to do the name proud. This is what Reb Saunders's father was doing. This is what every father must do.

Every son wants to live up to his father's name—every son wants to be so solid, courageous, tender, and capable that his father, beyond all others, will say of him: "You've lived up to our name, son. I'm proud of you." It is therefore the responsibility of every father to do his best to help the son do his best. If he does not, the son will take the father's name on paper but not in his heart and soul. The son will never quite know if he's a worthwhile man.

Even if father is dead or otherwise gone, mother and mentors must help him perceive the depths of the name he has taken. Throughout human evolution, one of the primary reasons marriage has been insisted upon by cultures as the preliminary event to the birth of children is to make sure a father will pass on his name to his children. With marriage, therefore, a man becomes a nurturing parent not only to their physical needs, but also to their emotional health. He thereby risks creating a vision of their destiny and then, when it is time, lets go.

From Daddy to Dad: Letting the Boy Go

A father and son came to see me. The father was sixty-two, retired. He had just gone through three years of treatments for cancer. He was cured, at least for now. The son was thirty-three, living with a woman, and about to have a first child—a son. Neither father nor son had been able to let go of each other. The father remained controlling, the son rebellious. They wanted a better life for themselves.

In their past were elements of father-son entanglements faced by so many boys and men. Wayne, the father, had been gone on and off quite a bit during Mick's first decade of life. When he was home, he wanted to be very involved with his son, but of course Mick had another life, with mom, siblings, and peers. Wayne got more and more controlling of Mick. When he bought him something, he wanted to see that Mick played with it "in the right way."

He would withhold money from Mick unless Mick "shaped up." Mick, for his part, felt angry at his father's absences and, as stubborn as his dad, did things to spite him. He grew into an adolescent who knew the very thing his father most feared—irresponsible behavior involving drugs and financial debt—and pursued it in spades. Wayne was careful with money, conservative in his ways. Mick navigated his teens and twenties rebelling against these shadows. Wayne navigated Mick's teens and twenties criticizing and judging his son.

But years had passed and now Mick was to have a son. The great circle of life was turning, giving everyone another chance. These two men took the chance. Through intensive work, Wayne discovered how controlling he had become and why. He took three months off from talking to his son and did intensive work on himself. Mick did the same. He saw how he had rebelled but never found his own vision, his own *raison d'être*. He had to separate his psychological journey toward maturity from dad's issues.

When the two men came back together, they worked out a new relationship. As you read this, Mick's son is growing up with a father and grandfather working together, in concert, to give him the best male models they can.

Father-son entanglements often go on throughout men's lifetimes. It's not every father and son who can do what Wayne and Mick did. Pride and stubbornness and the simple habit of being at odds keep fathers and sons entangled. They do things together, often work together, have family dinners together, even respect each other one moment and love each other the next, but they can't seem to make peace—they both live in a dull hard ache of anger.

Look for the following patterns between entangled fathers and sons. They'll show up very clearly just before or during adolescence, a time when so many dads do want to get more involved in son's lives, for the dads are awakening, at middle age, to the need to be intimate, and the sons, so often, want little to do with dad.

Control Systems. One of the two has set up a control system over the relationship. He withholds affection (which can include time, money, other resources) unless the other acts as he wants him to. Sons often withhold affection from dad unless dad gives them money, cars, etc. Fathers withhold affection unless sons act a certain way—dad's way.

Control systems are not to be confused with discipline systems (see Chapter 7). A discipline system is mutually covenanted between parent and child. Both parent and child understand the necessity of it. It becomes sacred between them, sanctioned and aided by their community. Control systems are imposed by one person on another for hidden reasons which are often not mutually empowering.

Compliance Systems. Father or son will at least appear to comply with the more authoritarian and controlling individual. Sons usually do the complying, building resentment against the control system and rage against the father. Sometimes, however, if a son is aligned with mom and mom is at odds with dad, dad will have to comply with a son's abuses in order to get time with him. This happens often in divorces.

Withdrawal Systems. Father or son will withdraw emotionally and physically from the other. Sons will spend almost no time with dad, dad almost no time with sons. Dad, once divorced from mom, will emotionally abandon the son. The son, after a divorce, will emotionally abandon the dad. Withdrawal systems exist on a spectrum from complete abandonment—never speaking again—to emotional distance—cohabitation without significant contact.

When a father or son is significantly dangerous, withdrawal needs to occur. How is "dangerous" defined? Carefully. So often a man is considered "dangerous," or his parenting style is considered a "crisis," when in fact neither is objectively true. For him to be dangerous, for a circumstance to be a crisis, the son must be unable to handle it, emotionally.

Once a mom came to see me about her son and divorced husband. The father was a hunter and was teaching the son how to operate and use guns. The mom was so adamant about wanting the son never to touch a gun, she was considering legal action to keep the father and son completely separate from each other. Part of my job was to help her see that her definition of dangerous had to change in order to keep her son and father in contact. There was no crisis here, nothing the son couldn't handle emotionally. The mom had a right to say, "I don't like guns," giving the son her input. But she did not have a right to kill the father-son relationship over her subjective dislike.

Rebellion Systems. Mick chose this course. It's rare a father rebels against a son, though it can happen, especially when a son and mother are enmeshed and the father feels the son has more emotional authority in the family than he does. The usual course, however, is for the son to rebel against dad. A little rebellion is a good thing, of course; it helps both father and son let go of each other. What Mick did was dangerous to him.

In all the patterns, the son and father are pushing at each other's shadows, not really relating to the whole person before them. They are in a power struggle. Even when they don't talk to each other for years, they still cannot be said to have "let go." One or both of them—more often the father-hungry son—is dependent on the other's image of him.

By the time the son leaves home, or soon after, the father-son relationship must shift to a relationship between two adult men—two emotional peers, of equal emotional power. Mentors help sons navigate out of dad's shadow. A few months or years away from each other helps. A son's journey into his own family pain helps. A father's journey into his mid-life changes helps him. If all this goes well, both father and son participate in initiation processes (see next chapter) through which the son accepts the father's imperfections and the father acknowledges the son's manhood. Without a three-family system to give the son other mentors and influences as he separates from father, son and father remain enmeshed and shadowy with each other. This is a great burden our society carries in it.

Wayne and Mick came out of the shadows. Wayne made a symbolic and tearful gesture to Mick as their work with me finished. Wayne had always been a great admirer of Douglas MacArthur. He had gotten a plaque made of a prayer MacArthur wrote for his son which reads as follows:

Build me a son, O Lord, who will be strong enough to know when he is weak and brave enough to face himself when he is afraid; one who will be proud and unbending in honest defeat, and humble and gentle in victory.

Build me a son whose wishes will not take the place of deeds; a son who will know Thee—and that to know himself is the foundation stone of knowledge.

Lead him, I pray, not in the path of ease and comfort, but under the stress and spur of difficulties and challenge. Here let him learn to stand up in the storm; here let him learn compassion for those who fail.

Build me a son whose heart will be clear, whose goal will be high; a son who will master himself before he seeks to master other men; one who will reach into the future, yet never forget the past.

And after all these things are his, add, I pray, enough of a sense of humor, so that he may always be serious, yet never take himself too seriously. Give him humility, so that he may always remember the simplicity of true greatness, the open mind of true wisdom, and the weakness of true strength.

Then I, his father will dare to whisper, "I have not lived in vain."

When Wayne gave the plaque to his thirty-three-year-old son he said, "I'm not a writer, so I hope you'll let this speak for me. You are the son I prayed for. You make me as proud as a father can be."

What a gift from father to son! Mick embraced his father and accepted the gift on not only his behalf but his son's too. I was honored to have been there to see life lived to its fullest by these two men.

chapter 6

A Boy's Second Birth: The Passage Into Manhood

> *Astronomers speak of the infancy, youth, maturity, and old age of stars and galaxies, acknowledging similarities with the stages of our own lives. For us, each life transition involves deep physical and psychological changes; the differences between one phase and another constitutes a new form or way of being. A former self dies and is replaced without disturbing the organic continuum of life.*
>
> —*Robert Lawlor,* Voices of the First Day

It is a clear day. An old woman and a young woman wander to an already chosen place at the outskirts of their aboriginal village. The young woman is in the early stages of labor, the old woman her helper. The old woman leads her to an acacia tree, directing the young woman to squat against it, propped by her arms, her face to the tree. The older woman massages her lower back. Under the young woman is a predug cavity. Around her swirls smoke from burning herbs.

As the baby boy begins to come, an observer might notice how the tree is aligned with the mother like the spine, both tree and spine giving birth to the child. As the boy is born, the old woman decides if it is well enough to live. If it is not, she will bury it in the hole beneath the mother. If it is, as this one is, she bites the umbilical cord with her teeth, and buries the placenta in the hole beneath the mother.

Robert Lawlor, author of *Voices of the First Day,* a classic study of Australian aboriginal life, says this about the tree and the hole: "This spot is the place of the child's birth; it will shape his identity and his ritual obligations to the surrounding land for the rest of his life." The mother, the old woman, and everyone else in the tribe know this, and know the importance of connecting this boy, from birth, to the spirit of nature that spawned him. The old woman rubs his body with ash and sand from this place. She twists his umbilical cord into a necklace for him to wear around his neck. She holds the child close to her face, breathing into his nostrils his sacred names. The birth of this boy is not just an ecstatic occasion for his family; it is a spiritually significant one. In this, his aboriginal experience is much like other tribal experiences all over the world; it is also like experiences our own ancestors had when children were born, experiences we've carried forward, barely, in christenings and birth circumcisions.

Ultimately, all birth rituals, whether for boy or girl, and whether burial of placenta or christening or the holding up of the baby to be shown off to society, are about spiritual connection. With the child's coming, all of spiritual life is reborn and ritualized. The more the child is valued by his family and culture, the more ritualized his birth will be—i.e., the more time the culture will take with bringing him into the world, naming him, showing him off, giving him early personal care, breathing names and knowledge into him, honoring and admiring him, teaching him to love himself, teaching him to know he belongs in the world because he is made of the very stuff of life, from the grandest human thought to the smallest atom of biological existence. Throughout his boyhood, as he celebrates his "birthdays," he gets presents, but more than that, he reaffirms that he was born into a world, a culture, a tribe and a family that knows he is essential.

Then, in adolescence, he will experience a "second birth." (His "third birth" occurs in middle age and his "fourth birth" at death). Puberty itself is respected by those peoples intimately connected with natural processes—for instance, the Australian aborigines—as similar to birth trauma. In terms of biochemistry, there are interesting similarities. Hormones rise and fall as they did during the womb time more than a decade before. Physical organs and body parts—from genitals to arms and legs—grow exponentially in a short period of time, as they did during the womb time. It is a boy's second birth, this one a birth not into boyhood, but into manhood. In a tribal culture, this second birth will be followed by years of initiation into manhood. After these years of initiation, the boy is seen to have become a man. His adolescence, in tribal life, is a conscious process of hands-on teaching and mentoring from parents and community members. Here are some of the primary experiences and lessons a boy goes through in tribal initiation:

▼ respect for the feminine: mother, women, female community
▼ anger management
▼ intimate mentoring
▼ life in an all or predominantly male community for a set period of time (some tribes have boys live with the males for three months, some one year, some more)
▼ spiritual connection to the divine through personal rituals of renewal
▼ religious rituals for communal protection and growth, and acceptance of fear and empowerment through it
▼ a male role and the important life work that goes with that role
▼ respect for one's own flaws and limitations
▼ integration of one's shadow side into one's life
▼ communication skills
▼ intimacy and sexuality training
▼ hobbies and crafts
▼ knowledge of the natural world, commitment to nurture it and live in concert with its rhythms
▼ values and morals

In and following his second birth, a boy in a tribal culture will go through and learn these lessons by making a supervised journey through his adolescent body and brain changes. The supervision is provided mainly by fathers and mentors. Mothers play a part in a boy's adolescence, as do female family members and mentors, but by the time the boy hits puberty, the mother and elder females tend to let the boy go to the elder males. One Kurdish mother in Eastern Turkey, who had raised nine sons and one daughter, had a simple standard for when to let her sons go: "When they get taller than I am, their father can have them!" No culture is without its share of absent fathers. In her case, her husband worked in Switzerland. She could not give her last three sons to him. These boys' elder brothers, however, partially filled in for their absent father, as did mentors from the village.

What is a boy's adolescence like in our culture? Of the experiences and lessons I listed, how many do the boys around you learn comprehensively? Most learn hobbies, some go to work, a few learn anger management, all learn something about sex and intimacy but not much they can really use, most never plumb the depths of their fears, many become alienated and lonely, all learn some values and morals but many not enough to make us feel safe in our communities, some learn respect for women but many don't learn enough, many never really touch the natural world that sustains life, few have intimate mentors to model their manhood after.

How many of our sons go through a second birth into manhood that is guided and honored by families, communities, the society as a whole, as a spiritual passage, central to the welfare of the boy, his family, community, and culture? Boys in our culture usually "become men" by joining an initiatory group, like the military or a gang. This applies to a minority of boys. For the majority of boys, combining disparate events—like shoplifting for the first time, getting a first car, playing sports, having sex for the first time—into a short-lived sense that they have psychologically advanced to manhood constitutes their introduction into manhood. For all boys, accepting physical manhood through maturation of sex organs and body hair, usually marked by shaving or a changing voice, is nature's way of telling them they are becoming men.

American boys generally "feel like men" through some combination of the three initiation structures, then report in middle age not knowing what a man is. In mid-life crisis, they may relive adolescence, to a greater or lesser degree, in order to initiate themselves into the psychological manhood they never actually reached during their second decade of life. They missed spiritual initiation into life at birth, then they missed the initiation into adult life because their family and society didn't realize a boy has to be taught, deep down in his spiritual core, what manhood is: he has to be rebirthed into manhood. In the absence of that initiation, they clung to the best image they could develop along with equally confused peers about what manhood should be: they made money, had a family, let women do the emotional work of the relationships, hoped for the best, and cut off their own feelings of confusion and vulnerability for as long as they could. In middle age, as men feel their mortality in their bodies, these confusions and vulnerabilities hit men hard.

We are, in large part, a culture that expects its boys to initiate themselves into manhood. But holistic or even minimal initiation into manhood through relatively unguided self-experimentation is rare. Boys cannot become whole men without men and women making them into men. In our late-twentieth-century culture, the lack of tribal initiation is an even higher risk proposition than it would have been a hundred years ago, for today's typical adolescence experiences more external stimulation to the brain and nervous system than a youth from our ancestral past or from tribal culture. Yet, ironically, a typical adolescence these days also experiences less supervision with which to absorb or integrate the increased stimulation.

Why is it that our culture does not initiate and birth its boys into a spiritually-rich vision of manhood? There are many reasons, of course. Many of us distrust the religions of our own upbringings so we've turned away from their traditions. Many of us distrust the concept of "initiation" because it reeks of tribalism and a social past in which individualism could not flourish. Many of us fear initiation of males because we think the more time boys spend with men, the more macho and destructive they'll be. Many of us are lazy or uneducated in how to raise boys or have other priorities; we'd rather someone else— like teachers or peer groups—get our boys through adolescence and into manhood.

All our reasons must be understood, then challenged. The key thing to remember here is that boys are naturally different enough from girls that they need boy-specific training in adolescence about who they are. Girls are reminded every month that they are girls. Should they choose never to have children, still they know what magic their body is capable of. Boys do not have a biology that initiates them, every month, into a sacred meaning for their existence.

If boys do not, during three to five years of adolescent initiation, learn how to feel connected to life and the life process through a sense of initiated spiritual security, they will act in ways that make us afraid for our own security. Wired and acculturated as they are for aggression and independence, we can expect that when they are raised through adolescence without a male group to test, challenge, and initiate them, male elders to help them explore the male mode of feeling, and a communal, religious, and spiritual construct in which to learn a masculine language of spirituality—they will become antisocial at worst or at least unable to commit to values of intimacy, community service, and personal boundaries.

We have heard complaints over the last few decades that "Boys get too much male-dominated religion, society, values, and initiation. Look at how the military initiates boys—to be killing machines, not men. Let's get the men away from the boys, let the women raise them, and the boys will be better off." Now we're realizing we've gone too far with this philosophy. The value of women's rights does not depend on getting boys and men away from each other. Rather, it depends on boys and caring men becoming closer to each other, especially in adolescence, so that boys learn from men how to be good, truthful, and brave. Women can't teach adolescent boys these things in the way the men can.

A mother's attachment to a son at birth is essential, whether out on the Australian outback or in a New York hospital, and the father's and elder men's attachment to the son is similarly essential at his second birth, his initiation. As the man stands slightly to the side while his wife makes a primary attachment to her son at his birth, we might say the woman must stand slightly aside while the father and mentor makes a primary attachment to the son at his second birth.

What does a healthy second birth look like? What does healthy male initiation look like? Let me tell a story that was told to adolescent boys as they were being initiated centuries ago in Central Europe. It was the model of healthy male initiation put in story. It is the story of Jack and the Beanstalk, the story of a single mother and a son who becomes, after a hard journey, a good, brave, and truthful man. Through this story, which is only one of thousands of initiation tales like it all over the world, we can see the basic steps of initiation, and discover practical models for our own integration of male initiation into our boys' lives.

Jack and the Beanstalk

Once upon a time there was a mother and a son named Jack. Jack was becoming older and his mother thought, "Well, it's time to give him a little more responsibility. Our cow is getting old and no longer gives milk. I'll ask Jack to take the cow to the market and sell it." Jack and his mother were poor people, so this was a big responsibility. If Jack failed, he and his mother would not be able to buy food to eat.

Jack set out toward town and met, on his way, an elder man. The man asked, "Where are you going with that cow?"

"To the market to sell it," replied Jack.

"Here," the man said, "look at these." He produced from within his coat a bag of magic seeds. They glowed, which intrigued Jack. The man said, "These seeds have more magic than money. Give me your cow and I'll give you these." So Jack took the seeds home and showed them proudly to his mother. His mother could not believe her eyes. She sent Jack to bed without supper, for there was no supper, and she tossed the seeds out the window in frustration.

SELLING THE COW

What's happening here? Is this just a simple tale of a boy who blows it?

Here is a mother who realizes that her son needs more responsibility. He's getting older. He needs to learn how to handle things when the very food they eat is at stake. So she lets him sell the cow. Mothers who let their sons mature into men do this in many ways: giving sons the responsibility for driving them places, sending sons shopping, giving sons the responsibility to deposit money in bank accounts. There are thousands of ways mothers give responsibility. At the same time, there are a few very important, symbolic ways that imitate the selling of the cow. If you are a mother, think of what these ways are: letting the boy go on his first one-week camping trip, letting the boy stay out all night for the first time, trusting the boy with your car, or some other very valuable family possession. When the mother gives the son responsibility over the cow she is trusting him to act like a man.

There's even more to this cow. It gives milk. This is a predominantly female image. The elder man gives the boy seeds, a predominantly male image. So the story is showing us how the boy must trade now some of the known and trusted female for the unknown, risky but magical male. Every aware mother has seen that look in her son's eyes when he reaches Jack's age (in stories we never know the exact age, so we can each fill in what fits for our lives). It is a look of a youth who has, for now, had enough of mom's milk and wants some different risk, some new magic, some male magic.

THE ROLE OF THE MENTOR

The elder man—the mentor—is the giver of the magic seeds. Those seeds will create for Jack his initiatory journey. This mentor is a guiding presence in the boy's journey. The role of the mentor in the initiation of the youth is the role of transitional parent—the parent(s) who helps the boy go from childhood in his parents' home to adulthood on his own. In tribes, the male mentor is often picked by the father. Just as often, he is a community member who forms a non-chosen affinity with the boy, and the boy with him. Always the boy knows he has a mentor when he receives from the mentor a skill or way of doing things that connects him to his own "magic."

This magic is difficult to name and different for every boy. Parents see it in their kids' gifts for music or drawing or talking. Mentors see it too, though they'll often see different gifts than the parents saw. As a transitional parent, the mentor's job is to guide the boy toward a path of initiation, support the boy throughout his initiation, and help him interpret his initiation, and thus integrate it into his manhood.

At the end of the initiatory journey through adolescence, the mentor joins the father in accepting the boy as a man. In saying "mentor" we don't necessarily mean to say there's just one. Boys will, hopefully, have three or four intimate mentors, supervisors, adolescent guides. These guides will be a part of their lives for months at least, and even years, long enough for intense attachment to occur. And by talking about mentors and fathers together we are not saying mentors and fathers have to agree on what's best for the boy. They'll have different visions of the boy. They must, however, agree on basic spiritual values—what's important in life, why the boy is on this planet, how he should treat others. Mentors and fathers, especially in our culture, in which boys often meet mentors in college, away from dad, don't necessarily accept the boy into manhood simultaneously, or in each other's presence. Hopefully, each does so on his own, in a way that reflects for the boy the cohesiveness of healthy male community.

MOM'S ANGER

When Jack comes home with the seeds, his mother has a very normal reaction—anger! She gave Jack responsibility and he appears to have failed. Should we interpret this as mom being stultifying and unable to see magic? That would sell her short. She is doing her job— her primary responsibility is to feed her son. It is not her primary responsibility to initiate him into manhood. She punishes him but, simultaneously, makes his journey possible by throwing the beans out the window.

When Jack woke up the next morning his room was nearly dark, for outside his window a huge beanstalk had grown toward the sky, cutting off much of the sun's light. He went to his window and peered upward. The beanstalk went toward the clouds. He put on some clothes and began climbing the beanstalk.

When he got to the top he was able walk on the cloud to a huge giant's castle.

THE BEANSTALK AND THE CASTLE

How much time has passed while he was climbing? We are not told. In the real life of an adolescent boy we can assume many months, even a year or two, have passed while the boy climbs up the beanstalk to meet the giant who will challenge him to his very soul. The boys we know climb beanstalks in many ways—those little rebellions, those hours spent alone in their rooms, away from family, that time spent with peer groups.

The beanstalk is symbolic in two very important ways. It is certainly a phallic, masculine image. It indicates the boy is exploring the male world very intensely. It is also a symbol for the tree of life. The tree of life appears in some form in most cultures and respresents connection with both the realm of perceivable nature and the realm of the imperceivable, life-giving spiritual world. The tree of life represents the very fullness of life. It is a symbol like milk—utterly nurturing—yet in this context, aligned more with the masculine world than the feminine.

When boys around us climb their beanstalks they spend more time in the masculine realm. Even when they climb the beanstalk by having sex with a girl—at say fourteen or fifteen—that sex is not, predominantly, about wanting intimacy with the feminine. It's mainly about wanting to explore the masculine, what it feels like "to get laid," to be a sexual male. They are processing their life experience in those early years of adolescence with an almost tunnel vision on what is maleness. Many of our sons climb this beanstalk—spend more time alone, watch action movies, play Cobra Attack, wander with other males, try to have sex with females—without knowing it is a magic beanstalk they're on. They may have started their adolescent masculine journey without meeting the mentor who gave them the seeds.

Every male is going to find some way to climb toward his masculine destiny. The question put to us by a story like Jack and the Beanstalk is, will he be led to see that the journey is magical? If he is not, he will abuse himself, abuse others, abuse the world. It is in his awareness of his own magic and the magic around him that he is taught both spiritual freedom and spiritual responsibility.

Jack walks to the huge castle. He knows it is a giant's castle because it's so huge. He is afraid. In some versions of the story, he also knows that it is a giant who killed his father. In those versions, he is walking not only to his own personal destiny as an adolescent male, but also toward the redemption of his own lost father.

When he gets into the castle, he comes to a room in which a goose is laying a golden egg. He watches the goose, mesmerized, as it lays egg after golden egg. He walks over to it and snatches it up, ready to go back down the beanstalk and show his mother his treasure. But then he hears a sound down the hall, so he pushes more deeply into the castle.

THE GOOSE THAT LAID THE GOLDEN EGG

In every growing boy there is this goose. There is in the boy a vision of the world, a set of gifts and talents, an ability to take risks or to play it safe, a way of doing things, core personality, gracefulness, athleticism, wit, intellectual prowess, sensitivity, toughness—indeed, there is in every boy some combination of all these that will be his foundation for strong self-image throughout his life. When he isn't sure who he is, he will return to what he knows as *his* gold. Gold in mythic stories is very often linked both to innocence and to future treasure, as if one's future treasure always lies somehow in one's integrated innocence. One must never lose one's basic trust in oneself. This is innocence. The cynic does not trust anyone else because, at heart, the cynic cannot trust himself.

So every boy's journey through adolescence must include the parenting and mentoring of this gold. The boy must spend a great deal of his adolescence becoming aware of and learning to manage all his gifts, talents, and personality traits. Except in cultures where he is trained for war from early on—in pockets of the Middle East, for example, we are finding youths trained for combat nearly from birth—he must learn both toughness *and sensitivity* in order to trust himself and exist in the world. By learning both, he learns to protect his gold and yet also how to share it. If he doesn't know how to share it, he will be lonely.

Adolescents show many gifts to parents and mentors. Which are the gifts represented by the goose that laid the golden egg? Only the parents, mentors, friends, and the boy himself can answer. Only those people intimate with the boy's inner life are qualified to speak. When we look into adolescent boys' eyes, we must look for that which is *core* to the boy. Sometimes we recall what we thought was the goose that would give us eternal success when we were young and we try to impose this gold on our sons. Instead our sons need us to help them find that energy within themselves that will always make *them* successful, no matter what blows life hits them with.

There is a very very small population of boys whose core is psychopathic, either caused by genetics or in boys who have been so abused that by the time they are adolescents they are incurably antisocial. Their core self has either become so twisted, or so buried, we can only keep ourselves safe from them. But even most boys in reform school, boys in gangs, boys on drugs have the gold hidden inside them somewhere. They need us and our social programs to reach inside them, through programs like Tough Love, through treatment programs, through renewed family involvement, to say directly to them: "What is your gold? What makes you tick? What can you base your future life success on?"

Boys who join gangs, boys who learn that money is the only gold, boys who learn that sex or drugs or another addiction is the gold that will sustain them—these are boys who have not been taught by intimate elders what their own gold is. These boys look outside themselves for the gold. In mythic stories, every piece of a story is actually a representation of something *inside* the person. What's outside is pretty obvious, what's inside is hidden. So mythic storytellers, who considered themselves responsible for the betterment of humanity, made sure to talk about the hidden stuff, the stuff people couldn't get at by just looking around. In the same way we are responsible to help boys look inward to discover the gold inside them, which won't be money or another addiction. It will be true personal freedom.

After Jack gets the goose that laid the golden egg, he goes into another room, for he has heard emanating out of that room a beautiful sound, like a chorus of gods and goddesses. When he gets to the room he finds a magic harp. It's playing of its own accord the most beautiful music that moves and mesmerizes Jack's spirit. Through the music, for a moment, he peers into his own soul.

THE MAGIC HARP AND SPIRITUAL LIFE

Part of what boys must learn from their three families during adolescence is spiritual connection to a sense of the divine. The sense of the divine gives them a lifelong grasp of themselves as spiritually grounded beings who belong in the great circle of life, beings who have a purpose and higher authority. In myths and fairy tales, music is often the symbol of spiritual connection. In Jack and the Beanstalk, it touches Jack as spirit and divinity.

Thomas Moore's classic bestseller, *Care of the Soul,* is useful reading for anybody involved in boys' lives. About a year ago I met a fifteen-year-old youth who had read it. He said, "I didn't get a lot of it, but, man, it was something." Boys have told me how they've read books like Chaim Potok's *The Chosen* or Hermann Hesse's *Siddhartha* and felt "changed." Other boys get involved in church youth groups and say things like, "I get it now, I know who I am." These moments of being changed, these moments of utter spiritual identity, do not last long, especially in a culture as distracting as ours, but they are moments of the magic harp for our boys.

Many boys feel spiritually connected to some mysterious world through music itself. Every generation has its spiritually challenging music. We often speak of a generation's music representing the "soul of that generation." From Bob Dylan to Led Zeppelin to Bruce Springsteen, the musical artists with spiritual depth sing spiritual themes—even common themes like love and loss, but in a way that embraces mystery and "moves the soul"—and even if that theme comes out as R.E.M.'s "Losing My Religion." Spirituality is not religion, though it includes it. Religion or religious music is not the only way to feel spiritual connection. Elton John's song "The Circle of Life," from The Lion King, is deeply spiritual, though not religious.

What, exactly, do we mean by "spiritual?" Spirituality is about connection of the self to the mystery. To experience spiritual connection, we must know ourselves at least enough to be unafraid of mystery. To truly know the mysteries of the world, we must never completely lose ourselves.

When we parent, mentor, and educate boys, especially adolescent boys, in spiritual growth, we are not trying to get them into cults, nor forcing our religion down their throats. We are showing them a magic harp and letting them hear, in its music, what they will. If we have helped them develop a strong enough self, they won't fear the mysteries of the music. They'll become spiritual men.

Practically speaking, the more adolescent youths spend time in nature, the more many of them will hear magic harps. The natural world, for all cultures, has been the longest-lived, most mysterious church. A boy who is parented and mentored to feel connected to all the mysteries of nature has a greater chance of becoming a spiritually responsible and dedicated man.

Church, synagogue, youth groups, church services in juvenile detention centers, all of these, under the leadership of spiritual adults, becomes places where some boys hear a magic harp.

If we want our boys to grow into spiritual men, our home must be a place of some ritual and some prayer. This is not to say that an atheistic home is by definition an antispiritual place. I am acquainted with an atheistic family that has dinner table arguments and discussions about God and grace and spirit that would put other homes to shame. That family is deeply spiritual in its own way.

When a mother and father disagree on religion, it can turn a boy off to spirituality. Before having children, it's very important mom and dad develop a "spiritual plan" for raising their kids.

Boys often learn spirituality from a mentor but not a father. That's just the way it is sometimes between a father and son. Fathers, if they are having no luck with sons, need to get out of the way and subtly help the boys find someone else to assist them. Boys learn a great deal of spirituality from moms before puberty but, for many boys, mom's insistence that they go to church provokes only boredom and rancor. Here fathers and mentors need to steer the boy into spiritual growth during adolescence.

A boy who leaves adolescence without knowing that prayer is an essential component to living leaves adolescence emptier than he needs to be. A boy who leaves adolescence without being on a path toward God (however he and his community define God—whether Buddha, Shiva, YHWH, Jesus, Allah, or another), lacks the ability to nurture his own growing spirit.

Jack finds the magic harp and puts it under his arm. Just as he leaves the room the harp calls out, "Help, master, help!" Jack stuffs the harp under his coat, silencing it, and hides in a third room. In that room he sees a beautiful maiden. As happens in fairy tales, the two immediately fall in love. The magic harp gets free and cries out again for its master. Jack hears lumbering footsteps. The whole castle shakes.

Jack and the maiden start out of her room. Running down a dark corridor toward them is a huge Giant. "What are you doing with my goose, my harp, my maiden?" the Giant yells. He attacks. Jack and his new friend run, carrying the treasures with them. They run across the cloud and down the beanstalk, the Giant following. As they near the bottom of the beanstalk, Jack yells for his mother to bring him the ax. She does and he chops the beanstalk down. The Giant, who hasn't made it all the way down yet, falls to his death.

With his treasures, Jack builds a new house for himself and his wife, and a new house for his mother. The neighbors and friends come around to admire what Jack has done. Jack takes the Giant's belt off the Giant's waist and puts it on his mantel in his new home. When the community is done admiring Jack's work with the Giant, a work party assembles and Jack and the party cart the Giant to a graveyard.

And everyone lives happily ever after.

FACING THE SHADOW

With a testament to joy, the story ends. You'll probably notice a lack of "fee fie foe fum I smell the blood of an Englishman" in this version. In some versions of the tale, Jack gets fed by the Giant's wife and the Giant's wife hides him from the Giant. In these versions, Jack goes back down to his mother's house with the goose, then the harp, informed by his mother that each treasure actually belonged to Jack's father. Jack discovers that his father was killed by the Giant, giving him all the more reason to end the Giant's life and take back his family's honor.

In all the versions, including the shorter one I told, Jack's journey through initiation includes a confrontation with what is called "the shadow" in myths and fairy tales. This shadow character—a giant in this tale, Ursula the sea-witch in Disney's *The Little Mermaid,* Scar in *The Lion King,* the villain in thousands of Hollywood action films— represents that part of each of us that is shadowy, destructive, hurtful. Every boy drags a shadow behind him. Every boy, during his initiation into manhood, learns to confront that shadow.

This confrontation is where parents, elders, and educators find their greatest challenge. When boys "act out," we could say the "giant is rising up in them." When they act irresponsibly—driving danger- ously, caring not at all if they get a girl pregnant, mouthing off disre- spectfully, destroying property, committing crime—they are exercising the shadow, crying out for direction, discipline, and leadership. Be- cause Chapter 7 focuses on a lot of this very specifically, I won't go into detail here. But it's essential to say here that every boy must learn—by experience, education, parenting, and mentoring—how to discipline himself, how to discipline the shadow.

Often parents see their son's shadow and become afraid of it, or lazy in the face of it. They just hope it will go away. They hope someone else will discipline it and give it structure. If parents—espe- cially male parents, including the transitional mentorial parent—don't take on the job of giving the boy structure and discipline, helping him understand his shadow in full, and helping him integrate its shadowy energies into his future growth, the boy will take that shadow into the society, his future marriage, his own future family, his workplace, and exercise it inappropriately. People will see that giant rise up in him as he sexually attacks or harasses them, loses his temper at ballgames, beats up his children. People will see the giant rise up and they will be afraid. When parents, mentors, and educators don't help boys confront their shadows in their adolescent years, those shadows become even larger giants, as the boy grows into adulthood, and in the end the law has to deal with them.

Among the Shavante of Brazil, the shadows in boys are honored and trained in a number of ceremonies. In one, for instance, boys are taught to work together to bring their anger, in the form of a huge log, into the camp. Through ceremonies like these, elders teach the boys the right boundaries for anger. Fear is another part of the human shadow that adolescent initiations deal with throughout Native America. Boys are mentored on three, five, ten, or fourteen-day Vision Quests in a dangerous and frightening wilderness so that they learn how to move through fear and find the self that perseveres. The essential idea in this questing is that if a boy's fear is not trained, he will not use it to further himself and his community—rather, he will, from his own position of fear, try to make others afraid.

Anyone who works with adolescent boys must teach them— through disciplines like martial arts and sports, through intimate and communicative family environments, through respectable authority— how to deal with their own angers and fears. A great deal of male self-discipline grows from flourishing in the face of the shadow sides of these emotions.

Many elders who teach boys, myself included, have turned to things like the Ropes Course as a way of helping boys work with their emotions, especially their fears. Ropes Courses exist throughout North America. They involve high platforms, poles run between trees. Boys have to push beyond their fears to walk across a thin pole (they are always harnessed for safety) thirty feet above the ground.

The world of sports is a world where many boys face large parts of their shadow. When a boy is playing team sports, he faces shadowy moments of fearful competitiveness, a need to humiliate another, the humiliations of others which he must combat or integrate. Through the sports experience, we see boys confronting shadowy egos, excessive pride, unchecked impulses, fears of failure, fears of success—"I can't do it! I'll always fail at the important things!"—how they navigate and are mentored to navigate these fears says a lot about who they become.

At home, boys must feel free to talk to parents about the shadowy feelings they are having—feelings about drugs, girls, violence, racism, sexism. Parents must use every opportunity to teach boys about their own shadowy prejudices, and give boys wise ways to do better.

The media is a place where a great deal of male shadow—from Power Rangers to Street Fighter and beyond—finds a mirror. As we'll discuss in Chapter 8, our laws will need to change so that we can better monitor and interpret for boys the imagery they take in.

The educational system is a major initiator of our youth. Teachers need to be trained in mentoring. When a teacher realizes he has become a boy's mentor, he and the boy's parents need to work together carefully, for now, in the boy's eyes, he is like a family member. What he teaches has become sacred. Much of what he teaches is how to handle the shadow.

Community centers, churches, youth centers all need funding, for they can all provide safe places for boys to face their shadows. More and more elderly men need to volunteer to teach boys boxing, archery, life skills, play videogames with boys, take boys horseback riding, and so on.

Rafting trips, ropes courses, and other rites-of-passage experiences need to become regular parts of a boy's adolescence. Through them, boys learn their gold, their spirituality, their shadow, and grow up.

Boys who are taught to move through fear thank their elders profusely. Once I joined a group of men on a rafting trip down the Salmon River in North Idaho. A seventeen-year-old youth came on the trip, a friend of one of the river guides. This youth asked, in many ways, for mentoring, and the trip became an initiatory experience. The men gave him wisdom he had not heard from a group of men, as well as healthy adult mirroring of himself as a young man. Many of his fears and confusions about being male found activity and audience on the river. One of his biggest fears was about how men would accept him. We accepted him in a way men never had. A year later he called me. He had gotten into a prestigious college based, he said, very much on his Statement of Intent which he had written after that river trip. He had not known until the trip what direction he wanted to go in. The trip helped him make his passage into manhood.

From initiatory experiences, boys learn not only to face the shadow as it appears to them in their hormone-driven adolescence, but also learn skills in their adolescence by which to face the shadow however and whenever it appears to them. Fate, crisis, the death of a child, a failed marriage, a lost job—these or other things like them are companions of every man's journey through adult life. It is in learning to face the giant in adolescence that the man gains the power and skill to face the giant—the outward giant and the inward giant—throughout life.

In the story of Jack and the Beanstalk, Jack takes the Giant's belt off the big waist and carries it into his new home. This is a representation of the necessity of a boy not only facing the shadow but also integrating it. Some mythologists call this "eating the shadow." Eating the shadow is about saying, "Yes, that's my shadow, that's my world of flaw, failures, imperfections, angers, fears, hurts, and now that I'm conscious of it and know how to walk around in it, I am able to be a man fully and truly." If we don't integrate the shadow but rather try to quash it, make it disappear, we face its uprising at sudden and dangerous times. We end up hurting other people and other organizational systems in our lives, at home, at work, at play—and thus hurting ourselves—because we have not let go of an infantile desire for perfection, and embraced a mature knowledge of the human shadow.

In Jack and the Beanstalk, the confrontation with the shadow—symbolized as a Giant who is Jack's own "giant world" of fears, shames, confusions—follows the sacred theft of the goose and the magic harp. In so many myths and stories, the confrontation with the shadow follows a similar pattern: it occurs *after* a boy's discovery of his gold and connection to spiritual growth. The mythic logic to this is good common sense. Facing the shadow is a very difficult task. A boy is better equipped for this if he has at least made good strides in feeling confident in himself and in his connection to the mysterious and greater world. Sometimes we don't have the confidence to face our shadow until we are well initiated into our spirituality and therefore feel grounded in life itself—feel like we are a unique self who absolutely belongs in this world.

In Jack's story, the whole community comes to admire what he has done. The man who sold him the beans comes to admire him. "I knew you would return from your magic journey," he says. "Now that you have, I'll be on my way." The mentor has finished his job—years of initiation have passed. Both move on.

The mentor in Jack's story moves back into a kind of communal background—he returns to being one of the tribe whose admiration Jack's work needs. Jack, like every youth, needs the communal group to say, "You are brave, you've done good." The youth on our rafting trip needed us to say, "We admire you for the work you've done to become a man." It's important to note also the timing of the community's admiration. The community gives Jack this respect not before he has faced the shadow but afterward. It is as if the community is saying, "We may have always cared for you as a person, but now you have earned our *respect*."

One of the terrible things we do with our criminals, most of whom are male, is to give them no respect or admiration after they do their time and face their shadows. We disrespect them when they leave prison. We don't give them jobs, we still treat them like criminals. And because some don't face shadows while in prison, we condemn all criminals.

We do the same thing with many boys in many ways. We don't notice the hard work they've done to grow up. We don't admire it. We don't help them cart away the carcass. We don't help them bury their pasts. Boys need their communities to accept the fact that they have a shadow side, to help them manage that shadow side, and then to give them respect for having learned self-discipline. That is the three-stage process of male initiation into the shadow—recognition of the shadow, aided by elders who see it, from the outside, often more clearly than the boy himself; confrontation with the shadow, aided by elders who themselves have been down the hard road of developing self-discipline; admiration by the community of elders for the shadow work done.

BOY MEETS GIRL

In just about every tale of a boy's initiation, there is a maiden trapped in the castle or cave of a giant, an evil sorcerer, a monster, a demon, a sea-witch, a warlock. The boy falls in love with the girl and must, in order to free her, confront the giant, the monster, the demon. Chapter 9 will focus primarily on boys and this maiden, discussing how to teach boys about sex, love, and intimacy. Let's just look here, as we end Jack's story, at how wonderfully interwoven is a boy's love of a girl with confronting his own shadow.

In Jack's story, he falls in love with the maiden and is immediately confronted with the shadow. It is rare in a boy's life that his sudden affection for a girl is not also accompanied by a confrontation with his own shadowy desires and impulses and, once he's rejected, his hurts. Mythic stories know biology very well. They know that, for instance, testosterone is the hormone that drives both sex and aggression. They know that in a boy, as testosterone surges, increasing his desire for sex and intimacy, so does his impulse to be aggressive and irresponsible. The deep confusion boys feel in their impulses to "have" girls is biologically grounded.

It is specifically when a boy begins to look to girls that we can expect him to face many shadows in himself, and thus it is essential we mentor him well at this time. A boy who "marries" the maiden before he has been led in confronting his own shadow—i.e., a boy who impregnates a girl before he has confronted much of his own irresponsibility, acting out, impulsiveness, and immature responses to hurt and rejection—does himself, the girl, his offspring, and his society future harm. A boy must kill the giant and take its belt off and put that belt up on the mantel where he can always be reminded of who he is before he takes on the most difficult relationship of his future life with an intimate mate.

Stories like Jack and the Beanstalk have tried to teach us this. The role of the fathers and elder males during the boy's early adolescence is crucial in keeping the boy from impregnating girls, abusing girls, using girls. If no elder male is around, the single mother often must change the way she has brought up and disciplined the boy to include diligent structure, lots of discipline, lots of communication about sex and about love. If the elder males are around, they must talk about the nitty-gritty—the impulses, the aggressions, the ecstasies—more than once.

As Jack's story ended, we saw that he built one house for himself and his mate, then another for his mother. His reunion with his mother included, initially, his mother bringing him the ax that cuts down the beanstalk. There's wonderful symbolism in all this.

The mother has let the boy go on his journey into masculine initiation, yet she is not tossed off or seen an unessential. She is essential again, the ax bringer. The son and mother are reunited, emotionally, in this gesture, for the mother helps the son, at least in some part, face the shadow. Respect for mother appears in this element of story. Respect for mother also appears in Jack's construction of a house for her. At the same time, separation from her is obvious. Jack no longer lives with mother.

And so Jack has gone on and been led on a masculine journey of initiation. It began with his mother's frustration and ended with Jack's acceptance by the community as a man. A journey like this one would be the ideal for every boy's adolescence.

The Hero's Journey

Jack's journey is what mythologists call The Hero's Journey. Boys love to be heroes. Boys want to be heroes. Boys needs to be heroes. They need to strive and be rewarded for their striving. They need to discover and accomplish heroic tasks and in turn receive communal respect. They need to develop, especially in adolescence, a heroic context in which they will live their lives. They need to make the heroic journey, first as an initiatory journey of adolescence, then, based on this foundation, as a spiritual journey throughout their lives.

Our culture has robbed boys of the hero's journey in myriad ways. Some among us have feared its warrior extremes and thus tried to teach boys to deny their need to perform and compete. Some among us, seeking to utterly destroy the male sense of role, have taught boys to avoid protecting and providing, to avoid that piece of their heroism. Some among us, too busy to help boys become the hero each needs to be, have neglected our elder responsibility. Most of us, feeling unheroic ourselves, have avoided looking into a boy's eyes and seeing his desire to be a hero.

Perhaps the most consistently available structure through which boys can do parts of the developmental work in the hero's journey is through sports. One father of four sons wrote this to me from Oakland:

"Never underestimate the importance of boys' team sports. This seems to me the most significant way that we provide a hero's journey today.

"I'm biased, of course, having three older sons and now a ten-year-old who's in the midst of an intense team sport experience which has lasted now for four full years and promises to continue indefinitely. We try to balance it with his piano and school (at which he also excels), but there's nothing to compare with the experience of playing on his ice-hockey team.

"I hear the same thing from other dads I know whose sons are in basketball, soccer, or baseball. Even lacrosse. Every game, every practice even is an opportunity for small or large acts of heroism. The bonding, the support of parents, extended family, and community is truly monumental."

This father's words capture the experience of so many parents and so many boys. In some ways, a viable structure for some of the hero's journey exists in team sports—camaraderie, working together to succeed, learning how to win and to lose with class and dignity, finding one's own skills and limitations, working for the entertainment and emotional responses of a community, feeling admired and admiring others, participating in events that bring people together.

Only to do sports would not, of course, do justice to the hero's journey, but I would not be surprised if soon we see a book come out that analyzes sports as a part of a young person's spiritual life, for it can be that.

BOYS WILL MAKE THE JOURNEY WITH OR WITHOUT US

Our culture has neglected to see that every boy will make the hero's journey whether we help or not. The question is, what kind of hero will he become? If we are intimate teachers who devote our soulful energy to leading that hero through all the possibilities of heroism— from protection to empathy to accomplishment to prayer—the boy will not need to beat up women, join a gang, hate his parents, or destroy his community to be a hero.

Boys become men by becoming the kinds of "heroes" we help them to be. Heroes become elders by moving beyond the hero and finding a new archetypal focus for life after middle age. Simultaneously, testosterone diminishes. Again, biology and spiritual growth are one. Because so many of our boys are not well initiated into the testosterone-driven hero's journey of youth and early adulthood, they never move beyond that journey into a new magic of eldership. They reach middle age trying to be the heroes they were supposed to be as adolescents and younger men in the first few decades of adult life. So we would get more than "good husbands and fathers and workers and sensitive partners" out of helping adolescent youths through the hero's journey. We would also end up with better elder men to lead us, years later. For when we guide our boys through the hero's journey during their second and third decades of life, we set up a society that will be led by elder men who gained that new magic—that wisdom that only the post-heroic, settled soul can provide.

Models of Initiation

Over the last decade, models of initiation have been created by people all over North America, without much attention by the media. Once in a while, something on the subject appears in a major magazine. Sometimes articles appear about new mentoring projects in the inner city. Numerous articles come out weekly on the sorry state of teenage life, but for the most part the grassroots movement to reclaim adolescence and make it a necessary and spiritual adventure has gone unsung.

Our overall neglect of grassroots resources exists in part, I believe, because of a cultural fear of men working together in grassroots spiritual community. Some people are afraid when men come together "the patriarchy" will be re-established. Some people are afraid that when men and boys spend time together "boys will learn macho values." Some people are afraid men who mentor boys will abuse or molest them, though the percentage of men who victimize is very low. Behind all this, I believe, is a kind of tacit individualism. It's subtle, but it's there. Leave boys alone, leave my family alone, leave me alone, we're doing just fine thanks.

For boys to be initiated into healthy manhood, our culture is going to have to look as carefully at its individualism as it does at its racism and sexism. Simultaneously, we have to look at our myth of the perfect institution. So often we say to the world, "I'm cynical. Government, schools, and other institutions aren't really very powerful." But simultaneously, we may say, "If my boy needs something, let school or the church provide it." Boys who need a tribe to initiate them do not care if that tribe of elders comes from blood relatives, from nonblood elder friends, or from institutions, or, most likely, from some combination of them all. Boys are simply hungry to become the best men they can be. A good way to monitor whether our boy is getting his initiation is by monitoring just how much we are hoping someone else will give it to him. If we're conscious enough to wonder, we're probably the person(s) who needs to take the initiative. Any of us can initiate them if we devote ourselves to being a part of a healthy group and bringing boys to that group.

DIFFERENT RITES OF PASSAGE

Initiation takes place over a period of years. It includes planned, institutional, accidental, incidental, and ritual rites of passage. A rite of passage is a part of initiation, not all of it, just as a bar mitzvah is only the beginning, not the whole, initiation of the boy into manhood. High school can be an initiation structure, so can college. Any educational structure that leads the boy through a social and personal journey of growth becomes an initiation experience.

When a boy makes a *planned* rite of passage, getting his driver's license, for example, we as elders need to help him see this in the context of his whole adolescent initiation experience. "This," we might say to him, "is like when you went alone on the airplane to visit grandma and grandpa the first time, remember? And remember the responsibilities that came with that. And remember how afraid you were. That's okay. Be afraid. I was afraid too when I got my first car, afraid people would think it was ugly . . ." Adolescent youths cry out for us to help them contextualize their life experiences.

Institutional rites of passage—like military boot camp, fraternity hazings, graduation day, and bar mitzvah—are essential parts of every boy's life. If no institutional rites of passage occur in his life, he grows up alienated from the institutions that run society.

These institutional rites have been argued over during the last quarter century. It is impossible for ideology and institution not to mix; thus so many of us came to despise institutional rites of passage, usually associated with rigid religious or social structures that appeared to countenance violence. Now we're having to look at our ideological misgivings again. Many young men benefit from the military—it gives them structure. Some parents are putting aside their ideological disagreements with the military and blessing their sons in finding a place of discipline and growth. Job Corp and Juvenile Boot Camps are becoming institutional places of passage for many other young males.

When a boy makes an *accidental* rite of passage, for instance, his first kiss, he will, hopefully, feel okay about sharing it with us. If so, we help him contextualize this into his whole heroic journey. We use it as a teaching tool, taking it seriously enough to give him respect and guidance without overreacting to it.

When a boy makes an *incidental* rite of passage, for instance, he is a participant in a larger initiation structure—like a sport, a workplace, a school—and accomplishes a certain big goal in that structure. Perhaps he does something at his part-time job that shows growth in him, or makes a winning basket after being considered too small to really play on varsity or wins a karate contest when no one, not even he himself, thought he could.

Some boys needs more supervision than others through their years of initiation. We ask them, as much as possible, what they need.

Initiation is befriended always by discipline. Every boy needs a minimum of one profoundly disciplining task and structure during adolescence—for some this is school, but for others who don't like school it might be playing on a team or in a band or working on a ranch or playing chess.

This task and structure may change during the years of initiation—one year the boy will play basketball, one year soccer. The more we are involved in facilitating the structure and task with the boy—i.e., the more we show it is valuable—the more self-discipline and self-value the boy will gain from it.

Sometimes the boy will choose a disciplining task and structure we are afraid of or despise—like a sport we despise. Our challenge is to search through our own fears and prejudices. If, after such a search, we cannot condone the task or structure, we must immediately seek tribal help—counselors, teachers, elders.

Boys risk, in their attention to singular tasks and structures, living out of balance. Our best strategy to help a boy live a various and balanced life is often not to restrict his time with his task but instead to invest ourselves in taking him away from it, at times, toward tasks and structures he might enjoy. It rarely works to say to a boy, "You're spending too much time with George. Go do something else." We have to say, "Hey, let's you and me go throw the Frisbee for a while." Or, "Do you wanna visit Uncle Frank next weekend, he's going to go fishing with your cousins." This gives the boy relationship as well as something specific to do and look forward to, thus giving him two incentives to try something different.

RITUAL INITIATION

Ritual rites of passage, the fifth form of initiation experience, is the one most rich in communal input. In its ideal, a church ceremony, a rite of passage adventure, an event a group or family creates for itself, has four main components.

▼ a safe place
▼ trusted elders
▼ a prepared ritual accepted by the community
▼ a ritual imbued with sacred energy and tradition

An example of a ritual initiation is the Vision Quest, a Native American ceremony in which a boy is led in making a spiritual journey into a potentially dangerous wilderness. Here he faces ordeals that challenge his defenses and fears. After a few days he slows his life down, learning the rhythm of the wilderness. Undistracted by others, he seeks visions—experiences and projections of his hidden inner life. His fearful, incipient goal—just to survive and tell the tale—gradually becomes a more important goal: to know himself. When he returns from the physical ordeal and the spiritual journey, he returns to the safety of mentors who help him interpret his visions. Even months or years later, he recalls the Vision Quest and feeds at the trough of that deep, personal experience.

Our boys have a few planned rites of passage, a lot of undiscussed accidental rites, vague institutional rites, even more unnoticed incidental rites, and almost no ritual rites. One of the ways many people are helping boys see all five kinds as essential in the context of initiation is by creating (or accepting, if one already exists in a church, like first communion, or in synagogue, like bar mitzvah) the fifth kind—the ritual—and through learning how it works with boys, seeing how the planned, accidental, institutional, and incidental rites can be used, acknowledged, and celebrated more consciously throughout a boy's years of initiation.

DO BOYS WANT TO BE INITIATED?

What do boys think about "being initiated?" I have helped many men's groups, churches, single moms, and school systems absorb "initiation" into their *raison d'être* and apply strategies for initiation. Often toward the beginning of one of these consultations, a parent, mentor, or educator will ask what the boys will think of all this "initiation."

A few boys, of course, will never care for it. Some will laugh at it. Some won't show up for the rite of passage adventure they signed up for. Some will leave their embarassed fathers behind, as they walk away from the hunting trip Dad carefully planned.

Yet I have found that most boys won't turn away from it. Most boys are so hungry to be challenged and admired by elder men that they'll put up with a lot of false starts, experiments with new male kinship structures, and confusing information about initiation. Most boys will listen—at least after a lot of investment from the elders—when the elders say, "You know, such and such that just happened to you, it's an initiation into manhood. So let's talk about what manhood is."

One way that boys come to enjoy the initiation experiences is by getting to know other boys better through them. One of the boys, David Edeli, in a ceremony Bernard Weiner captured in *Boy Into Man,* wrote this about his initiation experience:

"The consensus is that the initiation was most important because of the bonding among ourselves. We showed our friendship in bearing the freezing waters of the creek and exchanging knowing looks during the serious initiation, and we have decided that every year we should repeat the trip to the Sierra foothills to share a couple special days together."

David continues, ". . . we learned a reverence for masculinity and a dedication to responsibilities of manhood. And although our society dictates full manhood at age eighteen, and many of the things we learned are not applicable to us now, we will be prepared for the future.

"Looking back on the initiation, we initiates could say many sappy, tear-jerking things in private, but we all agree on one thing in public, best summed up by initiate Josh Magnani: 'It was fun.' "

Whether the initiation experiences are planned, accidental, incidental, or ritual, boys will enjoy them if we enjoy them with the boys. Boys will learn from them if we teach and learn through them too. When boys join gangs, they seek the camaraderie among peers. They learn a reverence for masculinity and a dedication to the responsibilities of manhood. They feel prepared for the future by their initiation into a gang. The question we face as people concerned for boys, and therefore for society, is not "Will boys like it?" They will like it in whatever form they can find it. The question we face is, "Will we do it? Will we do the hard work of making our boys into loving, wise, and powerful men?"

How to Raise a Boy

chapter 7

Teaching Boys Discipline

My parents made me respect them and held me to strict rules of discipline. I needed that, I can see it now that I'm a father. Good discipline is maybe the greatest gift I got from my parents.

—John, forty-six

We were together at a Wellness conference in a school district.

"My son is four," a mother said. "Should he hit me when he's mad?"

"My son is nine," a father said. "He doesn't listen to me. What am I doing wrong?"

"I have a twelve-year-old in my chemistry class," a teacher said. "He's ADD [attention deficit disorder], but it's more than that—he's so often so cruel to others."

"My stepsons," a woman said, "hate me, won't listen to me, won't let me discipline them at all."

"My grandsons," a grandfather said, "they just don't have the discipline we had to have when my brothers and I were growing up."

Professionals, parents, and other caregivers shared their exhaustion with trying to figure out what kind of discipline works with boys, which methods build character and which destroy it, what healthy models to follow. We talked, we workshopped, we made lists, we watched videos, we heard a great deal of wisdom.

Then a gutsy young teaching intern, still in her Masters of Education program, raised her hand.

"Maybe I'm missing something," she said, "but what exactly do we mean by discipline anyway? I don't think we're all talking about the same thing."

This comment sent us into an in-depth dialogue in which we recognized we all agree that most of our boys don't get enough "healthy discipline"; we don't have uniform standards for healthy discipline; as individuals in our culture we don't have agreement on what the word "discipline" stands for; we don't spend enough time generally with our kids so we certainly don't spend enough time teaching discipline; we're phobic about "abusing" kids and so avoid some important aspects of discipline; we aren't sure what "self-esteem" really means, but we all want to build it in our kids.

Following the discussion that led to these agreements, we explored material about how tribal cultures provide discipline to their boys. There is great variety, of course, among these cultures, but also a consistent element: discipline is provided not just for "bad acts"—i.e., "That was wrong, you'll be punished if you do it," or even, "That was the wrong thing to do, here are the consequences." Rather, discipline is constructed within the spiritual context of the culture. That is to say, the discipline a boy learns is part of his whole system of living in his community, on the land, in his world. Discipline, for a tribe like the Shavante, for instance, of Eastern Brazil, is part of *a spiritual system.* In the same way, our own ancestors used to make discipline a part of biblical religious systems.

In that Wellness conference, we were not building to the conclusion that we should become a tribe, or that we should return to a "spare the rod, spoil the child" philosophy. But we were noticing something that I believe is absolutely essential to the raising of kids, especially boys: how we discipline them must be woven into the whole social web of their development.

When we say to a boy, "Stop that," or hit a boy until he stops, then turn away from the boy back to whatever else we were doing, we are not giving the boy a discipline system to absorb into himself, live in, and navigate life by. We are, instead, teaching him to pay particular attention to certain actions which make us angry and get him in trouble. He learns to avoid those actions—something he certainly needs to learn, especially if they endanger himself or others—but he does not learn how he fits in the greater spiritual, emotional, and social plan of his family, his community and world.

When we say to each other, "At all costs, build that boy's self-esteem," we often forget that helping him to feel good about himself is only one of the jobs of discipline. Another very important one is the building of character itself. He must have a self to esteem. He must have a character to like. Fragmented acts of discipline can build some character, but more powerful is a boy's sense that he belongs in a consistent discipline structure in which to invest his energy and test himself. A family and community builds character primarily by providing that discipline structure, that discipline *system*.

What Is Healthy Discipline?

Where giving care to children is concerned, we shall let the word "discipline" stand for *a systematic approach to teaching a child appropriate behavior by building character, testing self-esteem, and teaching social skills.*

Discipline becomes systematic when it provides these ten elements:

1. Consistency
2. Leadership
3. Respect
4. Variety
5. Recrimination
6. Spiritual context
7. Choices
8. Respect for feelings
9. Authoritative structure
10. Early, ongoing, and adaptive use

Now let's look at these in more detail.

The healthy disciplinarian is *consistent* in reinforcing and punishing a boy's behavior. Consistency applies first and foremost to the question of when we should discipline. We must work out a way to be systematic, not random; thus our children will know when they are going to be disciplined. We don't discipline "just for the hell of it." Perhaps we decide: I will discipline my child when he breaks a rule that he knows and understands; endangers himself; endangers another person or living thing; endangers property; infringes on others' rights. Having decided on this structure, we stick to it consistently.

For discipline to be consistent, parents and caregivers must agree on basic principles and practices. One parent does not rescue the child when the other parent disciplines (abusive discipline is always the exception to this). One parent or caregiver doesn't undercut others' discipline, even if there has been a divorce. Turning a boy against one of his parents does even more damage to the boy.

Consistent application means we cannot make threats we won't carry out. Boys need to know the rules and know we will stick by them. If we show we don't believe in the rules, why should the boy believe in them?

Because so many of our own families were in gender and cultural transition during our upbringing, most of us were brought up in homes where discipline was somewhat experimental, and inconsistently applied. We have to look carefully at our own pasts when we are seeking consistency with our kids. Often we must not repeat the fragmentation of our childhoods.

Simultaneously, as disciplinarian, we must act with others in the boy's community—daycare providers, his friends' parents, neighbors, mentors, teachers—to ensure, as much as possible, adult consistency in applying standards of discipline throughout the boy's community. We can't be afraid of saying to our neighbor, "When Johnny's with you, you make sure he knows you're in charge. Here are some basic rules of discipline we follow. If you can discipline him using these rules, you'll be helping us as parents too."

Consistency in discipline applies to consistency throughout the *stages* of discipline. If you have not noticed it consciously, you'll probably have noticed intuitively that each incident of discipline is like a mini-journey, occurring in episodes. Here are the episodes, or stages, I've noticed.

Stage 1. If the behavior is immediately dangerous, stop it—with, for instance, a firm tone, or by removing the child from the danger.

Stage 2. Identify the boy's mistake. Identify to the boy what effect the inappropriate behavior has on self, family, community, web of life. This identification often works better when the caregiver says, "What was wrong with that behavior?" rather than, "Here's what was wrong with that." Letting the boy explain his error builds his confidence. If he says, "I don't know what was wrong," then the caregiver explains. If the boy is using "I don't know" as intransigence, then that action itself becomes a matter for discipline.

Stage 3. Provide a natural or punitive consequence if the behavior warrants more than Stage 1 or Stage 2. "You have chosen not to do the job I asked you to do. The consequence is that you will not be able to play with your friend Brian this evening as you wished to do." Often consequences just emerge spontaneously, but often consequences can be stated up front and the boy can have a voice in deciding what a consequence will be.

Stage 4. Consistently enforce the consequence. Don't give in too early, don't enforce the consequence longer than you said you would. This stage is the one in which so many discipline systems falter. "No you may not play with Brian, no matter how much you plead to. You made a decision earlier, it had a consequence that will not change."

Stage 5. Ritualize the end of the consequence with the show of renewed acceptance. Hugging a child after a moment of discipline—a time out, for instance—shows renewed acceptance of the child. If the boy is older and the punishment involves grounding, taking the boy to get ice cream to celebrate the end of the grounding is, for instance, a way of renewing the boy's acceptance.

Different discipline styles can be equally effective and equally important. Maternal and paternal discipline styles often differ. Mothers often see their children as extensions of themselves, whereas fathers often experience more distance from a child. In this situation, fathers are better at saying to boys—especially as boys get older—"I'll love you no matter what, but I won't respect you unless you do such and such." Mothers are often better at saying, "I'll respect you no matter what because you're my flesh and blood." Men and women can both misuse their own style, mothers sometimes erring on the side of letting boys get away with too much, fathers on the side of unnecessarily cutting boys off from a father's affection. (And, of course, some mothers are much harder on boys than fathers.) No matter their errors, each style is different and the boy flourishes by getting a balanced dose of each. He needs someone to say, "I won't respect you unless . . ." He also needs someone to say, "You can do no wrong in my eyes." Hopefully his parents, seeing their different nurturing styles, will work together to create a balanced and consistent discipline system for the boy.

The healthy disciplinarian consciously provides two forms of *leadership*—modeling and teaching—by which the child learns not only how to act with others but how to feel about his own worth as a person. When the disciplinarian models something she or he does not want the boy to learn, the disciplinarian is honest about the flaw in the behavior and verbally points the boy in another direction. "I shouldn't have yelled at you that way. I'm sorry. Sometimes I blow it. That's something I do that you shouldn't do."

The healthy disciplinarian teaches the child to *respect* the disciplinarian. The child is learning who he is, especially in the early years of life, by modeling and receiving mirroring from the caregiver (we will use "caregiver," "teaching adult," "elder authority," "parent," "mentor and educator," and "disciplinarian" interchangeably to mean any adult who is entrusted with disciplining the child). He must respect that person to be disciplined by that person and to build his own respect for himself. So the disclipinarian must act according to his values, walk his talk, and show himself to the boy. "This is who I am," he must be saying, "this is what I stand for, these are my values, these are my strengths, these are my vulnerabilities."

The healthy disciplinarian knows that crisis discipline and everyday discipline are not the same thing. Most discipline takes place as everyday discipline, involving, we hope, a systematic, authoritative way of meeting the daily challenges of guiding a boy's life. Crisis discipline applies when a sudden, dangerous situation has emerged and needs sudden intervention. When a child runs in front of a car, we must act instantaneously, sometimes yelling or even spanking the boy, in a way that is not consistent with the everyday system of discipline we have developed. When we discover that our sixteen-year-old son is trying to seduce a thirteen-year-old girl, and will not stop, despite all efforts consistent with our everyday system, we might do something drastic.

A father facing this situation told me he took out the battery, distributor cables, and alternator from his sixteen-year-old son's car. His son had no money and could not replace them. Without the use of his car, he became resentful, enraged, accused his father of circumventing his rights as a person. In fact, the father admitted that this kind of authoritarian theft of property was not consistent with the discipline system his son was used to from him. But the father also pointed out that this was a crisis. If the son got the girl pregnant, he could go to jail. Since the son would not listen to reason, crisis intervention was required. The son did finally stop seeing the girl, and the father gave back the essential items.

The distinction between crisis and everyday discipline is essential for people to recognize especially when they spend little time with their boys. People, especially parents, often think of most discipline as crisis discipline because it will seem the boy is often in crisis. Had they spent more time with the boy they would see that much of what appears to be "acting out" is normal behavior and does not need us to stray from the discipline system we employ.

The healthy disciplinarian avoids character attacks, focusing instead on behavior. "You're a piece of sh——" "You're stupid. . . ." "You couldn't get it right if I paid you. . . ." Shaming is usually an attack on character. It damages the child. The *recrimination tool* the healthy disciplinarian prefers is the teaching of moral responsibility. "Did you see how you hurt your sister when you teased her about her hair in front of her friends?" "I feel taken for granted when you just ask me for things, then show no gratitude, just more 'I want, I want.' "

The healthy disciplinarian shows the boy whenever possible how the discipline system fits within a larger *spiritual context*—religious, communal, social. One teacher at a Christian preschool told me. "Because we are Christian based, we can use the whole power of God to help us guide our children. I will often say, 'You are a piece of God and God is a piece of you. That's not the way the God in you wants to act, is it?' "

Whether one is Christian or not, the idea of utilizing the invisible spiritual realm to bolster one's discipline is hard to argue against. There is divinity in everyone, whether we define divinity as "God" or not. Often, using that divinity as a kind of higher standard within the child's self can help the disciplinarian in the task of guiding behavior.

Unitarian-Universalism, a religious movement for which Christianity is just one of many sources of wisdom, focuses its Sunday school students on the "inherent dignity of every individual person." Like the "You are a piece of God" at the Christian preschool, this UU creed gives children a guiding principle that is, for kids in this religion, larger than they are, something to respect as a high standard.

When a particular discipline system has history and tradition, let's teach our kids those, let's teach them the primary text of that tradition. In many of our homes, we have turned away from the institutional religion or tradition of our grandparents' world, and often for good reasons. Yet if we have done this, we have no real primary or sacred text to call on to give tradition to our discipline system. On the other hand, some of us, so desperate for history and tradition, have returned to old ways with fundamentalist, myopic energy. The whole question of how to teach a boy tradition is still an open one in our culture.

If we have turned away from all traditions, we must create our own: wandering through moments of discipline doesn't ultimately help the boy. We must actually create a new system (built from the best of the old values and best of the new values) that will become our family's "spiritual" tradition for the new millennium.

If we have returned to fundamentalist traditions, we must be very careful to avoid xenophobia and myopic application. The world is more complex than it was when the Bible was written. To try the literal application of biblical standards, all of which have been through many translations and are open to myriad interpretations, backfires with boys who rebel as soon as possible.

When we lack a written text to give history and tradition to our system of discipline, we can often use nature to help us. In taking a systematic view of discipline, caregivers work toward presenting standards of behavior—values, morality, etc.—that are necessary not only to guide the correct action in the immediate world but also to encourage his connection with the web of life. Caregivers show boys how discipline works in the natural world, how survival works, how everything in nature is a web of interdependence. "Watch those two animals fighting," a parent might say, as she and her son watch a nature program on television. "You know why they're fighting? Over food. That one will starve unless he protects his food. What were you fighting with your brother about? Was it like food? Was it worth hitting each other for? Was it really important enough to give him a black eye?"

Boys learn that consequences of behavior are seen as both microcosmic and macrocosmic—microcosmic in that they are specific incidents in a boy's everyday life, and macrocosmic in that the boy's everyday incidents fit within larger spiritual and natural context.

In helping children see larger contexts for individual acts of discipline, the disciplinarian needs to be honest about the ways in which what I call *the primary discipline system* differs from other social contexts, i.e., *secondary systems* of discipline like the media or peer groups.

No matter how hard we try to help our kids see that family, school, and community are trying to practice one primary and consistent discipline system, we are not a tribal culture. Our kids can see how our primary system gets undercut and contradicted by other systems. We need to keep our kids focused on the primacy of the system in which they were raised, helping them to see that the values of discipline and character building they get from media and peer groups should be tested by how they hold up to the primary system.

We can be afraid of "outer influences," like media and peer groups, or we can integrate them into our system. In being honest with our kids about how we have one system and our neighbors have another, the disciplinarian shows the child the choices available to the child, and helps the child make the right choice. The choices become a teaching tool. As disciplinarians, we generally cause more trouble than we solve by being reactionary toward those "other" people and images as if they seek to do damage to the primary discipline system. When we overreact, our children see weakness in us. When we say, "Oh yes, Mrs. Tanner believes that hitting is okay in that case. What do we believe? What do you believe?" We do some good. When we continue with, "Why do you believe Mrs. Tanner might want to hit in that case? What other choices has she missed?" we bring our child into a moral dialogue that matures him.

The disciplinarian teaches the boy right and wrong action, not right or wrong *feeling*. In teaching right and wrong action, the disciplinarian allows the boy privacy in his own inner world. The disciplinarian does not teach the boy that "this feeling is right and this feeling is wrong, this fantasy is right and this fantasy is wrong." A boy's feelings are not "right" or "wrong" nor are they the disciplinarian's object for control. (Exceptions to this exist in the cases of obsessive-compulsive, predatory or highly at-risk boys who lack the internal skill to distinguish fantasy from reality and act out from that position of confusion.)

Seeking to control a boy's feelings leads to more rebellion than the disciplinarian wants. In distinguishing feeling from action in the discipline system, the disciplinarian teaches the boy that his character is his own, cannot be and should not be taken away from him, and has boundaries. By adults not overjudging boys' feelings, boys learn how not to harshly and continually judge themselves, both as boys and as men, and thus to be more compassionate toward themselves and others. The quickest way to create a boy or man who lacks compassion is to judge and shame his feelings.

If a boy is given too little *structure* or too much, he will not flourish: neither permissiveness nor authoritarianism will create the boy and man we seek. An authoritative stance will. By authoritative we mean that we create a sense of wise authority in ourselves so that the boy believes we are the right leader to listen to. Boys need to know who is the authority. Authority figures hold power over a certain kind of magic. As long as the boy trusts that the authority—parent, mentor, educator, caregiver—is an empowered keeper of some magic, the boy will listen to that person and, when he steps out of line, accept punishment from that person (or persons). We become the authority not because we indulge the boy or because we make him intrinsically afraid of us. He believes we are the authority because we help the boy build his own inner sense of authority. The boy who has been disciplined in an authoritative way thus gradually learns self-discipline.

For a discipline system to be absorbed into the boy's psyche and functioning, it needs to begin early in life. Because the discipline system is a global way of teaching respect, strengths, and limitations we must introduce kids to the system early by giving them responsibilities early. We make them clear their own dishes, pick up their room, say please and thank you, and so on, as early as is possible given their individual abilities.

As the kids get older, the discipline system must *adapt* to changes in the lives of the adults and the children. A good standard for measuring where changes are needed is to keep track of what new pieces of independence the child needs year after year. The discipline system adapts as the child's urges for independence ask it to. In this, we can follow the child's cues, without ever needing to give up the core elements of the system—respect, moral choices, accountability, and integrity.

Discipline in the First Decade of Life

Clarice is a grandmother of five. When her grandson, David, was two and a half years old, he "was like the Ever Ready battery," Clarice told me. "He never ran down, and, my, did he hit." I asked her how she handled the hitting. She said, "At the time there was a lot coming out about hyperactivity, so I thought maybe that's what he was. We all talked about it, his parents, my husband, the school counselor. But we just didn't believe it was that. We all kept trying to work with him, trying time-outs when it was really bad, taking away the offending toy, giving him punitive consequences like taking away a movie or Barney.

"One day, we had a kind of breakthrough. Whenever he hit me I would say, 'David, you are hurting grandma,' or 'David, you could hurt grandma.' But this one day, after he hit me with a plastic hammer, I lifted my sleeve and pointed to a place on my skin that was a little off color near where he hit me. It wasn't a bruise from the hammer, but I said, 'David, look, you hurt me. I'm very sad.' "

"I was about to continue by asking for the hammer and taking away a privilege when he put his finger out to touch the discolored area. As he touched it I said again, 'That really hurt me.'

"He paused for a second, then looked up into my eyes and began to cry. He looked terribly upset and reached out for me. I hugged him and he hugged me hard, as if to say, 'I'm sorry.' I told him I loved him and I said, 'You're special to me, that's why it hurts me even more to be hit by you.' " He cried and hugged and finally, really, groked [a term from Heinlein's *The Stranger in a Strange Land,* which means to "fully understand"] the whole thing.

"He did hit me again, but not often. In fact, he was able to stop himself from hitting a great deal more. My daughter, his mother, reported a difference too. Something really happened for him that day."

Clarice's strategy involved continual love, explanation of natural consequences of the offending act—grandma's pain—as well as punitive consequences—taking away offending toys or other privileges—patient explanation and then, by accident, experiential learning. Hitting is a normal activity of independence for toddler kids. But that normal act turned into a valuable lesson once David touched the wound he caused, and thereby understood the pain he was causing. He truly had a neurological breakthrough.

TWELVE TECHNIQUES FOR HEALTHY DISCIPLINE

Clarice's strategy involves some of the common sense techniques of discipline that work best with prepubescent boys.

Technique 1. Show the boy in the external world the effect of his inappropriate action. When, for instance, he hits, show him with objects in space the consequence of the hit. Show the bruise. Make him pick up the broken plant. Showing works better, often, than telling does. The verbal component is not, often, a little boy's strength. When he *experiences* the consequence, it often is more powerful for him.

Technique 2. Redirect the boy's aggressive energies from an animate to an inanimate object. When a boy hits or pushes, show him that a living thing gets hurt, but he can hit a couch if he wants, or have a tantrum on the floor. If he wants to hit mom when he's angry, mom needs to redirect his fists to the floor. Boys who are given a ritual object to hit, i.e., the same part of the couch each time, or "their" place on the floor, benefit greatly. Toy punching bags or bean-bag chairs work well, too.

Technique 3. Use a stern tone of voice. Say please once, maybe twice, then become stern. Moms often report finding this difficult. One mom told me, "My three-year-old is scared to death of his dad's voice, but mine has no effect." Often a stern tone of voice, or a loud sound like the clapping of hands, get through to the boy where a pleasant tone of voice doesn't. Remember that boys can often hear less well than girls, so a modicum of increased loudness will help them hear you. The stern tone will show them you're serious. Sometimes just applying a loud, stern voice removes the need for more punitive interventions.

Technique 4. Give the boy (or you) a time-out when necessary. If time-outs start too early, they lose their power. For a boy under two, a time-out a day is too many. Time-outs need to be combined with the loss of toys and privileges. When you as a caregiver need a time-out, take it. Alternating caregiver time-outs with the boy's time-out can wonderfully change the whole dynamic.

Technique 5. Choose diversion and distraction first. Especially for toddlers, discipline is primarily about diverting attention from the offending object to another object. When we want the boy to put on his coat and he refuses, we often gain by handing him his Barney doll and then, his energy diverted, getting his coat on. So many toddler troubles are simply a matter of the toddler being fixated on one object or behavior for all it's worth—once we distract the fixation we get what we want.

Technique 6. Ignore his refusal, and give sixty seconds to do the task. We can all ignore our boys' whining refusals more than we do. When we ask a boy to pick something up and he whines, "I don't want to," we can ignore him and thus avoid a power struggle.

This ignoring should be accompanied by about sixty seconds of non-contact. Within that sixty seconds, he'll probably get to the task, especially once he sees we're not engaging in power struggle with him. Remember that power struggle is his normal separation-individuation-independence behavior.

If after a minute or so he has not done the task, we might remind him, offer to do a small part of it to help him, or explain what intrinsic reward he and the home or community will enjoy by his accomplishment of the task. For a boy who is living in a discipline system, this will often be enough. If, however, it isn't, then we punish.

The key here is to see that we have not been punishing him for the first couple minutes or so of this power struggle. By ignoring him, giving him time, even following up with explanation, we are saying to him, "I value you and your search for independence." By not picking up the toy for him, and by moving into potential punishment when we need to, we also show him there are rules to be followed. We accomplish a great deal in a few patient minutes.

Technique 7. Negotiate and provide choices. Give-and-take is a good strategy for boys as they grow beyond the toddler years. Negotiating with a boy does not show a loss of our authority. It shows the boy we trust that there is worth in his point of view and we are willing to explore that worth with him.

When the boy does not want to put on his coat, we might say, "Well, let's see, do you want to put the coat on yourself, or should I do it?" Very often, he will stop saying, "I don't want the coat on." Rather, he will say, "I'll do it myself!" By this strategy we are appealing to his continued and growing need to show his independent prowess.

Another way of providing choices is to offer to help the boy do something. "Hey, let's do it together." Sometimes he'll go for that. Sometimes he'll push away and want to do it himself. If he chooses that independent option, it's essential we don't take this as personal rejection, or react by entering a power/struggle. By giving him choices with which he can negotiate *his* options, we help him develop, whatever happens.

Technique 8. Take away privileges and toys. If the boy insists on disobeying, we can threaten to take away a coveted privilege or toy. If that doesn't work, we take it away for a defined period of time. "If you don't clean up the table as I asked you to, you will not be allowed to watch *Pocahontas* as you wanted to after dinner. You must help out with the work of the family before you can have the play." The privilege can be going to a movie, playing with a friend, watching a beloved program, eating a special meal. The toy can be a train set, a bike, a Power Rangers set. Every parent knows what a child covets most.

Making this work as a key element in the discipline system requires that the disciplinarian not give in once the privilege or toy is taken away. We need to set a time for "earning it back," and stick to that time.

Technique 9. Use positive expectations. Whenever possible, we need to say, "You can do it," or imitate a media model, like the little engine that could, "I think I can, I think I can," getting our boy to see himself as an innate success.

Technique 10. Make things into games whenever possible. When we create tasks that have a secondary play object, the boy often *wants* to do the thing he previously didn't want to do. "Can you set the table in one minute? I'll set the timer and let's see." When we choose this technique, it's important we don't overly reward the finished task. Sometimes we'll say, "If you do it within one minute I'll give you candy." This can cause worse problems, making the boy think he needs to get "paid" for every family task he's asked to do. The key to using games is to make the game fun enough without external reward to get the boy to do a task. We may not choose this technique too frequently, given our busy schedules, but sometimes nothing will work quite as well.

Technique 11. Focus boys on the specific challenge of tasks. When boys are inattentive, not doing what we ask, or rebelling, it often works to get them focused. They may need this task-focus. Sometimes the task itself is too big, or at least big enough to resist and rebel against. If, for instance, we say to a toddler who's resisting putting his coat on, "Can you get it over your head, can you get your arm in the sleeve," he gets refocused from the global task to the specific challenges within the task. When an eight-year-old doesn't want to clean up his room, we help him see the room in particular sections, with particular challenges. "Why don't you make that corner there the sports corner? Make that section the games corner."

Technique 12. Teach through mistakes and "failures." This is perhaps the technique we most often forget to apply. Perhaps it is more than a technique—it is a spiritual principle. We must let boys make many, many mistakes.

A mother told me about her five-year-old son who cut his one-and-a-half-year-old sister's hair. The mother, who had been in the kitchen cooking dinner, came into the playroom, saw the deed, was mortified, scared, enraged, and tempted to completely lose it with her son. Her daughter's head looked a terrible mess, and the mother had visions of the boy poking the toddler's eyes out with the scissors.

The mother confessed that she did "lose it," but then, after she calmed down and her husband came home, the two of them sat the boy down and said, "What did you learn from this mistake?" The five-year-old, of course, didn't have much to say, but the parents taught him, through his mistake, lessons about the danger of the scissors, respect for his sister's person, and so on. As the conversation ended, the mother said, "You know, my father told me when I was your age, it's okay to make a mistake once, that's how you learn. So you've had your 'once,' okay?" The boy, frightened himself by his mistake, was quite ready to agree.

This incident illustrates the commonsense notion that boys must be allowed to make mistakes. They learn experientially. Giving a boy two chances, as this mother did, or saying to a boy "three mistakes and you're out," works better than expecting perfection. In every case, when a parent, mentor, or educator expects perfection from a child, the expectation grows from the adult's sense of inadequacy, not from what is best for the child.

SHOULD WE SPANK BOYS?

During the early years, we are all faced with this question. Then, if we've chosen to spank, it comes up again as our boys get older and we wonder when spanking should stop. Our individual questions about spanking are being asked by many people all around us.

Murray S. Straus, founder and director of the University of New Hampshire's Family Research Lab, has fought for almost two decades to reduce or eliminate "the largely taken for granted family violence called spanking." His latest book, *Beating the Devil Out of Them: Corporal Punishment in American Families,* argues passionately that spanking does no real good as a discipline technique, and teaches kids violence.

On the other side of the fence is a resurgence of energy from people who want to find a dramatic way to end the "out-of-control" kids who populate our families and schools. This side of the camp wants to see more well-measured, "virtuous violence," in the form of spanking and paddling in schools.

Somewhere in the middle is a family psychologist like John Rosemond who argues that "spankings are not abusive and beatings are. A spanking is a swat (or perhaps two) swiftly applied to a child's rear end by means of a parent's open hand."

I sit in the middle. Those of us who sit here seem to agree that spanking is not something one "believes in." To say we believe in spanking implies that we believe that it is essential for the upbringing of a child. Because it can become abuse in the hands of a troubled parent, and because it can cause accidental damage to the child, both psychological and physical, we shy away from it. In any case, we have to understand *why* we spank, then if we still choose to use it, understand *how* to do it so it does its job.

Its job is to get a child's undivided and immediate attention; to quickly stop an undesirable or dangerous behavior; to get control of a situation that could quickly get worse, potentially causing more damage to the child, family and community than a swat would; and to remind the child forcefully who is the authority.

Hurting the child is nowhere in its job description.

If we apply a swat on a child's bottom for the four reasons, and apply it very infrequently, we are being responsible parents.

How many people spank? The National Family Violence Survey of 1975 and 1985 revealed that more than 90 percent of parents reported using corporal punishment with three-year-old children. They also revealed that parents who spank tend to do so often. Two thirds of the mothers with children under six said they hit their child an average of three times a week. Forty percent of parents said they still hit their fourteen-year-olds.

Many of these people are not spanking responsibly. If someone is spanking a child daily, even weekly, they are doing it too much. They are "believing in" spanking, they are not seeking other options, they are just plain lazy parents, or they have their own problems and use their children as objects to release frustrations. Studies indicate over and over again that consistent spanking does not change a child's acting out. In fact, it is often just the opposite. The child becomes immune to the everyday or weekly swats in the way his body becomes immune to an antibiotic that is taken too much.

For spanking to be an effective part of a discipline system that includes many of the features we discussed in the last section, it has to be used only a few times a year, in very dramatic situations. John Rosemond's "Rules of Palm" are very useful:

▼   Be quick about it. One or two swats, that's it.

▼   Do not ever spank as a "last resort." Parents who do this usually come to a point when the last resort becomes the first resort.

▼   Never, ever spank in rage. Take time out if you're raging. Count to ten. Get out of the room.

▼   Use your hand, and your hand only.

▼   Apply the hand to the child's rear end only. It's not necessary to pull down kids' clothes. Again, the purpose of spanking is not to cause pain—it is to get the child's attention.

▼   Follow through with a clear, stern message and, if need be, another restrictive consequence.

▼   Spank only in private, never in public. Corporal punishment in schools, if it is applied, must be applied with more privacy than is often practiced.

▼   Spank only occasionally; by the time a child is nine or ten, spanking should cease entirely. For a child entering the second decade of life spanking is a gross humiliation.

The whole issue of spanking points out how important it is for parents, mentors, and educators to have a conscious plan for a discipline system before they conceive children, become mentors, become educators. We must know how to gain the respect of the boys we care for from early on so that by the time they are becoming "unruly, testosterone-driven adolescents," no punitive physical intrusiveness from authority figures is necessary. The adolescents themselves will find, through sports, peer groups, the military, and basic male risk-taking, many ways to get wounded and learn boundaries. If we have not taught them strong self-discipline by then, they'll go in directions that hurt them and us worse than need be. If we've spanked them continually as boys, using few other techniques, we can bet they'll suffer profound difficulties becoming the men we want them to be.

HYPERACTIVITY AND ATTENTION DEFICIT DISORDER

All these techniques are well and good, someone will say, but what about my son who . . .

Kevin, eight years old, "bounced up and down the walls," according to his mother, who blamed herself for his behavior. Both parents had tried every form of discipline. In school, Kevin did some projects carefully, concentrating on them for an hour at a time; most things, though, he never really sunk his teeth into. He said things out of turn, teased girls, even stole pencils and other harmless items from fellow students. "No one liked him," his mother admitted. "Not even his parents."

Kevin suffered from attention deficit hyperactivity disorder. This disorder is the most common behavioral disorder in American children, afflicting close to 4 million kids. Boys are three times as likely as girls to be afflicted with it. It has been overdiagnosed, and so there is controversy about it. For a few years, just about any acting out a kid did—especially the acting out of boys from six through ten—got diagnosed as ADHD. Now, we're returning to some balance in the way we diagnose it.

The disorder is best known for these three symptoms: a child is extremely distractible, unable to concentrate, his attention moving from one thing to the next seemingly at whim; a child lacks appropriate impulse control, saying things out of turn, saying inappropriate things in social situations, doing inappropriate things whenever the child can; and a child's body seems to be in constant movement, from pencil tapping to getting up and down out of chairs.

ADHD very often coincides with a child's gross mismanagement of social situations, through blurted answers at wrong times to breaking rules to impulsive theft. The ADHD boy may be unable to stay seated for long, have trouble following instructions or playing quietly, be a know-it-all talker and an interrupter, have trouble listening, be prone to lose things, take unnecessary risks. ADHD kids will often be ostracized by other kids. ADHD does fade sometimes with maturity, but sometimes not. At least half of adults who, as kids, had ADHD, show symptoms of it in adulthood.

The suffering an ADHD boy goes through in boyhood can often pay off later. ADHD kids very often grow up with an intense love of life, great senses of humor, passionate ambition, a lot of smarts, intense creativity. But dealing with them when they are kids is difficult. One mother said, "We had years of hell. There's no other way I can put it."

If you know a boy who is particularly hard to manage, check into ADHD as soon as possible. You'll also find it called ADD (attention deficit disorder) or, as it used to be called when we were children, "hyperactivity." Drugs like Ritalin (methylphenidate) can be prescribed to combat the disorder, a disorder which is part of the brain chemistry of the child. Many experts believe it is particularly prevalent in boys because testosterone exacerbates it, and the male brain may be more susceptible than the female. Diet can affect it, heredity is a factor, illness can spur it on.

Boys with ADHD early in life are more likely to suffer emotional problems later. Some of this may be chemical and some may be damage to self-image done by themselves, their caregivers and their social world as a result of the disorder going undiagnosed and the boy being treated as emotionally deformed, wrong, or shameful.

If you know an ADHD boy, patience and careful discipline are the keys. Books like *Why Johnny Can't Concentrate* and *Driven to Distraction* are invaluable. Most important is to see a physician.

Be ready, if your child takes medication, for his personality and temperament to change. This is not an easy disorder and its "cure" has side effects. Learn about these before you begin medication. You might get advice and help from a national network called Children and Adults with Attention Deficit Disorders.

Discipline in Puberty and Adolescence

Adolescent males are some very difficult folk to discipline! If a clear structure and system of healthy discipline has not been in place during their first decade of life, or if it is disrupted by some trauma—death of a parent or mentor, divorce, parental addiction or disease, for instance—the chances that the adolescent male will become a "hard case" increase.

When, on the other hand, adolescent males have had, in the first decade of life, a first family that has been a secure base, second and third families that continue to be committed to mentoring and educating them appropriately, and a clear discipline system in which they've built character and self-esteem, they move into adolescence with a far lower chance of becoming antisocial. This is just common sense. If the first ten years have gone well, the second ten have a greater chance of going well too.

Yet the second ten can go utterly awry if disciplinarians change the rules too significantly as the boys enter the second decade of life. By "rules" I don't mean the incidental rules—who's responsible for taking out the garbage, curfews, appropriate dating. I mean the emotional rules. All too often, parents, mentors, and educators think that their emotional job is diminished at a boy's puberty. Often, because the boy wants more independence, the adults say, "Okay, let him go, he's gonna rebel anyway, I'll just let him know I'm there for him."

Often adolescent boys will try to seem tough, but they need an emotional center and secure base, more in some ways than ever before. The key to helping them navigate adolescence is not to let them alone throughout its process but to help them find new foci of energy for their discipline system. Mothers give sons over to fathers, emotionally speaking: this is a transfer of the emotional center but still keeps the boy emotionally centered. Divorced mothers, whose husbands are estranged, help the boy find male mentors to help guide them through adolescence. Single mothers who have no other choice create conscious dialogue with the boy to say, "I've been one kind of mother, now I'm going to become another kind, a mother of an adolescent, tougher, less malleable, more like the man you're needing right now." Schools set up day and evening programs, getting boys into as many activities—from sports to chess club—so that boys can direct their adolescent energy. Businesses create service programs for adolescent youths. The government tries to protect job quantity and quality for adolescent youths.

The list of necessary steps for giving adolescent youths discipline—focus, challenge, productive tasks—is endless. When a boy is roaming around with six to seven testosterone surges a day in his body, a brain that is often focused on physical activities and experiential learning, and life in a culture that trains him in boy-specific ways, we don't just throw him into the greater world. We give him structures for his energy. We give him constant activity and then time to recharge. We give him experiential learning through games and tasks. We give him work. We expect him to take up a lot of space in his gangly experiments with life, and we teach him, through task, work, game, activity, and experience how to use that space. Above all, we give him mentoring and supervision that respects and teaches his gifts, his visions, even his shadowy inner demons.

Except for very hard cases, most adolescent boys and youths I've dealt with have asked for more adult contact than they are getting, not less. Unfortunately, we have all had our own priorities. We have taken their youthful cries for more freedom and less adult restriction too superficially. We have assumed rebellion was enough to teach youth manhood. And we have been just plain lazy. Our youth want less adult contact if that contact treats them like boys. They want more adult contact that treats them like young men. Tired as they are of the former, they are hungry for the latter.

Just as we approached discipline as a systematic enterprise in the first decade of a boy's life, so we must approach it in the second. Here are some questions for us to answer:

What system have we had in place in the first decade and how can it be modified (not destroyed) in the second? We'll need to remain firm, keep clear rules, be consistent, yet give more freedom and responsibility.

How will elders play their roles and alter those roles in the boy's changing life? Our adolescent's emotional health depends especially on this element.

How will we help the boy find greater emphasis on second- and third-family groupings, especially peer groups and new mentors, without teaching him to make his first family and his peer group enemies of each other? This will require us to get as involved as he'll let us in knowing his friends, answering his questions.

What choices will we make to keep families intact and diminish family trauma? A certain amount of family upheaval is normal and even useful in an adolescent's growth, but divorce is very dangerous to the emotional life of the adolescent, especially when that divorce happens late in the first decade or early in the second decade of the boy's life.

If family trauma occurs, how will we get significant help for the boy, and how will we make sure the boy does not get caught in the middle of parental enmities?

Having said all this, let's listen to some adolescent males, in some of their own language. I asked a group of high school boys what they wanted from us as adults who provide discipline. The group was white, black, and Hispanic. We decided to put their requests in terminology from rap music and rap culture. It was a fun, disarming way to get the youth to talk freely. You'll hear nothing "new" in this list, but you'll hear it from this generation.

Cut the illin'. Illin' means absurd. In other words, they know when we're being absurd. If we're going to provide them with discipline, they need to know we're part of the real world. For them the "real world" is their world, so we'll need to learn as much as possible about their world.

When elders and youth all lived in the same tribe, their worlds were not so different. Now their worlds are very different. Many elders think "I'm the authority, I don't need to learn my son's silly fads." This is often a mistaken view.

Chill out. "You're all too tripped about us," one African-American youth, sixteen, told me. "You just gotta chill. We're not out to do you damage." An adolescent male, above all, wants respect. When we overreact to the media hype about "dangerous youth" by becoming hypervigilant toward our teenage males, they feel watched and threatened, not respected.

Hook me up. To be "hooked up" means to be introduced to someone or something important. Unanimously, the group of youths wanted help getting hooked up. They wanted adult help. They felt pretty abandoned. Since our topic was discipline, one of the youths said, "Why should we do what you all want when you won't help us get hooked up?" Youth need elders to open up work, people, and places to them so they can get the kind of work and experience with which to find respect and self-respect.

Don't dis' me. Don't disrespect me. "There's dissing and then there's dissing," one seventeen-year-old said. The dissing that hurt came often from elders who didn't try to understand the life of the youth but still wanted obedience—"very ill." This, to many of the youths, felt like the worst disrespect of all.

Be hard with me. To be "hard" means to be authentic. There is an element of toughness in it too. Young men want adults to be tough but not "extreme tough"—they want us to be tough in the way that's meant by authentic. They want us to know who we are and what we believe so that they can believe in us. When we have to be tough with them, they want to be able to respect us.

Be down with me. When you're "down" with something you support something. Teenage boys want support from adults. They want to be eccentric and still be supported. They want to be mainstream and still be supported. Their peer-group pressure and sense of isolation is so severe, they feel lost without our support. "I do one thing wrong," one youth said, "and my daddy's not down with me anymore." It seemed to me many of these boys felt parents and educators were often just looking for excuses not to be down with them anymore.

Be cool. Don't take what our youth do personally. The system of discipline we once had in place needs modification as our boys grow, but instead of modifying the system, in concert with the changing needs of our youth, we hang onto the past, then overreact to the present.

One fourteen-year-old told this story: "I came home with an earring and my mother flipped. I was grounded for a week. That was not cool. I looked like a wacko to everyone who mattered."

Our youth make demands on us. These demands might sound like youth trying to tell adults what to do. I haven't gotten that feeling except from the few really hard cases. Most of the youth who make demands are more than willing to work with adults. If we treat them with respect, they'll treat us with respect. Respect, of course, means giving our time, our energy, the discipline of three families, and standing back too, taking nothing personally, letting go.

Some specific techniques that work with youth are these:

1. Be *consistent* and clear about expectations and punishments.

2. Ignore the youth's acting out when it is harmless chatter and dissing. Keep in mind this is how some young men communicate with each other. Allow the little rebellions to wash off you, impose control over the big, dangerous ones.

3. Do not allow harmful disrespect to go unnoticed or unchallenged. Simultaneously, whenever you can, turn disrespect back on the youth through verbal gamesmanship, jesting, etc.

4. Give primary authority to the style of discipline that is most effective. Mothers often give primary authority for youths over to fathers. If this is done, let it be done in such a way that the mother is aligned with the father. If she undercuts, for instance, by going behind dad's back to give the boy rewards dad withheld, the discipline becomes not a system but a morass.

5. Build many of the expectations by talking with the youth. Some expectations are not negotiable, but many more can be negotiated than we allow to be. Negotiate whenever possible.

6. Take away privileges as a primary means of family discipline.

7. Let the youth choose his own punishment when possible. Let him mete it out to himself.

8. Never hit.

9. Spend as much time as possible with younger adolescents, doing what they like to do (which will often be what you want to do), so that in later years of adolescence they'll still want to spend time with you.

10. Help youths find games, sports, tasks, and other systematic structures in which to build their own discipline. Martial arts are an obvious example of this. Many boys will be better disciplined at home and school if they learn a structure or system that is separate from home or school but through which they can learn a new approach to self-discipline.

11. Follow stages of discipline, especially reacceptance of the youth once the punishment is finished.

12. Be *consistent*.

13. For every piece of freedom you give a youth, give him a similar piece of responsibility.

14. Always let him know you're there for him.

Difficult, Violent Boys

Here are some facts gleaned from polls, surveys and government reports about violence among teens.

▼ 40 percent of the teens said they knew someone in their age group who had been shot in the last five years;

▼ 13 percent said at least half the students in their schools carried knives or guns;

▼ Close to half said their parents were "sometimes or often unavailable" to them;

▼ Poor parents are twice as likely to break up as those with money. Once parents break up, a male child's probability of becoming a criminal and a female child's probability of becoming pregnant before the age of eighteen rise exponentially;

▼ More than three fourths of crime in America, both violent and nonviolent, is committed by male children born to single parents or following their parents' divorce;

▼ Half the teens reported the television being on while they ate dinners with their parents;

▼ 90 percent of the nation's prison inmates up to age thirty-five were born to mothers under eighteen;

▼ About 20 percent of all violent crime is committed by children under the age of eighteen;

▼ Most of these offenders, whether jailed or not, return to committing crimes;

▼ 90 percent of these offenders are boys.

This list of bulleted items make the head spin, doesn't it? They are windows on walls of a room we're sitting in. We're talking in the room about teens and violence. We keep talking about all the reasons a minority of our teens—nonetheless a frightening minority—commit crime and do violence. We've heard all the reasons before. We sit in the room exhausted from looking out the windows, exhausted from talking about boys and violence, frightened.

A final window in our list of facts is one of the reasons we're so exhausted: we keep putting more and more of these violent and criminal males in jail, but we feel less and less safe. In the last ten years, the number of federal and state inmates has doubled to almost a million. The local jail population has risen nearly three times to almost 500,000. In individual states, like Washington, where I live, we have seen a 79 percent increase in our jail population, an 86 percent increase in prison capacity, and yet our state population has only grown 18 percent! Said Governor Mike Lowry: "At this rate, everyone in Washington State will be working in—or in—prison by 2056!"

Males, especially in the hormone-driven teen years, are wired for increased aggressiveness. Cultures have known this since the beginning of time. Tribal cultures have made sure males were guided through these years with constant initiation and elder male attention. Even our own ancestral cultures knew that one of the society's most difficult and important jobs is to train male aggression toward socially useful functions and away from antisocial functions. Studies of other primates indicate similar social strategies among animals around us.

Things have changed. Writes Miller Newton, author of *Adolescence*, "Adolescence has become increasingly dangerous for a growing minority of teens. Unlike the ritual ordeals of primitive societies, which presented youths with challenges that enabled them to prove themselves and join adult society, today's rituals have become purposeless, dangerous, and threatening."

Young males need training and channeling. If they don't get it, a large minority of them will train and channel themselves to use aggression antisocially. Over the last few years, researchers in both the U.S. and Canada have been measuring testosterone levels among violent male criminals. The average testosterone level of the violent criminal is higher than the average testosterone level of a citizen without criminal record.

War was once a socially acceptable way of channeling male aggression. War training "kept men in line" and "channeled their natural aggression against the enemy." Most boys do not go to war as this millennium ends. Most do not join the military.

Sports is certainly the most obvious aggression-channeling venue in male culture today. In fact, studies indicate that boys who play organized sports have a lower frequency of involvement in drugs and violent crime than boys who do not. Martial arts is one of the best places for boys to get a wholistic sense of the physical, mental, emotional, and spiritual challenges of boyhood. Many boys, however, don't choose to play organized sports or get involved in martial arts, lacking the self-confidence, the resources, the encouragement, or the interest. Moreover, a minority of boys who do play sports or engage in martial arts can become more aggressive, uncompassionate, and violent. Despite this, I have never seen a study that leads me to believe the risks of getting more midnight basketball, more organized soccer, more martial arts training into the inner cities outweighs the benefits. The more we help our at-risk youth use sports to find camaraderie, discipline, self-image, bonding, personal challenge and a second and third family, the better off we will be at channeling their aggression toward structures they can grow in.

Many boys will act out—as they always have, in aggressive behavior—the shadow side of the culture that raises them. They will mirror, with gangly and violent and destructive bodies, the awkwardness they sense in adult life, the violence they feel and absorb, the self-destructiveness of the adult culture as a whole. This is what a frightening minority of our teenage boys are doing today, in gangs, random violence, crime. If they do not learn a dance of aggression through some organized activity from male culture that loves, nurtures, and trains their aggression into a disciplined dance, they will be more likely to take their loss of this training, their grief, their anger that they have not received it out on the world around them.

As I've suggested throughout this chapter, I also believe the key to stopping male violence lies in rethinking discipline to mean "a discipline system," following our rethinking of family to include a stable first family, an active second family, a welcoming third family, and constant discourse among the three families in order to achieve consistent application of the discipline system. Are we ready for this kind of solution?

I think we're closer to being ready than we were, say, five years ago. People who have kids are thinking twice again about getting divorced. More and more teens are abstaining from promiscuous and unprotected sex. The word "mentor" is back in the national vocabulary, especially in inner cities where boys are at such risk. Churches are reaching out again. Even the media is listening to calls for more kid-responsible programming.

We live in a wonderful, challenging time. Pinocchio has awakened, and stretched his testosterone level, but we have the resources to train and nurture him into whatever kind of man we want him to be.

DO BOYS NEED MORE DISCIPLINE THAN GIRLS?

"He sure needs a lot of discipline," we hear someone say about a boy. "He sure needs more discipline than his sister."

When we hear this, we are hearing judgment, aren't we? We're hearing negativity, as if his needing discipline indicates a flaw or defect, not only his, but our own.

Not all boys need more discipline than girls, of course. Yet many do. They seek to test limits, get hurt if need be, and learn through their wounds. Girls do this too, but the average boy does it more, often because his testosterone drives him toward more physical activity and other forms of risk taking.

To say a particular boy needs more discipline than a particular girl need not be a judgment of the boy. In fact, just the opposite: the boy is seeking the best way he knows to test the world for his limits, even if it means a great deal of pain, pushing and discipline.

Discipline as an Ongoing System

No matter how hard we try not to, our systems of discipline will hurt our sons. We will be imperfect in applying our discipline. We will be in bad moods and lash out at them. We will awaken, at various points in our boys' lives, saying, "I hurt that boy, I hurt him unnecessarily. I'm sorry." To be in relationship is to hurt others. To be an authority in the life of a child is somedays to hurt the child. As we teach our boys discipline our eyes will often see beyond what our hands and words have been capable of doing. To talk about discipline is to talk about ideal standards. To apply discipline is to come down from the sky and get muddy and bloody and sometimes confused.

Yet even in this our sense of discipline needs to continue in a spiritual context. For when our boys move through adolescence and then into adulthood, we have a choice about how to treat the shadow wounds we have given them along the way. We can watch their maturing lives in self-blame and guilt, intruding on them, in myriad subtle ways, with our many guilts. Or we can say to our boys, "Here are the mistakes I believe I made with you. I'm willing to talk to you about mistakes you perceive. Let me help you, or let someone else help you, discover now how the mistakes your parents, mentors, and educators made have become key elements in the heroic journey you're beginning as an adult."

If discipline is truly a systemic part of a boy's life, then that system is not finite or finished at age eighteen. Rather, it is more like an infinite circle. The discipline—both "positive" and "negative"—that we practiced with our boys creates a great deal of the energy of the life story they will live as men. As we let them go to their own adult path of self-discipline, our final job is to help them gain the adult tools to recognize the part we play in their destiny. As Carl Jung once said, "When an inner situation is not made conscious, it appears outside as fate." When our boys become adults, we become their inner situation. We become inner voices they often hear in their work, relationships, and spiritual practice.

The philosopher Sam Keen has written: "We all leave childhood with wounds. In time we may transform our liabilities into gifts. The faults that pockmark the psyche may become the source of a man's or woman's beauty. The injuries we have suffered invite us to assume the most human of all vocations—to heal ourselves and others."

The greatest gift a parent can give a youthful, then an adult child is respectable and trustworthy authority. The conversation between the parent and adult child that often leads to a great deal of mutual respect and trust between the two adults is the one that may begin in an adult child's anger at a parent for "negative" discipline. It may continue in an elder parents' apology and explanation: "Here's why I did those things and yes, I'm sorry for those mistakes." But it mustn't stop in anger and apology. It must also include encouragement on the part of the parent, mentor, or educator that now the adult child—the maturing young man—look back at the "mistakes" we made in his past, not to "fix" himself by looking back, but to find himself; not to end his journey but to continue it; not to blame the parent but to find his own soul. The elder authority never stops teaching the younger man.

Sometimes parents who have hurt a son think it helps if the offending parents become non-authorities. They will let the son verbally abuse them after he has become an adult. They will constantly apologize to the son. They cause more pain, rather than less, when they buckle this way. As the son looks back at the past he will reclaim parts of himself that he lost. When he comes through this phase of his life he will be most appreciative not of our indulgences and overapologies, but of our ability both to take responsibility and yet retain the power and strength we keep modeling for him, even on our deathbeds.

chapter 8

Teaching Boys Values, Morality, and Spirituality

*When I was young I was sure of the good of
the world, its beauty, and its ultimate
justice. And even when I was broken the
way one sometimes can be broken, and even
though I had fallen, I found upon arising
that I was stronger than before.*

—*from Mark Helprin's*
A Soldier of the Great War

There is a story told in the south of India about a boy who, as he becomes an adolescent, is sent by his mother and father to continue his growth in discipleship to a wise Brahmin. He remains with the Brahmin for some time, and then the Brahmin says to him, "Go into the world and ask those you meet this question: 'What is the greatest value?' Come back and tell me their answers. Come back neither too late nor too soon."

The boy sets off to his mission. Upon leaving the Brahmin's house he meets a mother with her children. The boy asks, "What is the greatest value?" She answers, "Take good care of the children, for they will feed you forever."

Further down the road he meets a goat. He asks the goat, "What is the greatest value?" The goat answers, "Take good care of the animals as if they are your own children."

Further down the road he meets some men at work in a ditch. "What is the greatest value?" he asks. A man answers, "Work diligently but do not lose yourself."

Further down the road he meets two lovers embracing. They answer, "When you fall in love, put all other work aside, and lose yourself."

So it went for this boy who was becoming a man. As he journeyed and asked his question, he got many answers. Some made sense to him. Some contradicted each other. All seemed like pieces of a puzzle, but he could not fathom how they came together.

One day, exhausted, he returned to the Brahmin. He said, "I am confused. So many answers. So many truths. What shall I do?"

"Maybe," the Brahmin said, "the question I gave you is no longer the right one."

"What is the right question?" the young man asked eagerly.

"How shall I know myself? That is the right question, for knowing yourself is the greatest value."

"Why did no one say that to me?" the young man asked. "Why did no one answer me, 'Knowing yourself is the greatest value?' "

"There are many ways of answering," the Brahmin said. "Go back out to the road, continue your journey, ask "How shall I know myself?" and listen well."

As parents, mentors, and educators we try to educate our children in these things in a vacuum that tribal cultures and our own ancestors did not face: without a concrete, universally accepted sacred text; without a guiding mythology; in a climate of cynicism, both among adults and youth; without a conscious, cohesive three-family system; without clear understanding of the stages of a child's moral development; without personal, intimate time with kids, while struggling under overwhelming materialist priorities to discover even meager spiritual ones; and within a social context that has become so politicized the clarification of values depends not on our soul's voice but on the politics with which we agree.

What follows are suggestions that do not require affiliation with a political perspective. The politicization of values these days and the propaganda each political camp throws out into the culture to push its values through its politics have nearly crushed the pursuit of truth and wonder in our children's lives. I will try to reinstate that pursuit, and hope my suggestions will help boys gain education in values, morality, and spirituality.

To Teach Values to Kids We Must Know Our Own

A wonderful anti-drug commercial plays on our television every few months or so. A boy of about thirteen is in his bedroom. His father comes in, irate, holding drug paraphenalia he had found earlier in the boy's room.

"Who'd you learn about this stuff from!" he demands to know from his son.

The son replies, "From you, Dad."

A foundation of our ability to teach values is our own self-understanding of the code of integrity, honesty, honor, responsibility, and soul care under which we live as adult individuals. I can best teach what I myself practice. I can best teach what I myself know. Kids will not learn from me what I myself am unsure of. I must clarify my own values so I can teach them to the kids around me.

What are your "values?" Forget for a moment that the word "values" has become as glib as the word "coffee" in the media and out of the mouths of politicians. What are *your* values? By way of simple definition: a value is a principle for living not only worthwhile for its own sake but necessary and fundamental to the progress of self, family, community, culture, *and* earth. The value, the principle of worth, can be semantically applied wherever anyone wants to apply it. It's a very malleable concept. But we can judge its application by whether, when we take *both a microcosmic and macrocosmic view* of the application, it still makes sense.

Some people will say, for instance, "Life should be the most important value to every human being." In the microcosmic view—focused mainly on personal and family survival—this makes good sense. If I didn't value life above all else, I would do great harm to myself, my family, and my world—I would not protect myself and my kin. However, in the macrocosmic view, "life" is not and has never been the primary human value: "quality of life" has always been the primary human value. We give and take the lives of plants, animals and even humans when human survival, social progress, and quality of community life requires it. So "life," which is of primary value microcosmically, is not necessarily of primary value macrocosmically. This often happens, for "values" have a highly complex logic. "Quality of life" is a value that applies both microcosmically and macrocosmically. We must always, in all circumstances, seek to assure that we have a good quality of life.

As we explore our own values, and the rhetoric that exists around the public debate over values, we do more for our children when we are careful to look for both the micro-truth and the macro-truth. Our children, of course, even if unconsciously, are looking at both kinds of truth.

Before going any further into this chapter, please take out a pad of paper and write about *your* values. I've only highlighted a few categories of values.

- ▼ What are your responsibilities as a human being?
- ▼ What is integrity for you?
- ▼ What constitutes the courageous position, in your mind, as you face difficult questions and situations in the world?
- ▼ To whom do you owe compassion and how should you show it?

Just your answers to each of these questions will probably take up a whole notebook as you notice all the people, issues, and needs you are challenged by in a lifetime. Here are some more questions:

- ▼ How are you responsible for yourself?
- ▼ How are you responsible for family?
- ▼ How are you responsible to friends?
- ▼ What's your role in the community and culture?
- ▼ How are you responsible for care of the earth?
- ▼ When is lying okay?
- ▼ What truths are relative for you and which are absolute?
- ▼ Whose ideas and modeling are you following, perhaps unconsciously, as you answer questions about truth—what prophets, seers, thinkers? Do their answers satisfy you?
- ▼ For what truths would you sacrifice your life?
- ▼ What activities show cowardice?
- ▼ How have you been a coward?
- ▼ How have you been courageous?

▼   To whom can you turn when you individually feel you have done something courageous but many others call you a coward?

▼   Who are the needy around you?

▼   Do you know how to be compassionate toward yourself, especially when you fail at something?

▼   Do you know how to soothe yourself and others when you are called to do so?

▼   What values, overall, are your priority values?

If you cannot answer these questions with rich, complex, and concrete replies, you will have difficulty teaching compassion, courage, integrity, and responsibility—and all the sub-values contained within them—to the boys around you.

The Stages of Moral Development

Earlier in this century, the theorists Jean Piaget and Lawrence Kohlberg, working separately but in similar fields, noticed that not only cognitive development but also moral development occur in stages. Initially, Piaget's insights saw two stages: objective and subjective. In the first, the child understands something as "immoral"—e.g., hitting his brother in the face—because it will incur an "objective" circumstance—e.g., a parent's anger. The painful consequence is what makes the act immoral to him. In the second stage, the child understands that subjective intentions are a large part of the equation: if he hits his brother by accident, he has not acted immorally; if he hits his brother out of spite, he has. In stage two of Piaget's model, the cognitive development of the child has evolved to where he has developed "moral rationality."

Lawrence Kholberg took Piaget's initial insights on stages of moral development much further, giving parents, mentors, and educators a six-stage model for moral development. Here are his three "levels" and six "stages."

I. *Preconventional Level.* At this level, the child learns cultural rules and labels of good/bad, right/wrong and follows these rules based on the pain/pleasure consequent to them. The amount and consistency of pain/pleasure (punishment/reward) is based on the power held by the provider of consequence. There are two stages to this level.

Stage 1. *Punishment and Obedience Orientation*. The child does not yet have a sense of an underlying moral order or design. All he knows is "Mom will be mad/hurt me if I hit Joey. I better not hit Joey." He cannot see yet that hitting Joey is not only wrong in, for instance, a parents' eyes, but in society's eyes as well. He avoids punishment and seeks rewards from the authority figure. These are his priority.

Stage 2. *Instrumental Relativist Orientation*. The child sees human relations as a kind of marketplace. His major priority is getting his own needs met. He thinks about fairness, reciprocity, and sharing but very pragmatically. "You give me a hot-wheel, I'll give you a whiffle-ball." His cognitive development does not make him capable of clearly understanding things like gratitude for its own sake, or any form of justice beyond "You took mine now I'll take yours."

All children differ, of course, so putting an age to these stages is risky. We associate the earliest stages with the early years of a child's life (*approximately* one to three for stage 1 and three to six for stage 2) and try to educate the child through and then beyond them as the child becomes capable of more advanced moral reasoning.

II. *Conventional Level*. The child advances cognitively to see that maintaining family, group, and even national expectations are valuable in their own right, even if the consequences cause pain. The child becomes loyal to family or group, actively conforming to, supporting, even justifying the social order to which he has given allegiance. The young person identifies with group orientation and authorities within groups for modeling of moral appropriateness. There are two stages in this conventional level of moral development.

Stage 3. *Interpersonal Concordance Orientation*. The child learns to be "a good boy," "a nice boy," "an appropriate boy." The child learns that the group will label him and he acts in search of the rewarding label. He wants approval and knows how to behave in order to get not only individual approval but group approval. "If I

steal, I won't be liked," he learns. "If I'm honest, I will be liked."
Of course, in some peer groups he may very well learn that if he
steals he *will* be liked! When this happens, he gains two competing
moral messages, and must, ultimately, pick between them. This
process of choosing refines his moral development.

In this stage, a boy often conforms to stereotypical images, thinking
that wearing certain clothes, talking a certain way, drinking a certain
drink are "natural" behavior or, at least, what the majority want him
to do.

Even while succumbing to stereotype, he works hard to clarify
intentions. When someone does something, he wonders about that
person's intention. When he himself does something, he often uses
intention to justify his behavior. So he is searching for group approval,
but he's also developing his own individual conscience.

Stage 4. *Law and Order Orientation.* The young person makes a
commitment to the fixed rules of a social order that he now realizes,
in his adolescence, is quite huge, even mysterious, and worth re-
specting. (This doesn't mean he won't rebel, too). "In our family,
we open the car door for mom," a father might teach. The son
follows this fixed rule. Right behavior is constituted, for him, of
doing his duty, showing authority figures ultimate respect, and
maintaining the social order for its own sake. "In a school classroom we don't speak while someone else is speaking." The boy
needs to know the rules in this stage, feel respect for who has made
them, and thus feel morally sound in committing himself to the
rules and the leader and, through them, the social order.

These two stages predominate late childhood and early to mid-
adolescence. By the time we are late adolescents and "adults," we will
hopefully have learned: morality by experiencing the rewards of acting
morally and the punishments for not doing so; pragmatic skills for
getting our needs met within moral boundaries; how to modify our
behavior to get approval from people and groups whose approval we
emotionally need; and how to do our moral duty within a social order.
With each stage of moral learning, we gain the power to mix elements
of previous stages, using each when necessary.

Our rebellions against parents and others will, if our three families raise us well, be *emotional* rebellions for the most part, not *moral* rebellions. We rebel against mom or dad by not doing what they say on a specific occasion, but we don't destroy the moral structure and authority of the family, group, or society.

III. *Postcoventional, Autonomous, or Principled Level.* At this level, we make the individual effort to define moral values and principles apart from authorities, groups, and our own need to identify with a group. We will often end up accepting a principle that a group or tradition accepts, but not until we've searched it out autonomously for ourselves.

Stage 5. *The Social Contract Orientation.* The person explores individual rights, both through the lens of what society has dictated those rights to be (i.e., "my constitutional rights") and through a less polished but deeply searching personal lens (i.e., "society says I have these rights, but I think individuals should have this other right too").

When my country is involved in a war in Vietnam but I don't believe I should fight that war, my moral reasoning will include this stage 5 element. I will see how complex a social-moral structure is—a structure that gives me the right to speak out against the war yet wants me to go fight the war. I will, in the end, have to choose *my* interpretation of what is the highest priority in my social contract with my culture.

It is this stage of moral reasoning that often gets laws changed, wars stopped, the lives of underprivileged people noticed and looked after. A young person in this stage feels great tension within himself about how to change a rule or law yet stay within the bounds of the procedural structures set up by social consensus.

In our families this sometimes shows up when a teenager is trying to get us to change a rule, arguing that he has new individual rights. Let's say our sixteen-year-old son drives our car without asking because he feels an emergency has come up. He has proven his responsibility already, but we haven't yet changed the rule. When he drives the car without asking, we go ballistic, imposing a stage 2 or stage 4 orientation on him. He has moved to stage 5, but we haven't. He knows he's capable of thinking out this emergency and making the right, conscientious decision. We get angry at his rebellion without noticing that it is not he but we who are stuck in earlier developmental stages.

When we see our kids rebelling, it's important to look at what stage they're in. Often they're way ahead of us. If we shifted as fluidly as our kids did, our kids wouldn't have to engage in as much moral rebellion. What they would often rather do is change the rule from within our family structure and not have to openly, painfully rebel against our moral authority.

Stage 6. *Universal Ethical Principle Orientation.* We choose ethical principles that appeal to a comprehensive inner logic, a sense of universal social values; principles that we seek to apply consistently. These are "principles"—like the Golden Rule—as opposed to concrete moral "rules, dictated by a higher authority"—like the Ten Commandments.

If I decide that I must do unto others as I would have them do unto me, I am learning a whole way of life, a way that gains its power and worth from my ability to let it permeate my personal, family, group, social, and natural interactions. If I learn "Follow your conscience at all costs," I will find myself becoming benevolent with no ulterior motives. I will give money to needy people without expecting anything back. I will become generous of spirit. I will do unpopular things and not feel my self-worth crushed by others' rancor. Instead, I may feel stronger from the blows.

We arrive at our sense of the "universality" and "ethicality" of our principles by having first understood, in depth, what justice is, reciprocity, equality of human rights, respect for one another, the dignity of individual persons.

Many young people never get fully into stage 6. Many adults in their forties, fifties, and sixties never quite get there, requiring recompense for every gift they give, making life a constant stage 2 give-and-take or stage 4 obsession with following tradition-based social rules.

These are the six stages according to Kholberg. Since his time, many people have modified them. Some have added stages. As our moral thinking continues to be studied by value theorists, we'll keep seeing the stages modified. Yet we'll also keep seeing that kids learn moral reasoning in stages, no matter what exact sequence and variety of stages a given parent, mentor, or educator sees in kids. If we are to assist our boys in learning values and morality, we have to start looking, in them, for what stage they're in at a given time.

THE PLUS 1 SYSTEM

One of the most valuable applications of Kohlberg's model is the "Plus 1" system. It works like this: if I see that my seven-year-old son is in stage 2, I help him evolve not by applying stage 6 thinking to him—his brain cannot cognitively handle stage 6—but I apply stage 3. Stage 3 is stage 2 "plus 1." His brain is developing to where it may be able to apply stage 3 now, so I challenge him with this next stage.

For example, let's say my seven-year-old, when he was younger, used to take toys away from his younger brother. I got him to stop by nagging, by getting mad, by punishing. This worked in its way—in stage 1 he didn't want to get punished, so he learned (at least for short spurts) not to do the offending behavior. But then, of course, once he forgot the lesson, he went back to doing it and I went back to stage 1 punishing.

Then, as he became four years old, I came to realize reciprocity worked. I did a plus 1. I showed him how to always offer his brother a toy in trade. I helped him move from stage 1 to stage 2. Now I didn't have to punish him as much because trading worked for him. He even started teaching his brother how to trade.

But now, he's almost seven and he's gone back into a toy-stealing mode. Maybe it's because we've just had a third child; he's acting out from insecurity. I could go back to stage 1, punishment; or even stage 2, trading, but I'll try a plus 1 again.

I'll bring in a few others from our community—grandparents, or his favorite uncle, or his godfather, or a parent of his best friend—and coordinate with them, saying, "I'm going to try to teach Johnny that stealing toys is wrong not just because he'll get punished and not just because trading is instrumentally more satisfying but because if he continues to do it he will feel that not only his behavior but even his *intentions* are not approved of by his community. So when Johnny does this, let's all try to talk to him about intentions—'Why are you stealing Mark's toys?'—and show him that he needs to really look at those intentions."

By bringing in community, the value-clarifying authority does not just rest with me now; it rests with the "group." This is essential for stage 3 moral learning. And the group focuses the boy on his intentions, also essential for this stage. Soon Johnny doesn't want to steal toys because doing so makes him feel "bad" in the group, and indicates "a mistake" to his developing brain—i.e., that he has proceeded from mistaken intentions.

When we look at the practicalities of applying the psychology of moral stages, we see that we, as value-clarifying authorities, need to be much more conscious than we have been about *how* to teach moral thinking. Just pushing values down kids' throats will not work, since they learn morals and values in developmental stages and need different tools and stimuli for each stage.

If we don't attend to stages, we can become angry at a boy for not understanding what we're teaching. Yet he may not be developmentally able to understand, or he may have regressed, developmentally, because of a trauma in his family system, like the coming of a new child, a death, a divorce, abuse, neglect. Abusive parenting is one of the most common ways to confuse a child's moral development. It forces a child to stay in early stages of moral reasoning. For instance, he may become an adult in physical, even social terms (he might already be married with kids), yet a great deal of his moral reasoning can be dominated by reward-and-punishment thinking because no matter what stage he moved through cognitively during childhood, he was punished by the value-clarifier, not helped to mature in moral reasoning.

Attending to the stages of moral development helps us develop healthy strategies for using moral tools, both parental and communal, to teach our children. Often because we don't realize the stages, because we hated being shamed as kids so avoid anything like it with our kids, or because we fear we'll lose our kids' love if we're "too hard on them," we neglect to apply what I call "surgical guilt." Surgical guilt is not shame—it does not attack a boy's character. It does surgery on *intentions*. In stage 3, for instance, which we modeled in the example of the boy who stole toys, surgical guilt is essential and appropriate. The community is empowered, in this stage, to judge a boy's intentions and, in the end, help him judge—feel guilty about—his own intentions.

Making him feel guilty is not, in this case, shame because we do not say, "You are bad" (i.e. your self, your character is defective). We say, "You stole for a reason you thought, at the time, justified the stealing, but in fact it was no good justification at all, and it hurt your sister." In this case not character but reason or intention is scrutinized. Sometimes when children are handled this way they will still confuse guilt and shame. It's important for us as adults to say, "You are a person I love unconditionally. What you *did* is not something I can respect."

When we talk about and work with these stages, we must be sure to remember that when an adult gets to stage 6, he'll still have the earlier stages within him. For instance, he'll avoid certain things simply because they will incur punishment. When we look at anyone at any given moment, we might see elements of many different stages at work. Yet we should also see that elements of one stage, the stage he's in, predominate his *moral* reactions. So in helping both kids and adults to clarify their values and learn moral reasoning, we need to look at the dominant stage but not judge harshly behavior that is reminiscent of an earlier stage.

MORAL DEVELOPMENT STORIES

When Kohlberg developed his insights about these stages he employed moral dilemma stories as a primary tool for assessing and maturing a child's moral reasoning. Here is one such story, given to me by Professor Armin Arendt, of Applied Psychology at Eastern Washington University.

"Joe is a fourteen-year-old boy who wanted to go to camp. His father promised him he could go if he saved up the money for it himself. So Joe worked hard at his paper route and saved up the $40 it cost to go to camp, and a little more besides. But just before camp was going to start, his father changed his mind. Some of his friends decided to go on a special fishing trip and Joe's father was short of the money it would cost. So he told Joe to give him the money he had saved from the paper route. Joe didn't want to give up going to camp, so he thought of refusing to give his father the money."

When parents, mentors, and educators use stories like this they utilize what are called "probes." This is another word for questions, very specific questions used to probe very specific moral content. Here are some standard probes Professor Arendt uses.

▼ Should Joe refuse to give his father the money? Why?

▼ Does his father have the right to tell Joe to give him the money?

▼ Does giving the money have anything to do with being a good son?

▼ Which is worse, a father breaking a promise to his son or a son breaking a promise to his father?

▼ Why should a promise be kept?

When we conduct a discussion with boys who are capable of understanding this story, we are not saying, "I'm right, I have the answer, here it is." We conduct the discussion to help the boy move through stages of moral development and, very practically, to determine ourselves what stage he is in. If he answers the third probe with, "Yes, a father can take his son's money and that's okay," we might find the boy is in stage 4 or, depending on his fear of the father, stage 1. Likewise, if the boy says, "Giving the money to dad is okay if the son gets something back, like his father pays for camp next year," we might find the boy is in stage 2. Determining the stage he's in— something which requires us to use more than one story—then helps us determine what "plus 1" would be. Engaging the boy in any kind of discussion using stories like this leads to wonderful results. It brings parents, mentors, and educators closer to boys and a boy's moral world; it helps the boy develop; it focuses the boy's attention on moral reasoning.

There are standard formulas for moral stories like the one about the father and son. Usually they involve people who have power or resources and people who do not, parents and children, governments and individuals, groups and individuals. There is often a crisis people are responding to. There is also, in just about every story, a choice that must be made, a choice that has ramifications for individuals, family and, often, culture as a whole.

One of the most famous of the "moral dilemma" stories is about the Joneses who have an air-raid shelter in their basement which only holds food for two people. A bomb is about to be dropped. Their neighbors knock on the door. Should they let the neighbors in and thus most probably die from lack of food, or not let them in and protect themselves but absolutely ensure their neighbors' death in the bombing?

Clearly, we are not after an "objective" answer. We tell this story to weave a subtle fabric of moral development for our youngsters.

When I look at Kohlberg's "moral dilemma stories," I'm always amazed at how his work resonates with the way many tribal cultures teach moral reasoning. Throughout tribal mythologies—East Indian, African, American Indian, Chinese, and just about anywhere you look around the world—there are "dilemma tales." These are stories that end with a moral dilemma the child, and the teaching community of parents, mentors and educators, must work through. Tribal cultures and our own educators are attempting the same thing.

Using Archetype and Mythology to Reach Boys

Stories are the world's oldest tool for teaching values and morality and still remain, I believe, one of the most powerful. Everywhere around us are thousands of stories that can teach. Wherever I go, I use stories—"Jack and the Beanstalk," "The Gnome," from Brothers Grimm, "The Huge Beings at the Bottom of the World," from Turkey, "Aladdin," from Arabia, the stories Disney puts out, like *The Lion King* and *Pocahontas*. Kids of all ages, adults too, often learn more from listening to the tale and its in-depth interpretation than they do from a lecture by a parent, mentor, or educator. Stories "speak to their souls" in a way nothing else can. The heros and other voices of these stories give messages that go right to the imaginations—the centers—of the boys' inner world. When your kids' eyes are riveted on Barney, they are listening to the story's hero teach them values. They learn to clean up, to care for each other and the earth, and so on—not as lecture but as story.

The kinds of stories I tell most frequently belong in the field of "mythology." They are, thus, "primal tales"—stories complex and deep enough to speak of everyday individual life (the finite world of what's happening on my street today), yet also to inspire wisdom about moral life (social values, ethics in flux, and moral responsibility), and go even further to generate spiritual energy (mysterious resonance in the infinite world).

Primal tales give no easy answers and know no exclusions. Every boy can understand a primal tale—he need not be a follower of a particular religion. The reason everyone around the world understands the same basic tales is because they are tales filled with archetypes. These archetypes—these rich, recognizable figures (heroes, lovers, warriors, crones, angels, prophets, kings, magicians, giants, maidens, heroines)—are the same no matter where they appear in the world. Carl Jung was one of the first to notice this phenomenon, followed soon by the mythologist Joseph Campbell, whose work is available in any bookstore around you.

Archetypes are not stereotypes. Stereotypes take a piece of an archetype, expand that piece into a large shell, and make a contemporary social imprint on that shell. For instance, Chuck Norris characters in his movies are one small aspect of the Warrior—the aspect of "protecting the established good and rescuing the trapped maiden"—made into a protagonist who fulfills this narrow role in the way society teaches him to do. Clint Eastwood's spaghetti western characters were much this same way. While Sylvester Stallone's first Rambo film was a powerful social commentary and anti-war film, his next two took singular aspects of the Warrior—"strong man rescues leader and weaker men"—and ran that through whole films.

Each human archetype is more like a wheel with many spokes than it is like a character in a movie who is focused on one social imperative. The warrior archetype, for instance, has these and many more spokes on its wheel: protector, rescuer, guardian, earth saver, asserter of needs, loyal follower, worshipful fighter, world protector, boundary watcher, servant to king or queen, or other society-focusing power source.

Each archetype exists in relation to every other. The archetypes are a map or record of the inner life of a human and a society, an interdependent web composed of individuals in connection. Here are just some of the archetypes boys sense, gain wisdom from, and model off of when we tell them primal tales:

The King
Service to Community
Leadership
Connection to the Divine
Self-Confidence
Healthy Conscience

The Lover
Emotional Openness
Sexual Love
Romance
Vulnerability
Delight
Joy

The Warrior
Loyalty
Discipline
Self-assertion
Protection of Personal and
    Communal Boundaries

The Magician
Vision
Magic of Work, Skill-
    Building
Inventiveness
Transformation
Focus on Mysterious
    Things

The Explorer
Experimentation
Channeled Restlessness
New Ideas
New Challenges

As boys hear stories, they can be guided to see archetypal elements in the story—"Why did the Hero do what he did?" "Did you notice the Warrior didn't just attack, he knew he had to act in loyal service to the moral power, the King." "Isn't there a part of you that's like that Lover? When you see a beautiful sunset, don't you feel total, absolute delight?" In this way the boy attaches his imagination to the archetypal element and gains a story for his existence.

Because our culture is nearly empty of archetypal stories, our boys turn to stereotypes for wisdom. Information may come to them from stereotypes, but wisdom will certainly not. Wisdom requires archetypal imagination, an in-depth thought and imaginative process that takes the boy on an ever-unfolding journey—no easy answers, a lot of positive modeling, an emphasis on courage and compassion, and goals that are filled with spiritual, moral, value-laden content.

Stories can be used with kids and teenagers of any age. The recent resurgence of interest in stories for adults—Joseph Campbell's *The*

Power of Myth, Clarissa Pinkola Estés' *Women Who Run With the Wolves,* Robert Bly's *Iron John*—indicate very clearly that no matter the age we are hungry for life-defining tales.

Chase Collins's *Tell Me a Story* is a wonderful resource for using stories with younger kids. Collins suggests this as a universal formula for making up your own wisdom story: "The hero has reason to set out on a journey and runs into difficulty. The capacity to overcome the difficulty is within the hero himself and once he realizes that, he is able to extricate himself. There is a happy ending and a return home."

Elisa Pearmain, a professional storyteller, uses storytelling in Boston schools, often to strengthen kids' language skills. At Lesley College, she trains teachers to tell stories. She says teachers are amazed at how telling stories changes the classroom. "One teacher told me recently that she'd never before had the attention of her children that way. Even the squirmy kids." Stories, especially archetypally charged ones, are magical for listeners.

Psychologist Jerome Bruner suggests that all adults try using stories with their kids. "Adults who don't use storytelling are missing out on a powerful ally." Indeed, I have found this to be true even with hardened teens, and even with boys and adults in detention, jail, and prison.

A STORY OF HEAVEN AND HELL

Often I have told this story and seen tears in hardened eyes. Once upon a time, there was a young man who had studied with all the great teachers. He had learned to be a warrior, he had learned to be a lover, he could fix anything, he had seen many lands. One day he came back to his village to seek out the man who had cared for him after his parents' deaths years ago. He found his mentor whittling wood on a stoop. He said, "Uncle, I have seen much, I am accomplished, I am married and have children, but still I want to know, 'What is heaven and what is hell?' "

The old man laughed at him. "What a stupid question." He giggled and laughed, humiliating the young man, who felt a terrible anger rise in him.

Calming himself, he said, "Uncle, why do you treat me this way after all these years? I am only asking a simple question, 'What is heaven and what is hell?' No one has been able to answer this for me. You have always been the wisest teacher."

Again the old man laughed. "That is the stupidest question I've ever heard. I expect more of you. If that's all you can ask, after all these years, you're pretty worthless."

This went on two, three, four more times. The young man became more and more and more angry. The old man laughed and whittled and laughed and humiliated. The young man felt his arm rising, his fist rising, he saw himself hitting the old man, hitting him for all the times the old man had hurt him, hitting him for all the hurts everyone had given him. He saw himself taking the old man by the throat and strangling him, crushing the life out of him. All the while the old man laughed and laughed.

Then, suddenly, the angry visions dissolved and the young man began to cry. He buried his face in his hands and wept, tears coming from a place deep inside him, a place of grief he had not touched, even when his parents died. The old man had stopped laughing.

As his tears dissipated, the young man looked at his mentor and saw the wise, comforting face again, no laughter in it, no humiliation in it.

The mentor said, "You wanted to kill me."

The young man said, "Yes, I'm sorry."

The mentor said, "Don't be. You asked what hell was. I have shown you."

The young man saw the truth of this. He had never felt more frightened, more enraged in his life. "But what is heaven?" he asked.

The old man walked to him and put his arms around him and the two hugged each other as they never had before.

"This," the old man said, "is heaven."

The power of stories, whether "simple stories" like this one or longer, more complex narratives like the version of Jack and the Beanstalk we told in Chapter 6, is immeasurable. It is a power anyone can harness. A home, a classroom, a yard is filled with potentially archetypal figures. A doorway can become an opening to a world. A closet can become a time machine. A towel can talk. An animal can be a magician. When children are afraid of something, story can be made of it to allay the fear. When children are overdoing something, story can be made to attract them toward something else. When children are unsure of themselves, story can be made in which the child is the hero.

All children need stories, yet there is a way in which I think boys are desperate for them. Boys, as they get older, feel less and less able to compete in the emotional arena. They feel less and less emotionally astute and mature compared to the girls around them. Their nature and their socialization tend to lead them away from emotional literacy, while both nature and socialization tend to lead girls toward it.

Boys need stories and archetypes to give them an internal, reflective language for their feeling experiences. They need help from stories in accessing their feelings. Often a boy won't be able to talk about his feelings unless he has analogs, metaphors, and stories through which to say, "I feel like the young man in the story when the old man laughed at him. That's how I feel a lot of the time."

The same holds true for issues of value and morality. Preaching to a boy that he ought to be responsible rarely does him good. Showing him what happens to a hero who isn't responsible empowers him, teaches him, guides him. He identifies with the hero and gains energy from the hero's journey. Preaching at a boy that "such and such is wrong" is less effective than showing, in story, the consequences of the action. Preaching at a boy to "change" rarely changes him. Showing him, in story, how to transform himself works much better.

HOW TO USE STORIES

Here are some important things to remember as you integrate storytelling into the daily life of your kids and the kids you serve. Set the stories in another time. "Once upon a time" is the perfect beginning for stories because it clicks the child's mind into the hidden world of his unconscious. The child is able to go to that world, gain gifts of wisdom and experience there, and come back to see his "own world"—the "ordinary world" of conscious life—differently.

This also holds true when you tell a story from your own life—i.e., not a self-composed fable or fairy tale from a book. The story you tell about how it was "when I was your age" can be just as powerful as the fairy tale. Your past is mythic story to your kids. They see you, often, as a mythic figure. You might begin a self-story with "Before you were born . . ." or "In Wisconsin, one really sunny spring day, back before the war . . ." You will naturally tell your own story well (though some of us can be boring!), filling it with mythic, archetypal elements (even if you never use the words "lover," "warrior," "magician").

It's best not to populate the stories with too many characters. Let the boy identify with one and get wisdom and experience from interactions with a few others. One of the ways that people telling their own stories rob them of wisdom is by overdetailing and becoming tangential. "Johnny was the first cousin of Jake who was the . . ." The same holds true for fairy tales. The ones that stick in the mind and really teach values, morality, and spirituality, are the ones that appear like simple dramas, at least on the surface.

Our stories should give recognizable details from the five senses. Sometimes a smell or taste will captivate the child's imagination. Colors are nice details to fill stories with, as are textures and sounds. The stories need to be simple on the surface but not without adequate detail to paint the scene as full, magical, important, recognizable.

Asking the boy to interpret the tale afterward is helpful. If he doesn't want to, don't insist. Give your interpretations sometimes but not always. Sometimes you have to tell a certain tale a few times before the boy will offer an interpretation, but that interpretation might be startling. The boy's own participation in the story can help it be even more real. Let him become the astronaut, the knight, the doorway to the other world, let him make up lines for himself.

Stories should balance archetypal elements. If the story is "too dark," without resolution, just a lot of people killing each other, the warrior archetype is unbalanced toward one extreme. The boy will learn unbalanced values. One of the oldest ways to keep stories balanced is to end them with joy, resolution. After a hard journey, the community celebrates the hero's return, or two characters hug, or there is a marriage that represents new union and balance.

Sometimes a teenager will talk about a relationship by your making a game of it. "I know we're not talking about you," you might say as entrée. "We're talking about some guy named Jim, right? Okay, so what did Jim want to do with so-and-so."

No matter the stage of moral reasoning a child is in, stories help develop that reasoning. No matter what values we want to teach, stories give those values life. Our greatest ally in teaching boys values and morality is the boy's own imagination. The vast majority of science fiction literature—from comic books about Batman and He-Man to videogames like Double Dragon, to novels like *The Hobbit* and *Star Trek*, to games like Dungeons and Dragons—are experienced by boys. Many parents use stories from science fiction, both self-composed and garnered from existing comic books and novels, to teach their boys. Other parents use fairy tales, historical, or religious figures. No matter the family, there are stories available right where we live, on our bookshelves, in our heads. The more time we spend with boys processing their experience through these stories, and the less time we spend exhorting, condemning, and lecturing, the more clearly the boys will learn the values and morality we need to teach them.

Teaching Boys Values Through the Media

The media—especially television, movies, and videogames—have become a part of most boys' third family. The average American child goes to school for 900 hours a year but watches television 1,500 hours per year. When a boy comes home from school and watches hours of television without input from elders, TV becomes an unmonitored influence in his second family. With the media becoming an influential family member, what should we do to monitor, or even use its screens, comic books, videogames, and stories for the betterment of our boys?

If a parent, mentor, or educator has no opinion of the influence of the media or a very benign one—i.e., "the media isn't something we need to worry much about"—I would caution them. While we know the brain is forming throughout boyhood and thus any input is important, we also know from common sense that any family member has an effect on a kid, no matter the age, sex, race or interests, even if that family member is on a television screen.

How do we enlist the aid of this third-family member in teaching our boys values? Common sense tells us that we teach universal lessons we *want* the boy to see through the story on television, but we also let the boy tell us what lessons he himself is learning. When we react to his lessons, we never overreact. We use his lesson as a doorway into his internal process of understanding values. When he seems to be learning a value that scares us, we tell him so, give him alternatives, and even take away his privilege of watching such-and-such a show, but remaining respectful always that he need not be ashamed of the lessons he's learning.

Sometimes, a story from the media can help a boy do a "plus 1" in his moral reasoning. Once I showed the first Rambo movie to teenagers. When we talked about it afterward it was clear that some of the kids understood the anti-war message in the movie. One seventeen-year-old said, "The war really messed him up. I saw this movie last year but until we kind of analyzed it today I didn't get how scared he was inside."

A MEDIA INTERPRETATION EXERCISE

Here is an exercise we can ask our kids to do. We ought to do it simultaneously ourselves. After we've both done it, we need to talk to our kids about the results. We also ought to do it many times for many categories of media and specific pieces of media—games, cartoons, movies, programs—that our boys are clearly very attached to.

This exercise gets the best results when done by the boy's primary caregivers, his first family. It can be modified for mentors and educators, but they would want to check with the first family to make sure parents, mentors, and educators are all seeking to teach similar core values through the media.

Buy a notebook, the kind your boy likes. Talk to him about the different categories and subcategories of media. For instance, "Movies" is a category and "Thrillers" is a subcategory. Your boy might want to subcategorize even further, i.e., based on stars ("Arnold Schwarzenegger movies") or kinds of thrillers ("Spy thrillers," "Urban street crime thrillers"). With videogames he may want to subcategorize based on brands and content both. Categorize with as much depth as you can with the boy. This can be very enjoyable, even illuminating. Sometimes we don't realize just how many subcategories of media are out there. Let the boy make a list of all these categories and subcategories in the notebook. Make this a game the boy wants to do. After your initial modeling of the process, don't do this *for* the boy.

When he's categorized enough, either having become bored or having finished the task, ask him to make a list of his favorite programs, movies, videogames, etc. Work with him to categorize these favorites into the categories and subcategories. Many of these will have already come up as you were categorizing earlier. Ask for a manageable list, perhaps two favorite movies, two favorite videogames, two favorite TV programs, two favorite TV commercials, etc. When he seems to be getting overwhelmed, just back off and work with what he has before him.

After you've identified favorites with him, pick one at random, or by asking him which he wants to start with. When you settle on one, ask him to re-create the story. Listen carefully as he retells the story. What you saw when you watched the program will not be exactly what he saw. It's very important you hear what *he* saw.

Paraphrase the story back to him. "So *True Lies,* that Arnold Schwarzenegger movie, was about a guy who . . ." After paraphrasing, ask if you got it right. He'll fill in details if you missed something.

Now ask him what he learned from that story. If he has trouble answering, be more specific. To prepare to do this part you will need to touch base with your own inner categories. You might ask, "What did you learn about what men should do?" "What did you learn about what women should do?" "What did you learn about how technology fits into solving life's problems?" Ask about as many aspects of the story as you can without overwhelming or making the exercise laborious.

As you do this process with your boy you are helping him be conscious of the values, roles, morals, and goals he's learning from the stories that so profoundly affect his life. As much as possible, encourage all parents, mentors, and educators in your boy's life to do some version of this interpretive exercise. Do the exercise many many times over a period of many years. This interpretation of media stories is a crucial part of the initiation of your boy into manhood.

Teaching Boys to Care for Their Own Souls

Thomas Moore begins *Care of the Soul* with this truth: "The great malady of the twentieth century, implicated in all of our troubles and affecting us individually and socially, is 'loss of soul.' When soul is neglected, it doesn't just go away; it appears symptomatically in obsessions, addictions, violence, and loss of meaning. . . . It is impossible to define precisely what the soul is. . . . When you look closely at the image of soulfulness, you see that it is tied to life in all its particulars—

good food, satisfying conversation, genuine friends, and experiences that stay in the memory and touch the heart. Soul is revealed in attachment, love and community, as well as in retreat on behalf of inner communing and intimacy."

In a sense, everything you've read so far in *The Wonder of Boys* has been about caring for the soul of boys and men. My suggestions right now, in this section, are no more about caring for soul than are suggestions about how to discipline boys, or teach them about sex, love, and commitment. Yet my suggestions now are about specific spiritual principles and practices boys would benefit from learning, spiritual principles and practices that help ground them in comfort with their own "soul," their own inner center. Remember that when we speak of "spirituality," we are speaking of universal connection, transcendent experience, our deep "sense of belonging" in the world. The spiritually alive person feels that he belongs where he is. A person's religion does not necessarily matter—these principles and practices are gleaned from all religions. In order to commit ourselves to them, and to spirituality, we ourselves must be people of faith. That is, we must know that to feel truly alive we must believe in—and touch through belief— force(s) greater than ourselves.

SPIRITUAL PRINCIPLES

What spiritual principles do you believe in? What spiritual principles do you live by? What spiritual principles do you nurture in the boys around you? In helping people work with spiritual principles I've found it useful to divide them into elemental categories of who, what, where, when, how, and why. I'll present a basic frame of what we can nurture in boys through these categories. This frame is gleaned from the wide variety of world religions and mythologies.

As with teaching values, before we nurture spiritual principles in boys we must know where we ourselves stand in relation to them. I hope the following material will inspire you not only to teach your children but also to sit back and come to grips yourself with what spiritual ground you stand on.

The WHO is about teaching boys who "God" is. I am using the word God here to denote the YHWH of the Jews, Jehovah of the Christians, Allah of the Muslims, Brahman of the Hindus, Godhead of the Buddhists, Creator of the Native Americans, Higher Power of AA, the Force of *Star Wars* and so on. Another word might be "the Universe." Teaching boys to see the world as a creation of "God" or "Universe" teaches them deep respect for mystery and meaning.

Not to teach boys some sense of Who created the world leaves them, I believe, with a kind of lie, for every child lives in a magical world where more powerful Being(s) create life. The boy knows deep inside himself that he is not capable of such creation. If we don't teach him the Who of existence—and teaching Who does not necessarily mean making God into a person—he cannot trust the deeply felt spiritual energy which pushes him to respect the Unknown creator.

If we do teach him some form of God or Universe, he comes, at some point, to the moment of faith. He believes in himself because he understands the continuity, universality, and security of all existence, and knows himself a part of it.

In asking parents, mentors, and educators to help boys focus on the Who of existence, I'm aware of religious boundaries between church and state, and between first families and other families. "I don't want anyone teaching my boys something I haven't taught them myself, especially about religion." It is every parent's right to have the final say, yet I hope all parents, mentors, and educators will come together to stretch their expectations.

Though my wife and I have taught our children a deep sense of Who, we have not taught them God as a person. Yet for a time they went to a daycare in which one of their favorite daycare mothers was a born-again Christian who spoke—never inappropriately, but simply as a part of her everyday language—about how God created people, and God watched us, and He sat in heaven. Her talk in this realm only helped my children. It never harmed them.

The WHAT is about teaching boys what life is made of. Boys need to be engaged in activities and dialogues that teach how to discover the basic elements of being alive. For so many cultures in our ancestral past these elements were Fire, Water, Air, Earth. Our ancestors' preoccupation with these elements, their creation of huge systems—like astrological charts, chemical charts, even, in the Middle Ages, human "humor" charts, to denote inner moods—indicates their need to learn what life is made of.

Boys (and adults) these days are no less hungry for this elemental knowledge. Each of us must glean from both the scientific community and the spiritual community information and wisdom about life's elements—whether "soul," "quarks," "molecules," "spirit," or a combination of all these and many more—and provide our boys with a *scientific spirituality* of the world they live in. I mean by this the same thing my Indian friend meant back in Haifa when he said that biology is spirituality. Science and religion are not opposites: they are potentially one and the same thing. When we teach our kids the intricate science of how insects live, how molecules move, how energy within human societies operates, we are teaching them spirituality as well. The simplest example of this is in saying to a boy who is watching a nature program, "Look at how beautiful is even the world of ants that God created."

Slightly more abstract is an example from the Marlon Brando–Johnny Depp movie *Don Juan DeMarco.* The young lover Johnny Depp asks, "What is sacred? What is worth living for? What is worth dying for?" and answers himself, "Love." Love, for him, is the primary element of existence. Love is both his science and his spirituality.

Boys want to wrap their energy around the elemental nature of their existence. They need to be taught the basic elements of their physical, mental, emotional, spiritual existence. What shall we teach them they are made of? Teaching them how their brains work, how nature is put together, how human societies work—all this can become spiritually alive for them.

The WHERE is about teaching boys a sacred sense of place. Boys' lives exist in the space of their home, street, community, natural surroundings. When we focus our boys' attentions on where they are, pointing out the bird songs, the many moods on peoples' faces, the architecture, the earth line, when we ask them questions about where they are and what intrigues them in their surroundings, and when we fill them with our own pleasures of place, we are helping them grow up with a deep sense of belonging.

For just about every boy, the natural world of forests and rivers and trees is a great cathedral. The more we can open the world of nature to a boy, the more spiritually various his experiences are.

The WHEN is about teaching boys to live in the Now. Little children seem to do better than adults at living in the Now, being right where they are, experiencing their feelings in the moment. Yet as their growing brains become more and more capable of complex thought, we notice in children's lives how quickly the Now becomes a complexity of hope for the future, future ambitions, past hurts, past neglects, the suppression of present feelings in order to gain ongoing approval. Children must do and have all these things, but as they gain ambitions and operate out of past hurts and suppress feelings we must always be there to remind them of the Moment.

As our lives speed up more and more, so do our children's. We forget and thus they forget that there is nothing more important than the present moment. We forget and thus they forget to relax, to find spiritual solitude, to let go of the past, to quiet ambition, to fully enjoy the eating of a strawberry, the scent of a rose, the touch of a hand on a cheek.

The HOW is about teaching creativity, and through it, mystery and faith. No matter the culture, creation stories are its bedrock. The fierceness with which certain cultures—even some of our own sub-cultures—adore their creation myths is just one indication of how elemental is our desire to know the unknowable: our origins, the How of our existence.

The urge that parents, mentors, and educators have to "enhance their child's creativity" is a spiritual instinct, for whether we realize it or not, every act of creation is an experiential "knowing" of what can never be rationally "known." We know the Great Mystery of creation by creating, not by solving its logic in our heads. Dan Wakefield has written: "Life is a lot more fulfilling when you see it as creation, and yourself as a co-creator of it (rather than as a victim or a passive passenger)—along with God or fate or the universe, however you understand the force that turns the world."

It is essential that we help our boys feel creative, be creative, respect others' creativity. It is essential that we talk to them about the mystery of World Creation, essential that we let them know it's okay to celebrate creation as a mystery that can't be solved. Whether through his love of nature, his curiosity about sex, his world of imagination, we find ways to show boys that creation and creativity are individual acts that fit within a larger tapestry.

The WHY is about teaching boys to search for meaning. As much as boys need to be engaged in creativity for its own sake, so must they be engaged in setting goals and finding ways of achieving them. The goals that are spiritually powerful—the ones that will help the boy feel most fully a part of the very life he lives—are the goals we and he invest with life's meaning.

Boys must be taught to ask:

▼ Why am I here?
▼ Why do I do . . . ?
▼ Why do I feel . . . ?
▼ Why does . . . occur in the world?

Often, especially as they get older, boys learn not by being provided answers but by discovering them for themselves. What boys need to be provided are stories in which they can make the search for answers.

When we tell a boy "the answer" we have limited his search for meaning to the answer we provide. When we tell a boy a story in which he can find a number of answers and doorways into a number of other stories, his search for meaning is infinite. As parents, mentors, and educators, we guide our boys' search for meaning based on the limitations of our own accomplished sense of meaning, and must accept that the boy will make his search into places we cannot take him. By giving boys more stories and less simplistic answers as they grow older, we better equip them to make their life journey with spiritual courage.

SPIRITUAL PRACTICES

What I have called spiritual principles are not worth much without practice. Here are some items for specific practice. Some of them will feel almost impossible to accomplish if a boy's life is not already guided by the "principles" we just talked about.

Try to develop traditions with boys—bedtime stories, dinner table conversations, camping trips. Make these traditions ritualistic, routine, so that boys expect them, respect their consistency, and feel safe to develop from within their structure.

Boys need us to help them begin to pray. Again, religion is not the issue here, though it can be a prayer teacher in a boy's life. Boys, once they realize how mysterious life really is, need our help in developing a language and method of prayer that connects them to the mystery. Initially, when very young, they may believe that by praying ("Please, God, give me a bicycle for my birthday") they have power to affect the mystery. Quickly, though, they'll learn they don't get everything they pray for ("O Lord, why have you taken her from me?"). Soon they learn they don't necessarily want everything they pray for ("I see Your wisdom now, that wasn't meant to be, no matter how much I wanted it"). As they grow, they ultimately learn that the deepest, most nourishing prayers they can make are prayers that change themselves, not others, not God ("Please help me to see the next step I must take. Please open up my heart. Please help me understand why I'm so afraid").

Prayer and the meditation that surrounds it constitute an inner language every boy must learn, no matter what specific words his parents' religion exhort him to use. Without learning this inner language, a boy is cut off from deep spiritual conversation. He is cut off from a large portion of his ability to feel transcendence, universal acceptance, and a sense of belonging in life itself.

To teach this spiritual conversation, we must model spiritual conversation, meditation, and prayer. In order to avoid crossing religious boundaries, it's always important for mentors and educators to augment their modeling with the statement that "I do it this way, but your parents may do it another, and you will probably do it your own way. There's no single right way to pray."

Boys can also record their life experiences in journals. The more boys make stories out of their lives, the more they learn from life. Getting a boy into keeping a journal is a wonderful thing. Some boys will include their dreams and get a great deal from that. Seeing a parent or other elder writing in a journal provides a model, so sometimes a parent will show a boy his or her journal. We must help boys make a story of their lives, both their hidden inner lives, which they often won't recognize unless they see it mirrored in a journal, and their outer lives whose record grounds them in time and space.

Boys need to learn the value of spiritual solitude. For the soul to grow, it needs those moments of no-stimulation, of wakeful peace. Because we adults don't usually practice enough solitude—because we are always "doing" things—we often neglect to teach our boys to find solitude.

One of the best ways to ensure our boy's continued interest in finding spiritual solitude is to attach that solitude to a place, his place, often hidden away out in nature, or in a fort he constructs, or in his part of the house. The reason that nature works very well is that unlike a boy's room, it has few material distractions like phones, Walkman, TVs.

Helping the boy to find different categories of hobbies is extremely helpful. Getting boys into model airplanes may nurture his already generous spatial abilities. Getting boys into music opens up parts of the brain otherwise closed—creative, abstract parts that are integrated with the sensory stimulation of sound. Music can be an incredible emotional release for boys, and a place to learn deep self-discipline. Hobbies, personal creative activities, and school activities like chess club or debate, to say nothing of sports, are some of the best ways for a boy to feel like he belongs, like he's accomplishing something wonderful.

The more we fill hobbies with spiritual content—using them to teach wisdom, spiritual centeredness, discipline, emotional life—the more they become spiritual friends to the boy, befriending him and helping him feel grounded throughout his life. The finest martial arts and basketball coaches all know this. They know that it is their job not only to teach the skills but also to teach the man. If hobbies, music, and other activities are opened up to a boy, he will be able to say as an adult something like, "My folks got me a guitar when I was seven. Now, when I need a place to go in myself, I still strum on that old thing. It feels like coming home."

Activities like these, as well as prayer and many of the other practices we're discussing, become what I call a boy's "watering hole." He goes to these places to replenish and renew himself.

Few things give a human being as much spiritual depth as relationship. If we teach effective communication and conflict-resolution skills to our boys from early on, we lay a foundation for spiritual groundedness. This means we must communicate effectively and resolve conflicts with them as much as possible. By our modeling and teaching, they'll gain the skill to go nearly anywhere and relate effectively, with appropriate boundaries, with good skills, and also with an ability to not take it personally when things go wrong.

I Don't Want to Feel Like a Stranger

Once a boy, fourteen, said to me: "I want to do what's right. I want to make people like me. But I don't know how sometimes. I feel like everyone else knows the rules and I don't. I feel like everyone else knows who they are and I don't."

I asked the boy, "What if I could prove that none of your peers really know much more about who they are than you do?"

He said, "That wouldn't matter. I know how I feel. I get together with them and I feel like a stranger. I feel this way in my family. I don't want to feel like a stranger, but I do."

So many young people feel like strangers in their own worlds. To some extent, their feelings are developmentally normal. It's difficult to meet an adult who didn't, during childhood or adolescence, go through a time of feeling like no one understood, no one cared, no one mattered.

Yet it may not be as "normal" as we'd like it to be. Our standard of normal may have been clouded by how individualistic our culture is. So many of our boys and teenage males feel like strangers for years on end. This is not "normal," except in a culture that accepts it as such; just as "oh well, he'll rebel," is only normal in a cultural context that has nearly given up on finding other ways than rebellion to guide adolescence.

To come to grips with "morality" among our youth we have to come to grips with how many youths feel like strangers, like aliens. How shall we do this? By rebuilding the three-family system.

What we've discussed in this chapter becomes difficult, often impossible, if we try to teach it in one family and the boy hears no echoes from the other families or, instead, hears contradictory messages from families two and three. I can teach my son values of integrity, responsibility, and respect, but families two and three must do so as well. The three families can disagree on some values, and that disagreement is often healthy. But if we politicize or overreact in our disagreements, our son is going to feel strange in each family: boy A—someone who respects elders but has the autonomy to question them when needed—in his nuclear family; boy B—someone who trashes any elder he sees—in his peer group; and boy C—someone who is taught to do anything elders say—in his church.

There is no way to build a three-family system overnight. I have seen small steps toward getting up the guts to be less individualistic and more communal wherever I travel around the country, but our society as a whole is still unsure of what to do. When it comes to teaching values, morality, and spirituality, each parent will have to take the lead. The initial structure for values-training must come from the parent. That parent must reach out consciously and verbally to a few other people the parent can identify as second- and third-family members—perhaps one blood relative, one nonblood relative (a mentor, educator, or godparent), a couple of church or neighborhood friends. The parent must ask: What values are you teaching, let's compare notes, let's talk about where the kids are at.

When parents, mentors, and educators come together in this way, they are creating what I call a Community Council. These Councils lead to conscious dialogue between the three families, making the teaching of values, morality, and spirituality more systematic in a child's life.

Often when parents and public educators get together in Council, there will be a few voices who cry out in fear of their child learning values the individual doesn't agree with. We can usually gauge the usefulness of these voices by their level of hysteria. If the offended parent cries out that learning about sexuality will cause her child terrible harm, or obsess on one particular political or religious value, we very often need to ask that person to find another Council. It's a hard thing to say to someone, but sometimes it has to be said. Our community cannot serve its children if its time is taken up dealing with the political or religious overreactions of one or a few members.

Community Councils often lead to parental commitments to get more adults involved in helping kids with a variety of projects. Often a Community Council brings parents together on a key issue, like what records are the kids listening to, what TV are they watching? The Council may agree to cut down on their children's television time. Thus my son doesn't go from my house to his friend Billy's house, watching three hours of TV there and only one hour at home. Just coming together to talk as parents, mentors, and educators on basic principles of values and rules can lead to wonderful, unexpected relationships between neighbors, new friends, parents, and teachers.

As we adults become less strange to each other, our boys can feel less like strangers themselves. Of everything we do, getting closer to each other and working more closely with each other is perhaps the most important step adults can take toward teaching boys values, morality, and spirituality.

chapter 9

Teaching Boys about Sex and Love

I want sex. Love, commitment?
That comes later.

—*Arnoldo, sixteen*

My father had the "birds and the bees" talk with me one Saturday morning while we watched Bjorn Borg and Jimmy Connors play a tennis match on television. I was fifteen.

Dad said, "Mike, you know about sex, right? You had sex education."

"Hmmmm," I murmured, mortified that we'd have to *talk about it!*

"And you and your friends got the rest figured out, right?" he continued, sensing my discomfort and experiencing his own.

"Hmmmm."

"And you know if you have questions you can come to me, right?"

"Hmmmm."

"Okay, then. Just be careful. Sex isn't something to mess with."

Silence.

"Wow, did you see that serve!"

My father insists this story is apocryphal, but this is how I remember it. I was still very much a nervous boy, filled with distresses and euphorias and more distresses, so I can't insist too much on the accuracy of my memory. But both dad and I agree on the symbolism of the memory. He, like most fathers, mentors, and educators in his day, did not teach, nurture, mentor, and initiate the boys around him into the world of adult male sexuality. When I was growing up, the idea was, "Boys will learn what they have to learn by figuring it out for themselves." On core issues like sex and love parents stayed out of the way. The pendulum is swinging back to a little more parental and elder involvement these days, but that swing is mainly ideological. Practically speaking nowadays, even if parents want to get more involved in initiating boys into adult sex, love, and commitment roles, they just don't have time.

Three quarters of today's boys have sex by the time they graduate high school, one half of today's girls do the same.

The median age for first intercourse is 16.6 years for boys and 17.4 years for girls.

According to the Sex and America's Teenagers' study, done by the Alan Guttmacher Institute in 1994:

▼ 9 percent of 12-year-olds have sex
▼ 16 percent of 13-year-olds
▼ 23 percent of 14-year-olds
▼ 30 percent of 15-year-olds
▼ 42 percent of 16-year-olds
▼ 69 percent of 17-year-olds
▼ 71 percent of 18-year-olds

These statistics only record the actual act of intercourse. They say nothing of other sexual acts nor of the amount of romance and love boys feel, even in prepubescence. Those acts and feelings are often the most confusing they encounter in the whole first two decades of their lives.

The statistics about sex are either good news or bad news, depending on how you look at them. Given that in a recent poll 62 percent of adults guessed the average teen has sex before age sixteen, the Guttmacher study might be good news. Kids are waiting longer than we think. Or, if we look at these statistics from the other side, we might be mortified to learn that 30 percent of our pre-sixteen-year-olds are not virgins.

Again in the good news category, the Guttmacher study also found that 70 percent of sexually active teens used some method of contraception the first time they had intercourse. On the other hand, most of that 70 percent did not use it every time they had intercourse. Given that 1 in 4 young adults has been infected with a sexually transmitted disease—that's well over a million—and that of all population groupings, AIDS is spreading fastest among teens and young adults regardless of sexual orientation—the fact that most sexually active teens don't use condoms consistently is very bad news indeed.

Whether the news is good for you or bad, we all know we have to do better by our boys when it comes to teaching them about sex, love, and commitment. So, what should we do?

Initiating Boys Into the World of Sex and Love

About the same time my dad talked with me over the tennis match, my mother, an anthropologist, had a videotape of a tribal culture in Africa. I watched it and discovered that in this tribe boys were initiated into sexual life just before puberty in a most unusual way. Led by the elder men, they hollowed out logs, took the knots out of the logs, sanded and smoothed both the logs and the holes in the logs, then practiced putting their erect penises inside the holes, imitating intercourse. I recall watching this tape with utter fascination.

Now, years later, my research has discovered numerous tribes that initiate sexual activity in this or some other physically demonstrative way. Often the teaching accompanies a series of ritual woundings of the boy and young man that take place over a period of years. Among Australian aborigines, for instance, many rituals surrounding circumcision, subincision, and thigh wounding teach the boy, then the young man, how important his sexual power is in the great cycle of life. The elders teach boys about love, sex differences, sexual activity, sex roles, commitment to mates, and even pleasure. These lessons are celebratory as well as instructive.

The difference between this form of teaching boys about sex and our own silent, puritanical way is stunning.

These tribal cultures want to make sure a boy knows how to use his body, both to control it and let it serve its natural purpose. These tribal cultures understand that purpose and that body as a sanctified and sacred force. Yet the tribal culture is not necessarily obsessed with "purity"—it does not see the experience of pleasure as oppositional to sacred commitment. And many of the tribal cultures that initiate boys into sex and love are as much or more monogamous in marriage patterns than ours.

Our culture may want to make sure the boy knows how to control his body, but we rarely teach him to learn, in depth and with elder help, his body's natural, sacred purpose. So the boy goes out and explores its natural purpose with girls, some of whom end up pregnant. We condemn the boy for getting the girl pregnant, yet we've done very little—little more than a sex ed class or a talk over tennis— to teach the boy the sanctity of the natural force he commands, his body. Why should he treat it as sacred when we don't?

Our culture tries to get a boy to control his sex drive and budding efforts at love by telling him that pleasure, at his age, will lead him astray. In yet another way we teach boys about themselves by teaching them that what they are experiencing is *bad*. From masturbation to coital pleasure we say, "There's something wrong with that pleasure you're feeling at your age, you're not allowed to feel it until you've reached X age." This is all well and good in a utopian world, but boys, at some point, see through our own adult fear of sexuality. They say, "Wait, my body is experiencing something and no scaredy-cat adult's gonna tell me it isn't. I'm gonna check it out." And they do check it out.

So not only do we spend little time initiating boys into who they are as sexual and loving beings, but when we do initiate them it's by trying to convince them what they're experiencing is bad. Boys don't learn the way in which they are sacred. Rather, they learn the way in which they are profane. We don't initiate them into sex and love as beautiful actions of self and soul. We initiate them into sex and love as dangerous acts of moral crisis.

This is not to say we shouldn't teach abstinence, celibacy, or virginity. I am as much a preacher of abstinence as anyone else. What I am saying, however, is that the *way* we try to teach boys the morality of sexual behavior and the psychology of human love is deeply flawed. It is based on our fear, not our sense of the sacred. It is not effective with too many boys who, even if they never get someone pregnant, grow up scared of themselves, do not understand who they are, and never learn how to love.

BOYS NEED MALE-SPECIFIC TEACHING AND MODELS

When I was growing up I often heard about boys of earlier generations, in New York, where my relatives all lived, who were taken by their fathers at sixteen to a prostitute. This was their act of initiation. The boy, supported by his father, lost his virginity in a controlled setting, was accepted by dad into adult male culture, then went with dad and maybe an uncle or two to a restaurant or some other place of celebration.

When I was in college I met a man who had experienced this kind of initiation. He told me he'd been scared to death, awkward; he had thought the prostitute wasn't very attractive; and he had trouble getting an erection. This form of initiation, in his words, "sucked." I mention it here not to suggest it as a proper course for boys but to ask us to look, through its lens, at a piece of common sense. Males and females view sexual initiation, sexual biology, and love itself as very different phenomena. Few elder females would even consider taking a younger female to a male prostitute to be initiated into female adulthood.

In a new survey of 3,432 adults eighteen to fifty-nine, the question was asked, "Why did you have your first sexual encounter?"

Fifty-one percent of males answered, curiosity/readiness for sex; only 24 percent of females answered the same.

A similar statistical result occurred on the other side of the coin. Forty-eight percent of females answered "affection for partner." Twenty-five percent of males, or about half, answered the same.

Different hormones and brain structures create profound differences between boys and girls that we must recognize if we are to understand how to teach boys about sex, love, and commitment. We must discover what works for *boys*.

As Barbara Dafoe Whitehead writes in an *Atlantic Monthly* cover article, "The Failure of Sex Education": "Despite changes in teenage sexual behavior, boys and girls continue to view love and sex relationships in different ways. Girls look for security, and boys seek adventure. Boys are after variety, and girls want intimacy. The classic formulation still seems to hold true: girls give sex in order to get love, and boys give love in order to get sex. According to one study, boys were more than twice as likely as girls to have had their first inter-course with someone they had only recently met. As Freya Sonenstein, of the Urban Institute, and her colleagues report, "A typical picture of an adolescent male's year would be separate relationships with two partners, lasting a few months each."

Beyond basic hormonal differences—that boys are dominated by testosterone, the sex-drive hormone, and that male reproductive biol-ogy is driven by the need to plant seed constantly—Robert Francoeur, a biologist at Fairleigh Dickinson University, points to brain structure as another hidden, essential area of difference. Because the female brain integrates more sensory and emotive material more quickly, its experience of sexual, physical, and emotional intimacy is grounded in the need for simultaneous stimulation of sex organs, five senses, and clusters of emotions. The female orgasm expresses this physically—in a whole body orgasm.

The male brain, with its structural differences, does not as often require simultaneous sexual, whole-body, and emotional stimulants. That brain, combined with the necessity of erection for sexual pleasure and ejaculation for the fulfillment of the male biological imperative, sets the male up to require sexual stimulation far more than other sensual and emotional stimulants, and to "check-out" of the coital and emotional relationship once the ejaculation is accomplished. For many boys, whose maturity level has not grown to a point of being capable of the emotional attachment they need for marriage, the sex act wants only to be that—penile stimulation, not emotional love. For a boy to go to a prostitute—despite our moral qualms—is indicative of his biology and brain structure. He does not attach much emotion to the physical act of sex itself, though like my friend, he will have certain feelings about the whole process of going to the prostitute.

All this is just common sense, isn't it? Boys and men tend to want penile stimulation and ejaculation for the sexual encounter to be a success. Girls and women are often more interested in emotional in-tercourse, cuddling, physical touch that is not sex-laden. Given that we all know this, why isn't this the foundation of how we teach boys and girls about themselves? The reason, of course, is puritanical, whether the puritanism comes from the political "far left" ("If we teach boys and girls how different they are we won't put a dent in male domina-tion of the female, male sexual objectification of the female, and the male sense of entitlement over the female") or from the political "far right" ("To talk about sex at all is to encourage it to happen, which will lead to the demise of civilization"). The puritanical view, from wherever it comes, is not serving our kids.

Male sexual biology, with its trillions of potentially fertile sperm looking for eggs, is not that interested in sticking with one mate too long. Male emotional life, on the other hand, is as needy for the attentions of a beloved female as any creature can be. And male social life has as many incentives to stick with loving commitment as does female. The trick with boys is to teach boys how to intergrate sex, love, and commitment so that they are equally important and integrated elements of mature male life.

This is what so many tribal cultures do so well. In these societies boys are taught that sex is sex, a natural biological act, not shameful in the least, in fact sacred; boys are taught that love, ardor, Eros is a mysterious emotional relationship with others, nerve-wracking but ultimately rewarding; boys are taught that commitment is a socially mandated role that allows for the male to have sex, experience love, care for his wife, children, and serve the great cycle of life.

Teaching a boy how to love does not necessarily mean we've taught him how to be committed. Teaching a boy how to be committed without teaching him how to love often leads to a hyperresponsible but resentful adult male. Teaching a boy to get sex whenever he wants it doesn't teach him much else.

Teaching these three elements simultaneously but with respect for the separate power and magic of each gives boys a great deal of insight into what is otherwise an undistinguishable, muddy mass of feelings and urges. It gives them a language. This separation of elements in our education of boys is a tack that girls benefit from too. Yet it is more essential to do the separation with boys if we want them to focus on the third, commitment.

Girls are, to a great extent, biologically wired to focus on commitment. They carry the child—they are committed. Societies acculturate them accordingly. Boys are not, to that extent, wired to focus on commitment. Societies, like ours, that have accepted the ideal of monogamy, have a huge acculturation job when it comes to boys. Hitting boys over the head whenever we can with the sanctity of the third element, commitment, but neglecting to teach them the complexities of the second or the acceptability of the first, is a terrible mistake. The number of boys who impregnate girls and then walk away is our best proof of the mistake. Unless we initiate boys into all three elements—sex, love, and commitment—we can expect the boys to do none too well. Tribal cultures have always known this. We're just catching up with it again.

WHAT BOYS WANT TO LEARN

When I ask boys what they would like to learn about in sex education—both in the home and in school—they respond first with tittering, nervousness, and even withdrawal. But when we get down past the nerves, certain themes come up again and again:

▼   How do I control myself?
▼   Why do I get so nervous around girls—does everyone, even athletic stars?
▼   How come he's got more hair than I do?
▼   Why do girls manipulate me so well?
▼   Will I ever get pubic hair?
▼   Am I big enough?
▼   How can I get more sex?
▼   Am I gay?
▼   Why do I feel ashamed of myself so much?

Boys ask specific questions and want specific answers. They need their nervousness about organ size to be heard especially by elder men. They need guidance on how to feel when everyone else has pubic hair and they don't. Boys need to talk to us and hear from us about strategies for sexual control—how to breathe, walk away, know one's own thresholds of physical stimulation.

A father once told me about teaching his son "the three P's"—that when the youth felt sexually stimulated he had to consider "Privacy, Person, and Penis." By this he meant: find a private place to express your sexual feelings, if you decide expressing them is even appropriate; consider the person you're feeling your stimulation about and whether that person shares it; remember that a lot of it's just about your own penis, and what it wants right now.

This is a father's clever way of teaching a boy some basics. It says to the boy, "What you're feeling is a private matter with social consequences—a sacred matter that is very much your own." It is honest with the boy about how so much of his experience is testosterone and penis, not emotion. It teaches the boy to consider the other—the female—as person not object, even though everybody, male or female, knows that when one is sexually stimulated, the stimulating "other" appears to some degree as a sexual object.

To the father's teaching I asked for the addition of another element, Process. "Can you also teach your boy that when he has figured out how to find privacy, how to respect his stimulation as physical, and how to see beyond the sexual object, that he notice whether and how an emotional process is kicking into place? He is then challenged to understand his own intentions in that process: rewards he will receive, gifts he can give, and his place through that emotional process in the cycle of life."

Sex has a functional, instinctive, and emotional aspect. It is about a body functioning in a defined physiologic way toward an *instinctive* purpose—to mate—which is laden with emotional content. In adding process to this father's teaching, a boy can see his sexual feelings as sexual (involving both the functional and instinctive aspects), can choose which sexual feelings become "emotional," and can learn, all the while, that whether remaining instinctive or becoming highly emotional, his feelings belong in a society that needs them to be controlled.

So often I've heard, "If I can just convince Johnny that what's important is love, not sex. He shouldn't want the girl unless he feels something deep about her." Closing our eyes to a boy's psychosexual reality and hoping that his biology will change does him and our whole culture a disservice. A great deal of his romantic drive has little to do with the emotion of love. We know this, yet we avoid its truth in our dealings with boys.

To bring all of this even closer to home, think about how we handle the topic of masturbation.

Masturbation

In late 1994, Dr. Joycelyn Elders was fired as Surgeon General of the United States. The "last straw" for President Clinton was her public comment that masturbation is a normal human function and ought to be taught as such. Not to do so, she claimed, creates problems for kids. She was fired for many reasons, yet this commonsense claim was the reason given. She tried to inspire us to become more responsible parents, mentors, and educators. She lost her job.

Why do we withhold dialogue and initiation from our children about masturbation? The two common justifications are well known: some fundamentalist interpreters of the Bible have used a few lines of that sacred text to convince the public God hates masturbation; and we're scared of dealing openly with anything having to do with sex organs. As with so many sexual issues, we adults give in to fears of our own mysterious sexual powers.

Meanwhile, our kids try to grow up. We know that our job as adults is to push through our fears so that we can be useful to our children, yet we don't. Showing kids by our silence how afraid we are of their normal functions makes them confused, even scared. When they go ahead and masturbate—as they will—they feel dirty, their self-image decreases, and we as a culture have gained absolutely nothing.

The facts. There is no reputable study that has ever shown that a male who masturbates becomes more promiscuous, more sexually or morally irresponsible or more irresponsible in his emotional commitments to his loved ones. In other words, there is no proof for the idea that masturbation makes one "immoral." In fact, studies show that, among other benefits, masturbation releases sexual tension among adolescents, cuts down on sexual promiscuity and, in some studies, rape.

Studies show that nearly every human male masturbates—not just in our culture, but throughout the world. Adolescent boys, whose bodies experience five to seven testosterone surges a day, often masturbate more than once a day.

The adolescent boys you know have probably masturbated some time in the last week. Even the average adult male (under forty-five years old) has masturbated some time in the last couple months. That masturbation is not illegal, if done out of the public eye. It is often medically advised—when, for instance, a male has a prostate infection and must keep the prostate cleaned out. It is pleasurable. It releases tensions that might get acted out inappropriately with a female who doesn't want to be the object of our son's tensions and frustrations.

Nearly everyone masturbates, even those people who cry out

against it. When will we grow up as a culture, and as individual parents, mentors, and educators?

One thing that might help would be to separate masturbation from sex. Moral condemnation of masturbation is fueled by the old idea that sex should not transpire outside of marriage. Since many people consider masturbation "sex," they can easily argue its moral turpitude.

Masturbation is not "sex." Masturbation has nothing to do with virginity. Masturbation in private involves no union between two people.

If we separate masturbation from sex, we may be better able to develop our moral thinking about it, and most of all, we'll be of more use to our children. They need us to be honest and caring adults. They need us to help them learn about their bodies. They need us to stop making them feel guilty because of our own confusions and fears. They need us to teach them about masturbation in the same way we teach them about menstruation, our changing bodies, what it is to be alive, what it is to be human.

What If My Son Is Gay?

Few things are more difficult for parents than hearing their son say, "I'm gay." Along with their love for their boy, parents react with varying degrees of disbelief, fear, even visceral hatred. In our communities and schools, the gay boy experiences the same disbelief, fear, and hatred without most of the love.

One way parents and communities deny the biological fact of homosexuality is to call it "a life-style choice." When a boy or young man comes to them and says, "I'm gay," they say, "You'll change." Most often, the gay adolescent knows this won't happen, though he may try to make it happen for a while, even marrying and having children.

One father, whose gay son was now twenty-four, said this to me: "Why do people go on about life-style choices? Who in his right mind would *choose* to be gay? You have a higher likelihood of getting AIDS, everyone hates you, it's harder to get a job, your friends are dying all around you. My son didn't *choose* to be gay. Like so much else in life, it was chosen for him."

Many people who react against gays use religious texts as their source of judgment. However, scientific evidence pioneered by brain researchers at the University of Pennsylvania and the UCLA School of Medicine and in England, at the London Institute of Psychiatry, makes it clear being gay is not just "a life-style choice." It is genetically and chromosomally influenced, with certain families having far more homosexuals in their generational lineage than others; and it is wired into the brain. This wiring has been measured by researchers on autopsied brains.

The hypothalamus is the mission control of the brain. In the hypothalamus is a bundle of neurons called the "sexually dimorphic nucleus" or "two-shaped nucleus" by biochemists and neurobiologists. It controls, among other things, sexual orientation. In a gay person's brain, this nucleus is half as large as the companion nucleus in a heterosexual person's brain, and although the research is far from complete it is now clear that somewhere between 5 and 10 percent of our boys have a smaller sexually dimorphic nucleus and a stronger biological tendency toward homosexuality.

The genetic tendency toward homosexuality and the smaller nucleus in the brain of a gay person are biological facts. The sexual orientation the brain tends the person toward is, from all best evidence, a biological fact. To condemn gays for being different is to condemn the work of their brains' Creator.

Despite this fact—and because this fact is not well enough reported in the media—mothers will ask—feeling terrible guilt—"Was it my fault my son's gay? Did I love him too much, or not enough?" Fathers will wonder, "Is it because he did all that sexual experimenting with boys, is that why? Did it stick? Should I have put a stop to it sooner?"

A mother's love does not turn her son into a homosexual. His own very normal sexual experimentation with other boys does not turn him into a homosexual. Sometimes very unhappy boys, from destroyed homes and confused childhoods, will go through a phase of months or even a year or two of "being gay," but it appears that if their brains are not already wired with the smaller nucleus in the hypothalamus, they will not "be gay" for very long.

Sometimes people will ask, "But what about pedophiles and sexual predators, the ones who want little boys? They're gay and look at the damage they do." For the most part, sexual predators are created by childhoods in which physical abuse, psychological abuse, and sexual abuse was so severe the neurotransmissions and other brain wiring of the boy get changed significantly enough to make him a pedophile and predator. He is not gay; he is mentally ill.

Myths about moms making their sons gay, pedophiles being gay, unhappy boys becoming gay are just that, myths. They circulate like rumors but have no truth.

LOVING OUR GAY BOYS

In the face of the new scientific evidence, we have three options:

1. refuse to listen to the evidence and continue our fear and hatred of our own gay sons;
2. accept the evidence and change our fear-based hatred enough to let gay boys and men be who they are;
3. go even further by actively helping our gay boys to find a special place in our society.

There is no compelling evidence that being gay leads to increased tendencies toward sexual abuse of boys. (In fact, straight men are more likely to sexually abuse a boy than gay men!)

There is no compelling evidence that being gay affects job productivity.

There is no compelling evidence that a straight boy can be turned into a gay boy because of a friendship with a gay boy.

There is no compelling evidence that being gay leads in any way to "the breakdown of society."

There is only, in the end, our irrational fear. That fear—our fear as parents, mentors, and educators—makes us turn away from the gay boy and hurt him and, thus, do God's work no justice at all.

Our own ancestors, and peoples from all over the world, have understood, even without knowing intricate biological systems, that gays are "different" and may possess unique gifts. These other cultures worked hard to help gays find their uniqueness, and integrate those gifts into the larger society.

In the Zuni tribe, gay members held the special role of "berdache." The berdache was a gay person, sometimes called a "man-woman," who counseled others and led religious ceremonies. From boyhood he was trained for this very important job. He was felt to be closer to the divine than the average person.

The Dagara tribes of North Africa train their gay members, from childhood on, to be "guardians of the gate." By this they mean priests and shamans who are so close to the divine, they can help people navigate between this world and the world of spirits.

Our European ancestors, especially the Greeks and Romans, had gay and bisexual rulers and emperors. Many of these were military generals. Gay boys have become gay men of spiritual, political, and emotional depth in every society ever recorded.

Another Mother Tongue, by Judy Grahn, goes through world languages with a gay lens. It points out hundreds of ways in which our very English language is linked to past gay cultures. Even many of the words with which we now degrade gays—like "fairy" and "faggot"— have their roots in sacred language: fairies were sacred beings, faggots were coals in sacred fires.

All around us, without our realizing it and in the midst of our prejudice against them, gay boys have become gay men who are integrated into the fabric of our culture, contributing to fashion, film, religious life, political office, family life, sports, and the arts.

Most difficult for some people to deal with, of course, is the fact that some of our gay boys grow up to be gay priests, ministers, and teachers. There is no evidence that our children are any more at risk with a gay priest or teacher than a straight one. Yet some people live in terrible fear. These people need our sympathy and good counsel. Perhaps a look at other cultures would help them see that for millennia gays have helped, rather than hurt, culture by being spiritual leaders and teachers.

I have given examples of how gay boys and men have spiritually fed cultures in hopes of helping change attitudes toward these gay boys. Gay boys have a very difficult life. Many realize they are gay early on and hide that fact. They live a lie most of their young lives. Worst of all, they feel betrayed by the very people—their parents and intimate community members—who purport to love them unconditionally. We can love them and accept them and utilize their special gifts, or we can continue to betray them, and bring more fear and hatred in our cultural life.

What are some of the practical things we can all do to help gay boys discover an accepted place in our society?

We can help dispel the myth that the majority of our society is anti-gay. Poll after poll shows anti-gay sentiment to be a minority opinion. Once we free our minds of this notion, we can reach out to gay boys. Ask how you can help them flourish in a society that is often dangerous to them. If your son or neighbor boy is gay, treat your own prejudice the same way you would treat your racial prejudice—as something you need to work on and push beyond so that you can reach out to the ones you love.

Faith and science do not need to be opposites. God gave us science too. Science has shown us that homosexuality is God's creation too.

And we need to work against "gay versus straight" polarization. Gays and straights are people, pure and simple, not polar opposites. The different ways they have sex are tiny parts of their lives.

Sex Education in the Schools

In Washington State, where I live, the following question was dropped from the newest state Department of Health survey of eighth-graders: "Have you ever had sexual intercourse (gone all the way)?" The 1992 version asked the question and discovered that 25 percent of Washington State eighth-graders said yes. When the question was going to be included in the 1995 version, a few very loud voices got the question axed. To ask the question, these voices argued, would encourage sexual intercourse among these young people. There was no empirical data to support this claim. In fact, common sense tells us that asking kids that young that question isn't going to lead them to go out and have sex.

Because the powers-that-be allowed these minority voices to rule the day, the question got dropped and now educators are even less able to develop educational resources to help kids manage sexual activities and hormones.

Our fear of discussing masturbation with our kids is similar to the fear of asking that question on the survey. We are afraid to talk to our kids directly, and often, about sex, so we give a lot of family power to schools. The schools are doing their best to be responsible educators and mentors in the face of parents who don't initiate boys into sexual life, but then we often hamper the schools by cutting out the important questions and answers.

It is a given among both parents and educators that deep wisdom and values-teaching about sex and love must come from a boy's nuclear family, extended family, and community. For boys, that wisdom-teaching needs to come most often from father and other intimate males first, then male teachers and others in the schools and community.

Lately there has been a great deal of comparative research on the effectiveness of different kinds of sex-ed programs. A consensus is developing that many sex-ed programs don't work. When we ask what the standard of effectiveness is, we usually get the answer, "They're not teaching abstinence. Kids are having sex. The programs don't work."

This is one worthy standard, but there are others. For many of these educators, cutting down sexually transmitted diseases is an equally important standard. For others, children's self-esteem is an equally important standard. Many sex educators are tired of hearing what a bad job they are doing when they are often the only people who educate children about sex with any depth.

Our social attitude toward sex education is comparable to our social attitude toward daycare. We treat it as a necessary evil when, in fact, it is an essential community activity. In order for it to come to fruition, we will have to apply many standards of effectiveness. As with daycare we'll have to connect its educational process with parental involvement.

When I was a boy I experienced two kinds of pedagogical sex education. In fifth grade we did the class with the girls and boys together. Then my family moved to another city and another school where we did the sex-ed class in sixth grade with boys and girls in separate rooms.

The second had more impact on me. In retrospect I don't see the extra year of maturity as the reason—I just felt less nervous and more comfortable with all males. Yet there were advantages to the first too. Both boys and girls had to listen to each other (on those rare occasions when someone would speak up).

For years to come there will be disagreement among politicians, sex educators, and parents about what "content" is effective. There need not be, however, disagreement on these principles, based on sheer common sense:

1. Our kids need much more honest sex education than they get.

2. Some of it needs to happen in sex-separate groups, some of it in cross-sex groups.

3. Elder male parents need to be invited into sex-education classes to tell stories, answer questions, provide echoes of what teacher or coach is saying, and generally help initiate the boys.

This latter activity means elder males need to come together as communities to train boys to see intimacy as a spiritual discipline. This has always been their job, wherever they have lived.

Love as a Spiritual Discipline

Love for adults is best when practiced as a spiritual discipline, a process of attachment for which there are rules of conduct, agreements about compassion and intimacy, tools available to fix what gets broken. Unfortunately, we adults barely see our own loving as a spiritual discipline, so it's very hard to teach our youth to approach it that way. Yet boys yearn to be taught by adults who have gone through the adolescent years of confusion that there is a discipline available to them through which and by which to navigate these dark, joyful, confusing waters. Boys, as in so much else in their lives, need to see the structures of discipline around them.

Often, seeking structures of discipline and given none or few to model or learn, boys will accommodate love to a structure they already know—sports. So they will discipline their confusions about love by making love into a sport. They will make having sex with a female like dunking a basket, something to work hard toward, then admire oneself for afterward, often in the company of comrades, with little follow-up concern for the ball or the basket or the court the game was played on.

Often, seeking structures of discipline, boys will recreate the most shadowy practices of their fathers', mothers' or other elders' ways of doing love, becoming abusive or passive like dad, abusive or passive like mom. When the elders don't talk much about the discipline structure they themselves are living, the boy will think he understands it, and recreate it, often with no real understanding at all.

Just as often, seeking discipline structures and not finding ones they can understand, boys will simply decide they can't love, and their self-esteem will be crushed for years to come.

Disciplined love—the kind we adults seek to practice and the kind our kids seek to learn from us—involves three kinds of spiritual work: Self work, Soul work, and Skill work.

Self work is the work of personal identity. In order to love with joy, compassion, and challenge, I must have a developed sense of myself, a personal identity from which to base my reaching out, my giving-and-taking of emotion. If I have little sense of my self-worth I will be unable to love well, for a person can only truly love another as much as he loves himself. To learn how to love well a boy must be initiated into his self. This, then, is about the process we spoke of in Chapter 6. As the boy makes the journey toward manhood, we initiate him along the way. If we don't, he doesn't feel like a man, a self, a whole person. Without this feeling, he can't love in a disciplined way.

Soul work is the work of individuals and couples seeking connection to spiritual mysteries, however they define them, and living in rituals and with stories that support the love of each other, children, community, earth. Deep love of one's own soul leads to deeper intimacy with partners, family, and others. If I as a boy am led to live a life devoid of spiritual content, I am not initiated into the rituals, ceremonies, prayers, feelings that my soul needs. Uninitiated into this part of my disciplined life, I will be unable to love another's "soul," another's core being. I will never completely see how worthy and sacred my lover is because I have not learned what sacredness itself is.

Skill work is individuals and couples working to be better communicators, better at getting issues worked through in conflict, better able to curtail judgments, to listen to each other, to make intimacy work, at a nuts-and-bolts level. If we are to fully teach boys how to love, we must say to boys, "Here are skills you must learn." Boys love a task. They love an objective. They love to learn skills. If we present intimacy to them as skills to be learned, we will have more success making them into loving men. If we don't, they will say to themselves, "Love is just something that happens." We need them to say, "Love is a spiritual discipline, the equivalent of other kinds of discipline—like respect for elders, martial arts, sports—and somehow love is the essence of all other disciplines."

Because we as adults may have forgotten that love is a spiritual discipline, with rules, codes, skills, profound responsibilities, and accountabilities not only to others but to the whole society, we have neglected to teach boys. They end up acting "undisciplined": getting girls pregnant, sleeping with as many girls as they can, lying to get sex, even raping. We condemn them for these things. Yet it is we ourselves who have not taught them the Self work, Soul work, and Skill work that it takes to be a lover.

Sex, Love, and the Media

The media has become both second and third family to many boys. It is the place where so many learn the "non-discipline" of loving. A recent study concluded that an American teen watches 14,000 sexual encounters a year on television alone. Most adolescents spend one second learning the discipline of intimacy for every hundred hours they absorb distorted images of intimacy from media and other kids.

A movie like *Pretty Woman* is a wonderful case in point. Here is a very entertaining Hollywood film which is purportedly about love. In fact, it's only about the first stage of love—romance of the mating ritual. Once the couple has mated, the movie ends. It is like 99 percent of the movies, stories, and books we read. Love, in this unreal model, is too easy, not a discipline but a series of conversations and little tiffs that lead to sex and marriage.

To an adult who knows better, *Pretty Woman* is just good entertainment. To a boy, *Pretty Woman* teaches not discipline but fantasy. In a boy's imagination, as in an adult's, there must be a safe fantasy world, where anything can be imagined, and rules are not important. It is in that fantasy world the boy creates new visions, experiments with new forms, moves through images quickly so that he then "comes back to earth" with the goal he really wants to follow in the world of disciplines. He needs the fantasy world.

But if fantasy is all or most of what his second, third and even, sometimes, his first family gives him, then the boy learns that fantasy is the largest director of life, and self-discipline a smaller one. Fantasy-dominated, boys will seek instant gratification, for that is a pillar of male fantasy. Fantasy-dominated, boys will seek fantasy objects, attaching their emotions to those love objects quickly, seeking some connection to them, usually through sex or quick romance, then leav-

ing them. Boys are already wired and socialized for quick gratification, female objectification, and lack of emotional follow-through. But
they are also wired and socialized for love and commitment. Discipline trains love and commitment, and fantasy engages the gratification, objectification, and lack of follow-through. Boys need both to be
whole, but to function in attachments to others, boys need more of the
discipline than the fantasy. Unfortunately, our media provides them
more of the fantasy and less of the discipline.

Politically, we're divided on what to do. Should we censor the
media? Of course we should, where children are concerned. Except
for quality children's programming the media is created to satisfy and
entertain the adult brain. Kids are not adults. Their brains, including
neurochemical stability, emotional activity, and hormonal stability,
have not matured to the extent an adult's has. It's generally agreed
that media for kids has to be different from media for adults. But who
will take responsibility? Parents or the media?

Again, common sense cuts through all the rhetoric. Both must take
responsibility. Parents must put limits on boys' intake of media imagery. The media must come to understand that it serves in our culture as second and third family—it is wearing many of the tribal
masks that tribal elders once wore—and thus must become a responsible member of the family. It must create programming that specifically teaches discipline to youth. Just as there are young adult novels,
most of which model and teach mature discipline structures, Hollywood must step up to the plate and create a similar genre of films:
Quality Young Adult Films. The media will have to hire consultants
who are developmental psychologists and other experienced parents,
mentors, and educators of young people.

When I "preach" this message around the country, I often hear,
"Yeah, right. Like the media's ever gonna do all this." When I hear
that response I'm struck by the tacit relinquishment of power. The
media creates what we pay for, what we lobby for, what we ask for. If
we prove to the creative people in the media that a massive subgenre
of adolescent programming would be useful, morally "right," spiritually nurturing, and *profitable,* they would create it. Proving this to the
media need not be difficult, in an age of AIDS, an age when many of
the media creators themselves have kids, an age when young adult
books and other activities already show great profits.

Some among us have hoped the media would go away, or have

hoped to convince the media to become puritanical—to cut out all sex and violence. The media is so much a creation of the male brain, so visually stimulating, so grounded in quick imagery, so completely a landscape of objects moving through space, it will never go away. It will only become a greater and greater part of the lives of boys and men. Now with computers and on-line communications going into homes and schools at breakneck speed, we need to learn how to mold the media to boys' needs rather than trying to get rid of it.

The media will never cut out all sex and violence because those two things are so much a part of adult life. Policy-makers would be better off taking the copious evidence available to them, studying it, seeing the connection between promiscuity and violence among kids and media imagery, and then making stricter rules for media output to *kids*—enforcing stricter movie ratings, training theater ticket sellers to turn away more kids whom they know to be too young, sanctioning them when they don't, blocking x-rated on-line electronic communications. Meanwhile we parents, mentors, and educators will have to lobby for and support this en masse. Cable networks will have to institute channel blocks. Parents will have to talk to each other and lay out media rules and ask their fellow parents to stick by them at their houses.

Our social response to the damage media does to kids—the overaggressiveness and promiscuity it feeds in boys—will lead to a wonderful community byproduct. We adults will have to talk to each other more, form more community, come together to tell the media what we want. And in this coming together we will create just a little more second and third family in our own schools, neighborhoods, on our Internets and CompuServes.

Boys and Sexual Abuse

Somewhere between 1 in 4 and 1 in 6 boys are sexually abused in the U.S. In over 90 percent of the cases, the victim knows the offender. In the majority of reported sexual abuse cases the offender is a male. Among those offenders, nearly all are heterosexual males. Almost to a person, an abuser was himself once abused.

There is confusion among students of boy culture about what exactly constitutes male sexual abuse. In one of the most helpful books

I've seen, *Protect Your Child From Sexual Abuse: A Parenting Guide,* Janie Hart-Rossi defines child sexual abuse as: ". . . when a child is used as an object for the sexual gratification of an adult through manipulation, exploitation, threats, or physical force. An example of *manipulation* is: 'If you take off your clothes and play with me, I'll let you have two desserts.' An example of *exploitation* is: 'This is just my way of showing you I love you.' An example of a *threat* is: 'If you don't let me play this game with you, I'll . . .' "

Hart-Rossi defines sexual abuse as primarily involving an offending adult, but it can also occur "when a child is used as an object of sexual gratification by a minor under eighteen years old who is temporarily taking on the parental role (for example, a baby-sitter)."

Hart-Rossi's definitions are to the point. They help us see through fears we may have that normal boyhood sexual play is abuse. Part of normal boyhood is a certain amount of sexual experimentation, very often with other males. When the males are peers—i.e., neither one is a parent, caregiver, mentor, or educator—that play does not involve the abuse of power that makes for sexual abuse.

Perhaps our difficulty with accepting boy-boy sex play as normal is our homophobia. If a boy and a girl involve themselves in consensual sex play we call it "sexual experimentation." If a boy and boy do it, we often worry that its abnormal or sexual abuse. As we grow out of our homophobia we'll be more comfortable allowing our boys their normal experimentation.

Our vigilance against real sexual abuse, however, has needed to become stronger and stronger in recent years. The more our first, second, and third-family systems break down, the more room there is for sexual abuse not only to occur but to go unreported and undetected. The less time caring parents and mentors spend with boys, the more boys will be lonely and susceptible to the wrong kind of "parent" or "mentor."

What are the signs of sexual abuse in a boy you know? Here are some questions to ask:

1. Does he show an unusual interest in or avoidance of all things of a sexual nature?
2. Does he have sleep disturbance and nightmares?
3. Is he withdrawing significantly from friends and family?

4. Does he have problems in school with grades and attendance, and/or refuse to go to school?

5. Is he depressed?

6. Does he use seductive mannerisms?

7. Does he make statements about his body being dirty or damaged?

8. Is he suicidal?

9. Has he become abnormally secretive?

10. Does he show uncommon knowledge of sexual activities?

Just because a boy shows some of these symptoms doesn't mean he has been sexually abused, but if he shows more than one, or one of those is 1, 6, 7, or 10, his chances of having been sexually abused skyrocket. Seek help right away.

The pain and legacy of sexual abuse is impossible for a nonsurvivor to imagine. The pain boyhood sexual abuse inflicts on society is stunning, for so many boys who have been abused become men who abuse and otherwise become antisocial. Bruce Kirkpatrick, a survivor of boyhood sexual abuse, described, in *M.E.N.* magazine, his abuser as a Charmer:

"When I was thirteen I met a man I liked immediately because he was funny, he paid attention to me, he complimented me, and he seemed to care about me." Bruce's parents were divorced, he rarely saw his father, the Charmer was "cool." A relationship developed wherein the Charmer became close second family.

Bruce continues: "One night I got drunk, with his encouragement, on some type of cherry-flavored drink. . . . The Charmer had conveniently let my mom know that I would be staying at his house all night long.

"He led me into the bedroom, took off my clothes, and raped me. Nothing physically painful, just emotionally devastating."

Bruce's relationship with the Charmer continued. Though this man hurt him, he was also a mentor, friend, and a cool guy. But years later Bruce would write: "I remember the pain I felt. I remember the terrible shame that filled me. I couldn't hide from that. He had scarred me in such a way that for the next twenty-six years that scar could not heal."

Bruce's experience is shared by hundreds of thousands of boys and men. Some of these men become predators on others—they get the headlines. Most of these men, like Bruce, cope in pain, fear, and crippled self-worth. Bruce has gotten help. Many men don't. Even if they've forgotten the abuse they received as boys, it affects them deeply, if subtly. According to John Gagnon of State University of New York at Stony Brook, whose study interviewed over three thousand adults, both adult males and adult females who had been sexually touched by an adult were more likely, as adults, to be above average in sexual promiscuity—have ten or more sex partners in a lifetime—and to experience more unhappiness.

Practical Principles for Teaching Boys about Sex, Love, and Commitment

Common sense about teaching boys how to love comes down to many principles. Here are twelve that I hope will help:

1. Teach boys and girls sex differences so they can have a dialogue with each other from a position of personal self-awareness and strength.

A fifteen-year-old girl reported that a male friend—not her boyfriend—asked her out. He told her honestly he wanted to lose his virginity and would she help? She called him shallow and shamed him. From her point of view, he was shallow, from his, he was just the opposite—he was honest, exactly the thing he thought girls wanted from guys!

Teaching boys and girls how different their perceptions will be, and that both perceptions can be equally valid, will help everyone in the long run.

2. Sons and fathers (or other intimate first-family elder males) must communicate constantly to prepubescent and to midadolescent boys about sex, love, and commitment. One talk is not enough. Dialogue about sex, love, and commitment must be a constant companion of a boy's adolescence.

3. Third-family involvement is crucial. Elders need to communicate constantly with kids in same-sex, intergenerational groupings. Have a group of trusted elder males instruct boys, tell stories of their own

fears around sex, love, commitment—e.g., at a family gathering, around a campfire on a hunting trip, in a men's group, in the locker room, at school, on men's poker night. Do this as often as spontaneity and ritual allow. Incorporate sex teaching into initiation processes and ceremonies. Boys will be less and less embarassed in this process the more comfortable the adults are.

4. For reasons of personal health and social stability, teach abstinence and virginity as much as possible, pointing out masturbation as a substitute for coitus.

5. Teach birth control. Teach safe and responsible sex. Teaching this requires we adults to be good sexual models—nonpromiscuous, birth-control users.

Numbers 4 and 5 seem contradictory, and they are. Yet one without the other means millions of boys will slip through the cracks.

6. Talk about pregnancy and its effects. Don't be afraid to instill fear in a boy about what would happen if he were to make a girl pregnant. Boys must learn what is expected of them as fathers should the girl get pregnant. Abortion should be discussed too—whatever your beliefs.

7. Teach the boy to respect his body, including his sex organs, as sacred. Help the boy see his body and biology in a spiritual light, as essential to the constant movement of the great circle of life.

8. Help boys develop their own language about their own sexuality. For example, we can teach boys to recognize the three elements of their own sex drive we discussed earlier—instinctive, functional, and emotional. By giving boys words to apply to their own confusing internal changes, they learn to gain insight and positive control over themselves. Literally, their brain development—through linguistic chemistry—becomes involved in helping them mature.

9. Teach boys that their paramount responsibility is to be honest about their sexual intentions. As they hit puberty and get many testosterone surges per day, their aggression increases far more than an average girl's. Studies indicate over and over again that the average pubescent boy gets more assertive as the average pubescent girl gets more demure. This natural aggression must be disciplined with elders' help; its discipline in the sexual-erotic arena has to do with letting girls know the object and intention of the romantic aggression: more often than not that object is sex, pure and simple.

Our cultural politics has lately included the notion that if we taught boys to do more of what girls wanted—cuddling, talking, giving flow-ers—they would be "less like boys," less inclined to take advantage of girls in the pursuit of sex. In fact, what many of the boys are doing is talking, cuddling, and giving flowers with no change in intention—they still want the sex, that's their primary goal. Even as boys learn new skills in relating to girls, they must be absolutely honest about why they're doing what they're doing.

Concomitantly, if a boy is honest about his intentions and a girl does have sex with him, those of us who view girls as born victims must see through this double standard and make them take equal responsibility for the act.

10. Teach boys and male culture that a boy does not need a girl to make him whole. He is not half a person without a girlfriend. Elders of both sexes have to work hard to teach this to both boys and girls who face a culture so obsessed with romantic love it teaches kids that a person must obsess about a mate to learn who he is.

11. Teach boys how to handle their rejections and sense of inade-quacy in the world of both boys and girls. Some of the most important lessons boys will learn about how to be men happen in the adolescent years as they face the terror of rejections. Even if they push us away on the surface, underneath they want us to be there to help them learn how to move through rejection.

12. Teach boys codes of relating. "When you approach a girl you . . ." "When you say this to a girl she may hear . . ." "If you do this with a girl she may think . . ." This kind of teaching needs to be a constant in adolescent male life.

Most of all, we must communicate with boys more than we do about sex, love, and commitment. We won't hollow out logs for the boys to practice with. But we can use the media, as in a new ad campaign for condom use: a computer-animated package hops into bed between a young, embracing couple. "It would be nice if latex condoms were automatic. But since they're not, using them should be," an announcer says. This ad is just one in a series that features Anthony Kiedis, of the rock group Red Hot Chili Peppers, Jason Alexander of *Seinfeld,* and other celebrities.

The "America Responds to AIDS" campaign, out of which the above series grows, and our government support of this campaign, indicate a growing awareness of a need to communicate to teens about sex, love, and commitment. It is unfortunate that it took the AIDS crisis to embolden this commonsense behavior of talking more about life's most important physical and emotional activity. Hopefully, each of us can devote ourselves to more communication and assistance for our boys, inspired by our budding national commitment to communicate. In doing this, we will be participating in very sacred work.

chapter 10

Teaching Boys a Healthy Male Role in Life

The universe is asking a great task of us today; it is extending to us a pressing invitation to reconnect our daily living to the Great Work.
    —*Matthew Fox,* The Re-invention of Work

In Eastern Brazil, among the Shavante, lives are guided in large part by the rhythms of the land, the wisdom of tradition, and the division of labor between women and men. Both women and men work, both do their share of child care, both have a clear sense of why they are alive, what the earth needs of them, what their roles are.

The role each lives out is not an easy one, but for the Shavante, as for most tribal peoples, the role each man or woman lives out is part of what gives indestructible meaning to individual and community life. Through the role, the person is connected to self, family, society, and earth. Without the role, the person would drift through life without purpose.

For millions of years, males in our culture knew their role in life: they were providers, protectors, and nurturers of children. This latter aspect of their role did not usually get fully activated until their children were no longer infants, for infant care was mainly the territory of women. But once the children got older, the men paid special attention to protecting and guiding the paths of their vulnerable daughters, and mentoring and disciplining the paths of their sons. When a battle needed to be fought, the men considered it their sacred duty to fight and die in it so the women, children, community, and value system were protected. When there was no food on the table, the men considered it their failure. Their sense of the sacredness of their role ran deep and long through the blood and DNA of every male born. These males were our ancestors, our grandfathers, even our fathers.

As we moved through the latter part of this century, it became clear that tumultuous social change had to occur as the three-family nature of human community gave way to individualism; the male role and men's work had driven fathers too far from their families; and the female role and women's work became, in the eyes of many, a second-class enterprise. Tumultuous social change has occurred and is occurring. It has been based, mainly, on deconstructing social systems that social thinkers believed restricted us as human beings.

As we enter the next millennium, the energy of deconstruction is gradually shifting to an energy of reconstruction, for we've noticed that much of what we threw out in our tumult has left holes in our society and in our souls. So we are revisiting the past not to toss out the good we've achieved over the last decades but to reclaim the good we lost and unite it with the progressive visions and systems we've discovered.

The search for a healthy male role requires this very kind of revisioning. As we enter the next millennium, our boys, young men, and our mature men are calling on us to explore with clarity what the role of males should be. For many people around us, talk about "a male role" is a scary subject; for many others, an abhorrent, unnecessary one. Yet given what we know about how a boy is built and how he is socialized, we have no choice but to notice that without a sacred role to grow into, he will, as he becomes a man, be more likely to join a gang, hit his lover, abandon his children, live in emotional isolation, become addicted, hypermaterialistic, lonely, and unhappy. He needs a structure and discipline in which to learn who he is. He needs to live a journey that has clear responsibilities and goals. He needs a role in life. Without these, without the role training that accompanies these, he does not know his sacred and important objectives in life. He only suspects he has some. People other than himself, often women, tell him what his emotional objectives are, something he'll resent at some point later when he feels he's being manipulated. He does not know how to obtain his goals, or how to feel grounded in his search for meaning. He may pick up strategies here and there, but never feels confident that he's living the right way. Without a structure a boy does not know why his goals are essential. In raising a child, for instance, he may sense how essential his presence is for a limited time, then, noticing that the child is more bonded with mom, and perceiving that conflicts with his wife trouble the child, he often leaves both mother and child, seeing himself as not only nonessential but in fact the problem. Without a disciplined role, a boy does not know how to gauge his success at his achievements. Especially in areas of responsible relationship, he will never quite know he has accomplished the sacred tasks of love, commitment, and caring.

The premise, then, of this chapter, and in fact the penultimate premise of this book, is that we must and can join together as a society to define a sacred role for our boys and men. What follows here is my attempt to do just that. It is only one attempt, only a model. I hope it inspires you to create your own "manifesto" of what you believe the male role should be.

A Sacred Male Role for the New Millennium

The male role, I believe, should rise from the seed of this word: husbandry. Boys and men at their best mature into a role in which they are not only required but want to be husbands: husbands of families, husbands of communities, husbands of culture as a whole, husbands of others around the world, husbands of the earth itself, and husbands of their own life journey. Boys, even in gangs, seek to husband something, some one, some energy, some spirit, some sacred goal.

The word "husbandry" comes from a combination of the Old English *husbonda* and the Old Norse word *bua,* which means to dwell. In these ancient cultures a husband was a household dweller who felt a deep masculine bond to his home and land. Husbanding implied generating and maintaining *stable* relationships with self, family, community, culture, and earth.

To define the husbandry role, I would suggest these ten principles. I have garnered them from study of tribal cultures, from historical record of the roles taught by our own ancestral cultures, and from our contemporary dialogue over values. For a sacred role, like the husbandry role, to become a life-giving and life-defining part of a boy's journey to manhood, we have to begin teaching it, in very conscious ways, from very early on. For its principles to take hold in a boy, they would have to be important parts of his discipline systems, his socializing structures, and the interweavings of his three families. Even when he is four or five, we would be pointing him in the direction of principles he couldn't yet fully fathom.

TEN PRINCIPLES OF A SACRED MALE ROLE

Principle 1.

Seek lifestyles, communities, and helpmates that afford you a balance of personal spiritual development, family devotion, and life-sustaining work.

A primary goal of an individual's existence is to live in balance between his responsibilities to his own soul's life, to his three families, and to whatever works in the world his talents, skills, and opportunities provide him. Working ten hours a day or seventy hours a week away from family or spiritual development does not afford balance. Nor does the kind of laziness that lets one be close to family, but becomes so quickly a source of shame and self-doubt. Where opportunities do not exist for the balance of work, family, and free personal life, society will have to make it a value to revision social structures so that balance can be achievable.

Principle 2.

Provide for, protect, and nurture those you are called to love.

A man, to the best of his ability, has the sacred responsibility to provide survival essentials—food, shelter, clothing, physical and emotional safety, unconditional love, respect, hands-on nurturance, and paths of exploration to those in his care. To provide, protect, and nurture requires as much lover in a man as warrior. When a man creates a child, he can have no more important responsibility on this earth than that child.

Principle 3.

Actively participate in not just one but in three families.

A man's responsibilities to human society do not begin or end with his own blood kin. Each man stands at the center of three concentric circles. The closest circle is his immediate family, the next one his extended family (including nonblood kin), the next one his community. To fully participate in life he needs to have one or more specific foci of energy in each of the three families. He needs not only to raise his own children but to mentor others' children. Should he find himself without a mate and not a father, the energy he would devote to the first circle needs to be redirected into the other two circles, so that those men who are partnered and who are fathering can spend more of their energy on the heavy demands of partner and children.

Principle 4.

Live in concert with the natural world.

As much as possible, and even if it requires the diminishing of material acquisition, a man is responsible to and for the natural world he lives in. He is a part of the interdependent web. His integrity as a man is not only judged by how he relates to other human beings but also by how he relates to the body and spirit of nature. Nature is, after all, the place from which he came and to which he will return, long before and long after his human relations have ended. A man's interactions with the natural world are interactions filled with gratitude.

Principle 5.

Seek equal partnerships with women and female culture.

A man respects a woman for who she is. He does not give her power over him nor does he seek power over her. He knows that he has a tendency to want to give her whatever she wants, then exact from her whatever he wants. The urges toward domination and compliance are two sides of the same coin. Men who are isolated from women and female culture, or dominating of them, or enmeshed with them, or subservient to them are all charged with the responsibility of discovering balance. When forming relationships with romantic partners, a man discovers deepest love by practicing his love as a mature spiritual discipline, with rules and codes of conduct, spiritual paths, boundaries to keep safe.

Principle 6.

Seek a male kinship system.

Among first, second, and third families, a man will discover a male community in which to support and be supported, achieve and help others achieve, admire and be admired, husband and learn to better husband. In this emotionally and spiritually vital male community, he will feel a part of something elemental, something humbling and empowering at once, and in ways he cannot quite define. To belong to a community of men is as much to grow by osmosis as by conscious plan.

Principle 7.

Be an agent of service, social dialogue and, when necessary, social change.

A man must participate in his society's evolution. He must serve others. If he is without compassion for the underprivileged, he is not whole. If he does not understand the social dialogue around him, he seeks out information and wisdom. A man who claims to know it all is dangerous. True heroism is courageous service.

Principle 8.

Know the story you are living.

A man needs to remain ever conscious of the life journey he is on. Part of a man's focus must be on what stage of life he is in, what season of manhood he has reached, what are its demands and rewards. A man needs to know where his bloodline came from, what its traditions were, even if he adheres to few of them. Individual freedom swiftly becomes emotional isolation in a man who does not know who he is. He is responsible to seek mentors all through his life who will act as mirrors and wisdom-teachers, people and places that will help him remain conscious and awake through life. He is responsible to live in concert with rituals, ways of praying and communicating with mystery, that show him life is a spirit-filled journey.

Principle 9.

Enjoy the fruits of your labors.

A man who cannot play ecstatically is not wholly a man. A man cannot fully embrace life unless he loves not only his labors but the fruits they bear. Manhood is a role filled with joy and dance, relaxation and excitement, mischief and good fun.

Principle 10.

Be open to change, especially changes in values.

A man is fully a man when he is able to let go. When rigidity is required for courage to flow, he remains rigid. But when rigidity leads to mistaken loyalties, dangerous relationships, and unnecessary struggles over power, a man must return to a stance of wonder and anticipation, working for a new path, a new way, a new focus of personal energy. Because he is an adult, and therefore has accepted personal responsibility for his life, he knows that he alone is ultimately charged with making his life worthwhile. Change cannot defeat it. Rather, it forces new, rewarding challenges.

Can we bring the husbandry role into the lives of even our small boys? Among the Shavante, specific role training starts when the boys are four. They are brought out into the center of a meadow where, in the words of one Shavante father, "they are taught to become like trees." Much of what holds us back from beginning our role teaching in the early years, and much of why we neglect teaching it all through a boy's life, is simply the fact that we haven't defined what we want it to be. I hope the husbandry model provides you with a foundation for defining a sacred male role, then from there, adapting and implementing role teaching in the lives of the boys you know.

One of the primary institutions through which role teaching occurs is the workplace. In a sense, all talk of providing boys with a sacred role is dependent on understanding the role of work in a boy's life, a man's life, a husband's life.

Giving Boys Important Work

An essential element of happy boyhood and happy manhood is the love of work—not all work but especially those few and important tasks through which boy and man learn intimacy with others, physical and mental maturity, self-confidence, the ways of the world. Males are both hard- and soft-wired to work at tasks, achieve definable objectives in the tasks, and gain self-image from working at the tasks. Without constructive work, men often feel terribly lost. That the same can be said of girls and women in their way takes nothing away from the fact that for so many boys and men working often feels as important as breathing.

Through work the individual boy seeks that which sets him apart from others yet that through which he belongs with others. His push-pull between needing to be independent and yet be with others is often resolved in work. He can do his own thing in the workplace yet feel he belongs in the collective effort. He finds a method by which, as a male, to walk safely the razor's edge between freedom and responsibility.

"You are giving people the news," my father taught me when I started my first paper route. "The news, the advertisements, the schedules for movies, all these things," he said, "bring people closer together, help people form opinions about how to vote, give people a place to call when they're hurt. You're not just giving them paper, you're giving them *the news*."

Listening to my father one would have thought I was giving people the "good news" of a gospel. Well, wasn't I, in my own way? Didn't I, as a boy, need my elders to show me that the drudgery of what I was doing was also combined with the greatness of my role in the world?

From toddlerhood, boys need important work. It focuses them. It builds self-confidence. It helps them belong. It helps them become husbands. When a two-year-old drops a fork on the floor, we bend to pick it up for him. Better yet would be to have him do it himself. When a three-year-old leaves his tricycle outside, we carry it in on our way in from work. Better yet would be to make him do it himself. When a seven-year-old has to choose between his homework and playing with his friends, we are sometimes tempted by our love to do the homework for him. Better yet would be to help him manage his time. When a twelve-year-old wants to do three different activities in one day, we are tempted to keep him happy and stimulated, and so run him around to all three. Better yet might be to help him choose one or two, and show him how to do those with depth.

Boys don't just need work, they need important work. That means they need us to be involved with them in that part of work where we can give wisdom and blessing. They need us to show them how the work is a vehicle for experiencing deep joys and sympathies other than the work itself. They need us to explain the importance of the work to them, putting it in a context of importance to themselves, their family, their community, and their society. They need us to show them how essential it is in their husbanding, sacred role. When the work is drudgery, we must help them find meaning in it. This is especially important as so many boys are faced with dead-end, underpaid, mindless jobs. Somehow, we must help the boy find the piece of the job that is sacred.

Work is not something to protect boys from; it is something to lead boys toward. Sports can be work for athletic boys, computers can be work, newspaper routes, housecleaning, visits to a parents' workplace, schoolwork. All these are "work," and all are potentially important.

As boys are led by parents, mentors, and educators into a rich life of work and play, they need a language too for "inner work." From very early on in a boy's life, we need to show the boy that his managing and soothing of his own fears, pains, griefs, and angers are "the *work* of being human, the internal work of being a boy, then a man, a lover, then a husband." How wonderful it is for a boy when the adults around him ask, "What are you learning about yourself, your friends, your community as you do such and such work?" For a boy's work to be important, it needs the dialogue of elders constantly around it.

When I was fourteen, I worked at a Greyhound station, sweeping up, cleaning toilets. My family had very little money. I was "forced" to work by these circumstances, but even if I hadn't been, I hope my parents would have encouraged my working there anyway. One of the clerks become my chess-playing friend. He often talked to me about who I was, what I was doing, what I hoped for. Once he even said to me, "You've cleaned toilets at a bus station, Mike. If you can do that, you can do anything."

WHAT ITS REALLY LIKE FOR MEN IN THE WORKPLACE

One of the impediments in our culture to fully understanding the needs of boys and men in relation to work is the gender myth that males have it easy and females have it hard. In order to regain a sense of a sacred male role, we'll have to see through this myth. Both males and females have it hard in the workplace.

In fact, as we enter the new millennium we live in a society in which the female role grows in opportunity and sacredness—women now not only raise most of our kids but also hold more than half of our jobs—and the male role diminishes. In the workplace, except in the most visible high-hierarchy jobs, to which the most competitive, high-testosterone males—aided, at times, by sexism—usually ascend, women have gained economically in the last thirty years and men have lost.

Economist Stephen Rose conducted a twenty-two-year study for the National Commission for Employment Policy. He found:

In the 1970s, 24 percent of men were income losers. In the 1980s, 36 percent were income losers. Women were consistent winners in earnings during these time periods. White males on average lost earnings and black males lost very big. In the 1970s, three quarters of black men were able to maintain a full-time job year round throughout the decade. In the 1980s, only half could do so. In the 1970s, of young men between twenty-two and twenty-six, only 9 percent suffered declining earnings during the decade; in the 1980s, 26 percent lost. The number of income losers among similar women declined from 40 percent to 30 percent.

Economic changes have done much to "even the score" between women and men, though in certain corporate areas that score still may need to be equalized. As a family feminist, I work toward the goal of equality in the job world. But that single goal—"equality in the workplace," which has become an obsession of many feminists—is only one of the important goals in human community. What we have not noticed as we've vehemently pursued the economic ascension of women is the danger that change holds for men, and thus for the society as a whole. The millions of men who have lost their jobs or large chunks of income have not gained in comparable access to children—in most divorce cases the children go to the mother for primary custody. Nor have the income-losing men gained in access to health care or other social services. Ninety percent of the homeless are male. The vast majority of adults on welfare are female. The health-care system *when taken as a whole* provides nearly twice the care to women, on a day-to-day basis, as to men.

By focusing so obsessively on the safe ascension of women in the workplace and neglecting the work role of men, we are teaching most boys that they don't really have a clear path to self-respect anymore;

their job is to make sure women and girls have a clear path to those things. Herein lies a bitter irony. Boys and men have always, in whatever culture, known that their primary job is to sacrifice themselves so that women and girls can be safe. The last thirty years of feminism, for all its good, has not noticed that feminism is preaching the same old message to male culture when it asks male culture to see how victimized women are, and make sure women are taken care of. Male culture has been biologically and socially based on this principle for millennia.

Teaching Boys a Sacred Role

David Sawyer, one of the country's leading experts on Youth Service, is director of Students for Appalachia, a community service program at Berea College that won the Thousand Points of Light award. He has testified before White House and Congressional committees on national youth service. Speaking about the National and Community Service Act, he recently said, "The thousands of grassroots programs that preceded and precipitated it have begun to do something more critical than create service opportunities for youth and service benefits for those in need. The Act creates a new structure of roles and meanings in which the heroic search can find legitimate and healthy expression."

The role of husbandry is, I believe, getting taught all over the country. We do not have to look too hard to see programs, such as the ones created under the auspices of the Act, and the ones we've looked at throughout this book, that involve parents, mentors and educators in close life with youth.

How can each of us join this effort? You will know of many ways to teach boys and youth a sacred role. My suggestions here are toward a model for implementing and teaching husbandry which is by no means exhaustive. Many, if not all, of the practical strategies here are not "new" at all. They are common sense.

Join me in an exercise for which you'll need only a pencil or pen, and some paper. I will list categories inherent in the Principles we delineated earlier, then ask you to write on a separate sheet of paper how you can help. The blanks you will write in are:

▼ *Who* you will enlist to help you teach _____ (fill in the blank) to a boy you know.

▼ *What* exact tenets you want taught.

▼ *Where* the best locations are for teaching these tenets and finding your three-family assistance.

▼ *When* are the right times to accomplish the teaching.

▼ *How* the teaching will take place.

▼ *Why* you believe the teaching is important.

This exercise will help you focus your energies on specific principles, places, and people around you that can help teach sacred roles to the boys you know. This exercise is not only useful to parents but also to mentors, educators, grandparents, neighbors, anyone who takes a particular interest in the healthy nurturing of a child in his or her community. This exercise can be done on sheets of paper for as many children as you wish. With the first category, I'll model the format of the exercise. With the subsequent categories, I'll just list Who, What, Where, When, How, and Why.

TEACHING BOYS TO HUSBAND THEMSELVES

How can each of us help a boy gain self-respect, insight into himself, personal and spiritual growth? Focus on a boy and fill in the blanks. Who will help me help this boy in this way?_____

_____

What specific principles in this category does this boy need to learn better at this time in his life?_____

_____

Where are the best places to teach these principles? In nature? In church? In school? With more time spent at home?_____

_____

When are the best ritual or spontaneous times to teach these things? At the dinner table, on a camping trip, during a rite of passage ceremony, on grandpa's farm?_____

_____

How should I and my community teach this? With what experiences, what games, what sports, what tools? In what format, by taking away or giving what?_____

_____

Why is it crucial these things be taught to this boy? Write down what behaviors you've seen that indicate he is not husbanding himself well._____

_____

Having written all these things, you not only have focus for your own and your allies' efforts but you also have things to talk to the boy about, should you choose to do so.

TEACHING BOYS TO HUSBAND THEIR FIRST FAMILY

Focus now, whatever your present first-family system, on a renewed commitment to teach the boys to husband everyone in that first family and, if a member of the first family has been replaced by a blending of families, include a blended family member too.

▼   Who will help?
▼   What needs teaching?
▼   Where should it best be taught?
▼   When is the best opportunity?
▼   How shall it be taught?
▼   Why must it be taught now?

TEACHING BOYS TO HUSBAND KIN AND COMMUNITY

From very early on boys sense their responsibility to second-family kin (whether blood-kin or nonblood) and third-family community. They revel in the attentions with which they are rewarded by nonparents. They want more of those attentions and will do what they can to gain them.

Focus on different members and groups of your second and third families. Who might you direct your boy toward now, in a conscious way? What role does this person(s) teach? Where are you willing to send the boy to learn this from this person(s)? When is the best time? How can you help it be taught? Why is it essential?

TEACHING BOYS TO HUSBAND THE EARTH

There are so many venues around you to choose from if you decide to consciously focus on teaching boys to husband the earth. There are places that show the boy the awesome grace of nature. There are field trips. There are Sunday drives. Decide Who, What, Where, When, How, Why?

TEACHING BOYS TO HUSBAND MALE COMMUNITY

We often assume boys automatically learn how to take care of other boys or men because they are themselves male. Yet don't they need our help in focusing their energies on how to act and be with other males? Boys often feel great confusion about the community of men. Fill out the blanks on your separate sheet of paper, perhaps as you recall a question your boy asked, or a misgiving or even fear you've seen him experience lately in the world of males.

TEACHING BOYS TO HUSBAND FEMALE COMMUNITY

Even if he is not "in love" with "a" girl, a boy is always challenged by the massive force of female community around him. That community often feels to him like the Holy Grail—other times it feels like a disaster area. Some moments, he wants to join it, other moments to destroy it.

Focus as much as you need to on who can help you teach your boys a healthy role in relation to that community, a role in which his self-respect is never sacrificed, yet opens him up to female energy. Focus on where the best opportunities are for this teaching. A year ago it may have been in your home; now, as the boy grows older, there may be another place that needs equal time. Focus on When, How and Why. As you answer this last question, see the world through your boy's eyes rather than your own. Why does he need to learn how to husband female community? How will it make him a better person?

TEACHING BOYS TO HUSBAND A LIFE PARTNER

Parents, mentors, and educators cannot invade much of this part of a boy's quest. Yet we can guide some of it better than we do. Sometimes we don't ask for help from an appropriate person, place, or source of wisdom. So our boys don't learn the very lesson we want to teach: how to love intimately. Instead, they learn how to dominate, to control, to withdraw; how to feel like failures at love; how to define themselves by what their lovers think of them; or even how to avoid love altogether. As you explore the Who, What, Where, When, How, and Why of this teaching, you might end up putting yourself as the Who, for perhaps it is you who is modeling something that the boy needs more of, or, perhaps, you are modeling something that harms the boy.

TEACHING BOYS TO HUSBAND (FATHER) CHILDREN

What elements of the fatherhood role are you teaching? Boys also want to learn, from early on, their role as mentors to nonblood kin. Are you mentoring others so that the boys who model off you are learning to mentor? Who, What, Where, When, How, Why?

These are just some of the categories of "husbanding" we can explore in an exercise. I hope you'll do the Who, What, When, Where, How, Why exercise for every category you think of—work, schools, blended families, gay families, churches, synagogues. After you've done it, I hope you'll commit to putting some of it in action. It is a tool you can return to at various stages of your boy's life. Use it over and over again as a means of focus, and as a foundation from which to generate new parenting, mentoring, and educational energies.

Epilogue

When I sat watching the movie *Pinocchio* as a boy, I could not have known what a journey through my own boyhood I would make. I did not know how generously my own biology was propelling me toward a very male way of coming out of my awkward boyhood woodenness and discovering my own male flesh, blood, and spirit. I did not realize how difficult it would be to learn how to be brave, truthful, and good. Nor did I realize how many parents, mentors, and educators I would need to help me truly learn how to live. I knew only, at that time, that I, like Pinocchio, felt wooden, and wanted to feel real.

I hope this book has inspired you to feel the profound importance of what you do for boys, whether as a member of their first, second, or third family. No matter who you are, you are charged with the care of boys. You are their Blue Fairy, you are their Geppetto, you are even, at times, the mean boy-merchants on the false island paradise. You love the boys, you challenge them, you disappoint them, they disappoint you. In all of it, you are, nonetheless, helping them feel real.

Despite the various experiences I had as a boy, I confess to not having felt like a man until I was in my thirties. I remember saying to a men's group, "I don't know if I'm a man." This was in the mid-1980s. Following that confession I discovered that they, then many others, then over the years, hundreds of thousands, even millions of other adult males felt the way I had. We were adult males but still felt wooden. We didn't know who we were, what a man was, what a boy should learn, what we as men should teach. Even as "grown men," we still had one foot back in Pinocchio's journey.

In writing this book, I hope not only to help us raise better boys, and not only to help the human community come closer together by focusing on its huge role in that task, but I celebrate too the lives of every adult female and adult male who wakes up one day asking the spiritual question, "Who am I?" and turns, in search of a good answer, toward the boys and girls around us who need us now more than ever.

Additional Resources and Community Agencies

SUPPORT FOR MOMS

Moms continue to tell me the value of *The Little Boy Book* as a primer and resource by Sheila Moore and Roon Frost. Published by Ballantine, in New York, 1986.

If a mom (and, of course, any parent or caregiver) of a young child has not yet discovered the "What to Expect . . ." books, now's the time! Written by Arlene Eisenberg, Heidi Esenberg Murkoff, and Sandee Eisenberg Hathaway, they are perennial bestsellers. Put out by Workman Publishing in New York, they have the "What to Expect" theme and words in their titles.

Another wonderful resource for the early years of life is *Caring for Your Baby and Young Child: Birth to Age 5,* put out by the American

Academy of Pediatrics, Steven P. Shelov, Editor in Chief. The academy also puts one out for the years 5 to 12 and the years 12 to 21.

If parents have any questions at all about early attachment theory, T. Berry Brazelton's books are essential reading (see the Notes for Chapter Four and the Full Bibliography). Brazelton believes that millions of mothers are not attaching well enough with their children in our culture. I have seen no reason to disagree with him.

Mom's Project. Boston, Massachusetts. 617-638-5160. Women ex-addicts help pregnant women fight drug abuse.

FATHERHOOD RESOURCES

Institute for Responsible Fatherhood. Washington D.C. 202-789-6376. Teaches parenting and responsibility skills primarily to single fathers. Supports single fathers generally.

Mad Dads. Omaha, Nebraska. 402-451-3500. Provides volunteers who serve as positive role models. Dads patrol drug markets to report dealers.

National Fatherhood Initiative. Lancaster, Pennsylvania. 800-790-DADS. Provides information, research, and other resources to teach and understand responsible fatherhood.

For statistics, information, and issues relating to the fatherhood crisis facing society today, David Blankenhorn's book *Fatherless in America* is an invaluable resource.

STEPPARENT SUPPORT

Stepfamily Association of America. Provides a free catalog of educational resources for people who want to pursue stepparenting issues. Dept. P, 215 S. Centennial Mall #212, Lincoln, Nebraska 68508.

BOYS AND DISCIPLINE

Thomas Gordon. P.E.T., *Parent Effectiveness Training.* New York: Peter Wyden, 1970. Still a classic on how to more effectively communicate with kids, including positive discipline.

Myrna Shure and George Spivack. *Problem-solving Techniques in Child-Rearing.* Oakland, Calif.: Jossey-Bass, 1978. Still a classic, filled with tested techniques and common sense.

BOYS AND SEXUALITY

Bruce S. Glassman. *Everything You Need to Know About Growing Up Male.* New York: Rosen, 1991.

Robie H. Harris. Illustrated by Michael Emberley. *It's Perfectly Normal: Changing Bodies, Growing Up, Sex and Sexual Health.* Cambridge, Mass: Candlewick Press, 1995.

Wardell Pomeroy. *Boys and Sex.* New York: Delacorte, 1991. Honest, packed with information, a must-read for anyone trying to help boys understand themselves.

For preteens with questions about what to expect as puberty comes, Dial Plus Health and Beauty Awareness Council publishes a free booklet, "Coming of Age," which discusses the physical changes taking place in boys and girls, and many other passages. Call 800-258-3425 for a free copy.

ADOLESCENCE

Both the Notes and the Full Bibliography include resources about adolescence. Here I'll call special attention to two valuable books:

Elizabeth Fenwick and Dr. Tony Smith. *Adolescence: The Survival Guide for Parents and Teenagers.* Dorling Kindersley, 1995.

Pat Palmer with Melissa Alberti Froehner. *Teen Esteem: A Self-direction Manual for Young Adults.* San Luis Obispo, Calif.: Impact Publishers, 1995.

Impact Publishers in general is a good resource for books on child and human development. Their address is P.O. Box 1094, San Luis Obispo, Calif. 93406.

BOYS, EDUCATIONAL SYSTEMS, AND COMMUNITY EDUCATION

Center for Collaborative Education. New York City. 212-348-7821. Studies school systems and advocates for smaller schools and more educational choices.

Teach for America. New York City. 212-425-9039. College grads seeking to teach for two years in understaffed public schools are recruited and matched with schools.

Parents as Teachers. St. Louis, Missouri. 314-432-4330. Promotes parental involvement with kids' education.

Caring Communities. St. Louis, Missouri. 314-231-3720. Helps schools function also as community centers.

VALUES TEACHING

Building Character School-wide. Dayton, Ohio. 513-224-7364. Provides information about classroom character education.

GENERAL COMMUNITY BUILDING

Who Cares Magazine. Washington, D.C. 202-628-1691. info@whocares.org. A resource and information center for community activist groups which are founded by young people.

CHILD-CARE COMMUNITY BUILDING

Child Care Action Campaign. Dept. P, 330 Seventh Ave, 17th Floor, New York, NY 10001-5010. A place to start looking for strategies and information about the business/child care collaboration.

CHURCH COMMUNITY BUILDING

One Church–One Addict. Washington, D.C. 800-451-3500. Educates churches on how to run drug and alcohol rehab programs.

MENTORING AND INITIATION

National Retiree Volunteer Coalition. Minneapolis, Minnesota. 612-341-2689. Helps companies establish programs that bring retirees into useful charitable work, including mentoring work.

Initiation Resources.
There is a wonderful book written by Bernard Weiner called *Boy Into Man.* In this book, Weiner, a father of two sons, records the coming-of-age ceremony he and his men's group, with the support of spouses and community members, created for eighth-grade boys— their sons—who were entering the time of the hero's journey, the adolescent stage of maturation. This book provides the most detailed model of how to build tribal community in the center of busy American life I have ever read.

Stan Crow, co-founder of the Institute of Cultural Affairs in Bothell, Washington, puts out the magazine *ICA Journeys,* and has led rites of passage adventures for over a decade. The ICA can be reached at 22421 39th Ave. SE, Bothell, Washington 98021. For anyone interested in delving more deeply into rites of passage, initiation, and coming-of-age work for adolescent youths, Stan is an invaluable resource.

A number of magazines have grown out of the men's movement. *Wingspan,* the largest among them, has carried stories by men and youths of the rites of passage and initiation adventures they've worked on together. In the book *Wingspan: Inside the Men's Movement,* many men's magazines are listed, with addresses and phone numbers.

Marianne Williamson, the bestselling author of *Return to Love,* recently published *Illuminata,* a book of insights, prayers, and ceremonies. In it she shows how a community can create its own prayers to bring pieces of initiation experience together.

PROGRAM FOR AT-RISK YOUTH

Bureau for At-Risk Youth. Huntington, New York. 800-99-YOUTH. Puts out a catalog, called *At-Risk Resources,* which in itself is an invaluable resource for families and others working with at-risk kids.

GAY ISSUES

The White Crane Newsletter. P.O. Box 170152, San Francisco, CA 94117-0152. A newsletter featuring spirituality from a gay male perspective. Robert Barzan, who puts out the newsletter, has recently published a book on gay men's issues, entitled *Sex and Spirit: Exploring Gay Men's Spirituality.* San Francisco: White Crane Press, 1995 (same address as above).

WORK AND SERVICE

Jobs for Youth. Chicago, Illinois. 312-782-2086. Provides job training in the tough-love format.

Strive. New York City. 212-360-1100. Provides young adults with training and follow-up for entry-level jobs.

City Year. Boston, Massachusetts. 617-350-0700. A one-year intensive community service for young people ages seventeen through twenty-three.

For information and training on youth service, David Sawyer, Director of Service Programs at Berea College, is a good resource. Contact him at Berea College, CPO 1842, Berea, Kentucky 40404.

Notes

Introduction

Pages xvi–xx. Moving Beyond False Myths
Sources for the statistics in this section include:

The Bureau of Justice Statistics.

David Blankenhorn. *Fatherless in America.* New York: Basic Books, 1995.

Warren Farrell. *The Myth of Male Power.* New York: Simon and Schuster, 1993.

Aaron R. Kipnis. *Knights Without Armor.* Los Angeles: Jeremy P. Tarcher, 1992.

Aaron R. Kipnis and Elizabeth Herron. *Gender War/Gender Peace.* New York: William Morrow, 1994.

Jon Pielemeier. "Man Is the Fellow Victim, Not the Enemy," *Seattle M.E.N.* magazine, reprinted from *Seattle Times,* February 1992.

Chapter 1: Where It All Begins: The Biology of Boyhood

The material about the effects of sex-different brain and hormonal systems is very controversial. One physiologist will come to one conclusion about pieces of it, one endocrinologist to another. Researchers argue vehemently over the quality of sources of research. The only thing all researchers agree on is that human beings are each individuals, with sex differences existing on a spectrum rather than at polar oppositions.

My own research into the biology of boyhood relies on three primary sources: biological material, anthropological material, and personal observations. I have been able to resolve the ambiguity and controversy to my own satisfaction by taking specific items of brain research and comparing them individually with historical and anthropological trends, then confirming those "hard science" and "soft science" facts with personal observations of 1990s' boys and families.

When, for instance, brain research tells me a boy will tend, because of his testosterone and brain structure, to process emotive information in a certain way, I will see if anthropological information indicates that tribes and societies have set up cultures and left cultural residues that support that biological trend, and I will observe boys in my life and work for that trend. If all three confirm each other, I feel comfortable that the brain research is robust.

Page 4. Nature Versus Nurture

Many researchers in the fields of evolutionary biology and brain science have discovered the same things simultaneously. The facts in this chapter about how testosterone and the male brain work are gleaned from a number of sources the reader might want to pursue simultaneously.

The most valuable resource I've discovered—packed with information and delightfully readable—is *Brain Sex,* by Anne Moir, Ph.D., and David Jessel. *Brain Sex* culls information from endocrinology, neurology, and numerous other medical journals. I suggest it as a place to begin if you are looking for a book-length work. The material on pages 14 and 15, as throughout chapter 1, is primarily from the following sources:

Mary Batten. *Sexual Strategies.* Los Angeles: Tarcher/Putnam, 1992.

T. Berry Brazelton, and Bertrand G. Cramer. *The Earliest Relationship.* Reading, MA: Addison-Wesley, 1990.

Helen Fisher. *Anatomy of Love.* New York: Fawcett, 1992.

Lynn Margulis and Dorion Sagan. *Mystery Dance.* New York: Summit Books, 1991.

Anne Moir and David Jessel. *Brain Sex.* New York: Laurel, 1989.

Sheila Moore and Roon Frost. *The Little Boy Book.* New York: Ballantine, 1986.

Robert Pool. *Eve's Rib.* New York: Crown Publishers, 1994.

Carl Sagan and Ann Druyan. *Shadows of Forgotten Ancestors.* New York: Random House, 1992.

Robert Wright. *The Moral Animal.* New York: Vintage, 1994.

In presenting research of this kind, textbooks in the medical field become essential, as does the assistance of individuals trained in the medical sciences. Darl W. Vander Linden, Ph.D., and Jeff Hedge, D.O., were of invaluable assistance in helping me interpret medical information, and in providing me the use of their textbooks:

Eric R. Kandel, James H. Schwartz, and Thomas M. Jessel. *Essentials of Neural Science and Behavior.* Norwalk, Connecticut: Appleton & Lange, 1995.

Constance R. Martin. *Textbook of Endocrine Physiology.* New York: Oxford University Press, 1976.

Arthur. C. Guyton. *Textbook of Medical Physiology.* Philadelphia: W.B. Saunders and Company, 1976.

Since *Time* magazine ran an article on brain differences as its cover story on January 20, 1992, other magazines have followed suit. More recently, *Newsweek* ran a cover story on brain differences (March 27, 1995). The November 28, 1994, issue of the *New Republic* featured an article by Robert Wright, "The Moral Animal," comparing feminist views with evolutionary theory. These articles are well worth looking at if you don't have time to go through whole books on the subject.

Page 6. The Prime Mover: Testosterone
Don and Jeanne Elium. *Raising a Son.* Hillsboro, Oregon: Beyond Words, 1992.

Moore and Frost, *The Little Boy Book.*

Page 8. Testosterone and Aggression
Margulis and Sagan, *Mystery Dance.*
Sagan and Druyan, *Shadows of Forgotten Ancestors.*
Batten, *Sexual Strategies.*
Brazelton and Cramer, *The Earliest Relationship.*

Page 10. Testosterone, Puberty, and Beyond
Moir and Jessel, *Brain Sex.*
Wardell B. Pomeroy. *Boys and Sex.* New York: Delacorte, 1991.
Holly Nadler, "My Life as a Man," *LEARS,* December 1993.

Page 11. Testosterone and Tension
Elium and Elium, *Raising a Son.*

Page 12. How a Boy Thinks: The Male Brain
Moir and Jessel, *Brain Sex.*

Page 13. Structural Differences in the Brain
Moir and Jessel, *Brain Sex.*
Moore and Frost, *The Little Boy Book.*
The Learning Channel, "Brain Sex" (a three-part video series based on the book)
Michael D'Antonio, "The Fragile Sex," *LA Times magazine,* December 4, 1994.

Page 15. Brain Differences and Your Children.
Brazelton and Cramer, *The Earliest Relationship.*
Moir and Jessel, *Brain Sex.*

Page 16.
Moir and Jessel, *Brain Sex.*

Page 18. How the Different Brains Were Created
Margulis and Sagan, *Mystery Dance.*
Sagan and Druyan, *Shadows of Forgotten Ancestors.*
Wright, *The Moral Animal.*

Page 20. The Way Boys Feel: Feelings and the Brain
Moir and Jessel, *Brain Sex.*

Chapter 2: The Culture Boys Create

Page 29. Boys and Competition
Deborah Tannen. *You Just Don't Understand.* New York: Ballantine, 1990.
Myriam Miedzian. *Boys Will Be Boys.* New York: Anchor, 1991.
Moir and Jessel, *Brain Sex.*
Helen Fisher. *Anatomy of Love.*
Marv Braunstein, of the Washington State Criminal Justice Training Commission, was very helpful in giving me information regarding boys, sports activities, and crime prevention.

Page 34. Principle 2: Task-Specific Empathy
Eleanor Maccoby. "Gender and Relationships," *American Psychologist,* April 1990.

Page 37. Principle 3: Large Group Preference
Tannen, *You Just Don't Understand.*
Victor Turner. *The Forest of Symbols: Aspects of Ndembu Ritual.* Ithaca, N.Y.: Cornell University Press, 1967.

Page 39. Principle 4: The Search for Independence
Fisher, *Anatomy of Love.*
Lillian B. Rubin. *Intimate Strangers.* New York: Harper Colophon, 1983.

Page 42. Principle 5: Personal Sacrifice in the Collective Experience
Woodrow Wilson. *When a Man Comes to Himself.* New York: Harper Bros., 1915.
David Sawyer, of Berea College, called to my attention the PIP program. Sawyer is a national trainer in Youth Service and can be reached at Berea, in Kentucky.

Page 44. Principle 6: Male Role Models
David Blankenhorn. *Fatherless America.*
My training videos are put out by Big Brothers and Big Sisters. For information, call them at 509-328-8310.

Page 46. Principle 7: Making Sport of Life and Life of Sport
Katherine Martin. "Is Winning Everything?" *Parents,* 1986. I've quoted Tutko from her article.

Page 50. The Early Years
Pielemeier, *M.E.N.* magazine.
Brazelton and Cramer, *The Earliest Relationship.*
Daniel Stern. *The Interpersonal World of the Infant.* New York: Basic Books, 1985.

Page 52. Puberty and Adolescence
My videotape, *Understanding the Mother-Son Relationship,* put out by Big Brothers and Big Sisters, and my book, *Mothers, Sons and Lovers,* deal with this transition, as it relates to mother-son separation. For information about the training video, call Big Brothers and Big Sisters at 509-328-8310.
Kathleen Berger and Ross A. Thompson. *The Developing Person Through Childhood and Adolescence.* New York: Worth Publishers, 1991.
David B. Wexler. *The Adolescent Self.* New York: Norton, 1991.

Page 53. Can Boys Be Boys and Feminists Too?
Aaron R. Kipnis and Elizabeth Herron. *Gender War/Gender Peace.*
Katie Roiphe. *The Morning After.* New York: Little Brown, 1993.
David Thomas. *Not Guilty.* New York: Morrow, 1993.
Christina Hoff-Sommers. *Who Stole Feminism.* New York: Simon & Schuster, 1994.

Chapter 3: Boys Need a Tribe

Page 64. Boys and Gangs
Geoffrey Canada. *Fist Stick Knife Gun.* Boston: Beacon Press, 1995.

Page 70–73. Daycare and Child Care
"Daycare Often Grim, Study Says," *Spokesman-Review,* from wire reports, February 6, 1995.

Page 73.
T. Berry Brazelton. "Families Today" column, *New York Times* Syndicate, February 6, 1995.

Page 73. Creating Extended Families of Your Own
Jay P. and Julia M. Gurian. *The Dependency Tendency.* Lanham, Md: University Press of America, 1983.

Page 77. What It's Really Like for Boys in the Educational System
Sadler and Sadler. *Failing at Fairness.* New York: Scribners, 1994.
Mary Pipher. *Reviving Ophelia.* New York: Grosset/Putnam, 1994.
Thomas W. Marino. "Sexism in Society: How Both Genders Suffer," *Counseling Today.* July 1995. See also, Lawrence Beymer's *Meeting the Guidance and Counseling Needs of Boys.* Alexandria, VA: The American Counseling Association, 1995.
Fiona Houston. "The War on Boys," *Men's Health,* October 1994.
Gordon Clay. *The National Men's Resource,* Winter 1995.

Page 81. Energizing Community Programs
Martha S. Hill, at the University of Michigan Survey Research Center, is one of a handful of researchers who studies work hours put in by women and men. See Pielemeier, *Seattle Times.*

Chapter 4: Love You Forever: What Boys Need From Their Mothers

Page 85.
Robert Munsch. Illustrated by Sheila McGraw. *Love You Forever*. Willowdale, Ontario: Firefly Books, 1986.
Paul Olsen. *Sons and Mothers*. New York: Evans, Co., 1981.

Page 86. The Right Conditions for "Good" Mother-Son Relationships
A number of good sources exist for these statistics, including Barbara Dafoe Whitehead's 1993 article in the *Atlantic Monthly,* the U.S. Census Bureau's "Household and Family Characteristics: March 1993" study, and the National Fatherhood Initiative (800-790-DADS).

Page 91. When a Divorced or Single Mother Brings Home a Boyfriend
Evelyn Bassoff. *Between Mothers and Sons*. New York: Dutton, 1994.

Page 94. Mother-Son Wounds
Pielemeier, *Seattle Times.*
The Journal of Social Work, November/December 1987.

Page 94–95.
Jay R. Greenberg and Stephen A. Mitchell. *Object Relations in Psychoanalytic Theory*. Cambridge, Mass: Harvard University Press, 1983.

Page 95–96.
If you think this might apply to you or someone you know, you might want to read my book *Mothers, Sons and Lovers,* which focuses on impingement quite comprehensively.

Chapter 5: From Daddy to Dad: The Father-Son Relationship

The lines by Loren Pederson are quoted from Charles Scull's anthology, *Fathers, Sons and Daughters*. Los Angeles: Jeremy Tarcher, 1992.

Page 108. Of Princes and Kings
Aaron R. Kipnis. *Knights Without Armor*

Andrew G. Kadar. "The Sex-Bias Myth in Medicine," *The Atlantic Monthly,* August 1994.

Page 111. The Father a Boy Needs

Page 112. Why Fathers Disappear
The National Fatherhood Initiative is a current and high-quality source of studies and statistics dealing with family issues. They can be reached at 800-790-DADS or by writing them at 600 Eden Road, Building E, Lancaster, PA 17601.
Page 112.
David Blankenhorn. *Fatherless America.*
Wallenstein, Judith, *Second Chances* Ticknor and Fields, 1989.

Page 117. What Fathers Need
Books like *A Circle of Men* by Bill Kauth (New York: St. Martin's Press, 1992) teach men how to start their own group. Books like *Wingspan: Inside the Men's Movement* by Chris Harding (New York: St. Martin's Press, 1993) list different agencies and men around the country who know about groups in different regions.

Page 123. From Daddy to Dad: Letting the Boy Go
For access to these categories I am grateful to Al Turtle, a certified Imago therapist, trained in the work of Harville Hendrix, and the therapist Kari Wagler.

Chapter 6: A Boy's Second Birth: The Passage Into Manhood

Robert Lawlor. *Voices of the First Day.* Rochester, VT: Inner Traditions International, 1990.

Page 135. The Role of the Mentor
In his novel *Body and Soul* about Claude, a musically gifted boy who is mentored by Weisfeld, Frank Conroy writes, "As [Claude and Weisfeld] walked along the northern rim of the reservoir Claude felt a sudden wave of love for Weisfeld, a kind of melting sensation in the chest. He moved closer, and Weisfeld, without breaking stride and in the most natural way, took his arm." Weisfeld has been Claude's mentor for five years. This moment between them is the moment when their intimacy becomes conscious, for a moment, and all powerful. Claude loves Weisfeld like he loves a close parent, a best friend, and an elder, all at once; Weisfeld loves Claude like a son, a

friend, a student all at once. Every boy who has had a mentor, and every mentor who has had a mentor know the beauty of this mentor love.

Page 148. The Hero's Journey
Joseph Campbell. *The Hero with a Thousand Faces,* 2nd edition. Princeton, N.J.: Princeton University Press, 1968.
While parenting books on boys' lives are invaluable, I have also found that books on the hero's journey are also invaluable for anyone raising, mentoring, or educating boys, for these books grow mainly out of male vision and masculine culture, and they give deep, often mysterious, insight into the archetypal world boys live and strive in.

Page 149. Boys Will Make the Journey With or Without Us
The new archetypal focus men seek in middle age is what mythologists call the "trickster" or "the magician." Allen Chinen's book, *Beyond the Hero,* is a wonderful study of this midlife shift.

Page 150. Models of Initiation
Mothering, Summer 1993.

Page 153. Ritual Initiation
Hyemeyohsts Storm. *Seven Arrows.* New York: Ballantine, 1972.

Page 154. Do Boys Want to Be Initiated?
Bernard Weiner. *Boy Into Man: A Father's Guide to Initiation of Teenage Sons.* San Francisco: Transformation Press, 1992.

Chapter 7: Teaching Boys Discipline

Page 161. What Is Healthy Discipline?
In general, adequate caregiver contact time is in short supply these days, yet without it, all talk of a "discipline system" is just that, talk. We cannot expect to raise well-disciplined boys unless we as individual parents and we as parents, mentors, and educators spend adequate time with the boys. This time must include a great deal of conscious conversation and cooperation about what our mutually agreed-upon discipline system is, how it's working, how it can always be improved. Often we can ask the growing boy his opinion. "What discipline would work better with you?" We need to spend this conscious talking time because we adults grew up in different discipline traditions or in few discipline traditions.

Page 170. Twelve Techniques for Healthy Discipline
There are some wonderful resources on disciplining children in the first decade of life. Some appear in the Bibliography and in the Notes of this book. A very useful non-book resource is the newsletter *Parents' Time-Out,* subtitled: *The Quarterly for Busy Parents of Young Children.* It's put out by The Parent Education Resource, Box 578932, Chicago, IL 60657. The resources focus on general child-discipline, not on "boys." In the next few years I would not be surprised to see a book come out whose whole focus is on what discipline strategies work with boys.

Page 173. Should We Spank Boys?
Murray S. Straus. *Beating the Devil out of Them.* New York: Lexington Books, 1995. Straus utilizes the National Family Violence Surveys of 1975 and 1985.
John Rosemond. *To Spank or Not to Spank.* Kansas City, MO: Andrews and McNeel, 1994.

Page 176. Hyperactivity and Attention Deficit Disorder
Robert Moss and Helen Huff Dunlap. *Why Johnny Can't Concentrate.* New York: Bantam, 1995.

Page 178. Discipline in Puberty and Adolescence
Moir and Jessel, *Brain Sex.*

Page 183. Difficult, Violent Boys
These statistics are gleaned from AP and UPI wire reports, the Silence the Violence campaign, the Bill Moyers report "What Can We Do About Violence?" and his article in *Parade* magazine, January 8, 1995, *Time* magazine, February 7, 1994, as well as private conversation with Ken Kerle, Ph.D., editor of *American Jails.*

Page 186.
Steven Goldberg. *Why Men Rule.* Chicago: Open Court, 1993.
Moir and Jessel, *Brain Sex.*

Chapter 8: Teaching Boys Values, Morality, and Spirituality

Mark Helprin. *A Soldier of the Great War.* New York: Avon, 1991.

Page 193–197. The Stages of Moral Development
Lawrence Kohlberg. "Moral Stages and Moralization: The Cognitive-

Developmental Approach." In *Moral Development and Behavior,* ed. by T. Lickona. New York: Holt, Rinehart and Winston, 1976.

Richard M. Lerner and Graham B. Spanier. *Adolescent Development.* New York: McGraw-Hill, 1980.

Page 202–205. Using Archetype and Mythology to Reach Boys

Robert Moore and Douglas Gillette. *King, Warrior, Magician, Lover.* San Francisco: HarperSanFrancisco, 1990.

Michael Gurian. *The Prince and the King.* Los Angeles: Tarcher/Putnam, 1992.

Page 204.

Joseph Campbell. *The Power of Myth.* With Bill Moyers. New York: Doubleday, 1988.

Robert Bly. *Iron John.* Reading, Mass.: Addison-Wesley, 1990.

Clarissa Pinkola Estes. *Women Who Run with the Wolves.* New York: Ballantine, 1993.

Chase Collins. *Tell Me a Story.* New York: Houghton Mifflin, 1992.

Barbara F. Meltz. "Storytelling Adds a Little Magic to Your Child's World," *Boston Globe.* In the *Spokesman-Review,* April 30, 1992.

Page 209. Teaching Boys Values Through the Media

Lena Williams. "Group Wants Nation to Pull the Plug on TV," *New York Times,* appearing in the *Spokesman-Review,* February 20, 1995.

Harry F. Waters, with Daniel Glick, Carolyn Friday, and Jeanne Gordon, "Networks Under the Gun," *Newsweek,* July 12, 1993.

Page 211. Teaching Boys to Care for Their Own Souls

Thomas Moore. *Care of the Soul.* New York: HarperCollins, 1992.

Chapter 9: Teaching Boys About Sex and Love

Page 221.

Alan Guttmacher. "Sex and America's Teenagers Report," Alan Guttmacher Institute, 1994.

"Teenagers Not as Sexually Active as Adults Believe," AP wire, appearing in *Spokesman-Review,* and Cox News Service wire, "Some Prom Memories Best Avoided," Marilyn Geewax, in *Spokesman-Review,* April 16, 1994.

Michele Ingrassia. "Virgin Cool," *Newsweek,* October 17, 1994, quoting John Ward, chief of the Center for Disease Control's AIDS surveillance branch.

Page 225. Boys Need Male-Specific Teaching and Models
John H. Gagnon. "The Social Organization of Sexuality Report," reported in *Spokesman-Review,* October 7, 1994.

Page 225–226.
Barbara Dafoe Whitehead. "The Failure of Sex Education," *Atlantic Monthly,* October 1994.
Joel Aschenbach. "Why Things Are," *Spokesman-Review,* March 5, 1995.
James Weinrich, author of *Sexual Landscapes: Why We Are What We Are, Why We Love Whom We Love,* echoes Francoeur's findings.

Page 231. What If My Son Is Gay?
Brain Sex details a number of studies which explore the biological link. They make interesting and controversial reading.
The controversy surrounding this information was beautifully captured in the *Harvard Medical Letter.* In the *Letter* of January 1994, Michael Bailey, Ph.D, and Richard C. Pillard, M.D., argued that homosexuality was innate. See their article, "The Innateness of Homosexuality." In their response, entitled "Biology and Human Sexual Orientation," in the February 1994 *Letter,* William Byne, M.D., Ph.D., and Bruce Parsons, M.D., were unable to argue against the biological link. They had to be satisfied to call the studies "inconclusive."
As with all brain research, anthropological information about tribal cultures is a useful secondary source. When we look at the Dagara, the Zuni, and so many other cultures which honor homosexuality as an intrinsic part of the web of life, we come even closer to "conclusive evidence" that the brain researchers are correct in finding a link between homosexuality and the natural order.

Page 233. Loving Our Gay Boys
Judy Grahn. *Another Mother Tongue.* Boston: Beacon Press, 1984.
Malidoma Somé. *Of Water and the Spirit.* Los Angeles: Tarcher/Putnam, 1994.

Page 235. Sex Education in the Schools
Anne Windishar. "Sexual Denial is a Dangerous Game," *Spokesman-Review,* December 28, 1994.

Page 237. Love as a Spiritual Discipline
Michael Gurian. *Love's Journey.* Boston: Shambhala, 1995.

Page 241. Boys and Sexual Abuse.
Janie Hart-Rossi. *Protect Your Child From Sexual Abuse: A Parent's Guide.* Seattle: Parenting Press, 1984.

Page 243.
Bruce Kirkpatrick. "The Charmer," *M.E.N.,* February 1994.

Page 244.
John H. Gagnon. "The Social Organization of Sexuality Report," reported in *Spokesman-Review,* October 7, 1994.

Page 245.
Sadler and Sadler. *Failing at Fairness.*

Chapter 10: Teaching Boys a Healthy Male Role in Life

Page 248.
My information about the Shavante comes from the "Millennium" series on tribal cultures, created and narrated by David Maybury-Jones, and repeated often on PBS.

Page 250. A Sacred Male Role for the New Millennium
Robert Mannis. "Husbandry," *Utne Reader,* May/June 1991.

Page 257. What It's Really Like for Men in the Workplace
Anthony Carnevale, "Trickle-down Causes Flood of Ills," *Washington Post,* November 29, 1994. Carnevale, Chair of the National Commission for Employment Policy, advises the president and Congress on employment issues. The Stephen Rose study, which he quotes, tracked 5,000 families.

Page 258.
"Family Feminist" is the term I've invented for those of us who pursue equality for women as *one* of four equally important social goals. These four are: children's security, men's issues, community development, and women's equality. "Feminism" needs, in my view, to remain highlighted because without the efforts of twenty-five years of feminism much of the work we do to blend the four goals would not have its present power. Yet the bottom line for a family feminist is that the desires of women as a political bloc need to be seen as equally important to, not more important than, the urgent need in our society for family stability.

Full Bibliography

Abbott, Franklin, ed. *Boyhood, Growing Up Male.* Freedom, CA: The Crossing Press, 1993.

Abrahams, Roger D. *African Folktales.* New York: Pantheon Books, 1983.

Afanasev, Aleksandr. *Russian Fairytales.* New York: Pantheon Books, 1945.

Ames, Louise Bates and Frances L. Ilg. *Your Four-Year-Old.* New York: Dell, 1976. See the yearly books in this series from "Your One-Year-Old" to "Your Ten- to Fourteen-Year-old."

Bartimole, Carmella, and John Bartimole. *Teenage Alcoholism and Substance Abuse: Causes, Consequences and Cures.* Hollywood, Florida: Frederick Fell, 1987.

Barzan, Robert. *Sex and Spirit: Exploring Gay Men's Spirituality.* San Francisco: White Crane Press, 1995.

Bassoff, Evelyn. *Between Mothers and Sons.* New York: Dutton, 1994.

Batten, Mary. *Sexual Strategies.* Los Angeles: Tarcher/Putnam, 1992.

Berger, Kathleen, and Ross A. Thompson. *The Developing Person Through Childhood and Adolescence.* New York: Worth Publishers, 1991.

Beymer, Lawrence. *Meeting the Guidance and Counseling Needs of Boys.* Amer. Counseling Association: Alexandria, VA, 1995.

Blankenhorn, David. *Fatherless in America*. New York: Basic Books, 1995.

Bly, Robert. *Iron John*. Reading, Mass.: Addison-Wesley, 1990.

Brazelton, T. Berry, and Bertrand G. Cramer. *The Earliest Relationship*. Reading, Mass.: Addison-Wesley, 1990.

Campbell, Joseph. *The Hero With a Thousand Faces,* 2nd edition. Princeton, N.J.: Princeton University Press, 1968.

————. *Historical Atlas of World Mythology*. New York: Harper & Row, 1983.

————. *Myths We Live By*. New York: Bantam Books, 1988.

————. Commentator. *The Complete Grimm's Fairy Tales*. New York: Pantheon Books, 1972.

————. *The Power of Myth*. With Bill Moyers. New York: Doubleday, 1988.

Chinen, Allen. *Beyond the Hero*. Los Angeles: Tarcher/Putnam, 1994.

Clarke, Jean Illsley. *Self-esteem: A Family Affair*. San Francisco: Harper & Row, 1978.

Coles, Robert. *The Moral Life of Children*. New York: Atlantic Monthly Press, 1986.

Collins, Chase. *Tell Me a Story*. New York: Houghton Mifflin. 1992.

Conroy, Frank. *Body and Soul*. New York: Dell, 1993.

Crary, Elizabeth. *Without Spanking or Spoiling*. Seattle: Parenting Press, 1979.

de Chardin, Pierre Teilhard. *The Creative Imperative*. Millbrae, Calif: Celestial Arts, 1986.

de Gaetono, Gloria. *Television and the Lives of Our Children*. Redmond, WA: Train of Thought, 1993.

Dominguez, Joe, and Vicki Robin. *Your Money or Your Life*. New York: Viking, 1992.

Dorsett, Tony, and Harvey Frommer. *Running Tough*. New York: Doubleday, 1989.

Eliade, Mircea. *Rites and Symbols of Initiation*. New York: Harper & Row, 1975.

Elium, Don and Jeanne. *Raising a Son*. Hillsboro, Oregon: Beyond Words, 1992.

Erdoes, Richard, and Alfonso Ortiz. *American Indian Myths and Legends*. New York: Pantheon Books, 1984.

Erikson, Erik H. *Identity: Youth and Crisis*. New York: Norton, 1968.

Estes, Clarissa Pinkola. *Women Who Run With the Wolves*. New York: Ballantine, 1993.

Eyre, Linda and Richard. *Teaching Your Children Joy*. New York: Fireside, 1984.

Farrell, Warren. *The Myth of Male Power*. New York: Simon and Schuster, 1993.

Fenwick, Elizabeth, and Tony Smith. *Adolescence: The Survival Guide for Parents and Teenagers*. London: Dorling Kindersley, 1995.

Fisher, Helen. *Anatomy of Love*. New York: Fawcett, 1992.

Fox-Genovese, Elizabeth. *Feminism Without Illusions.* Chapel Hill: University of North Carolina Press, 1991.

Gilmore, David. *Manhood in the Making.* New Haven: Yale University Press, 1992.

Glassman, Bruce S. *Everything You Need to Know About Growing Up Male.* New York: Rosen, 1991.

Goldberg, Herb. *The New Male.* New York: Signet Books, 1979.

Goldberg, Steven. *Why Men Rule.* Chicago: Open Court, 1993.

Goldstein, Sam, and Michael Goldstein. *Hyperactivity.* New York: John Wiley & Sons, 1992.

Gordon, Thomas. *P.E.T., Parent Effectiveness Training.* New York: Peter Wyden, 1970.

Grahn, Judy. *Another Mother Tongue.* Boston: Beacon Press, 1984.

Gray, John. *Men Are From Mars, Women Are From Venus.* San Francisco: HarperSanFrancisco, 1993.

Greenberg, Jay R., and Stephen A. Mitchell. *Object Relations in Psychoanalytic Theory.* Cambridge, Mass.: Harvard, 1983.

Gurian, Jay P., and Julia M. Gurian. *The Dependency Tendency.* Lanham, Md.: University Press of America, 1983.

Gurian, Michael. *Mothers, Sons and Lovers.* Boston: Shambhala Publications, 1993.

———. *The Prince and the King: Healing the Father-Son Wound.* Los Angeles: Tarcher/Putnam, 1992.

———. *Love's Journey: The Seasons and Stages of Relationship.* Boston: Shambhala Publications, 1995.

Hamilton, Edith. *Mythology.* New York: New Directions, 1942.

Hanh, Thich Nhat. *Peace in Every Step.* New York: Bantam, 1991.

Harding, Chris. *Wingspan: Inside the Men's Movement.* New York: St. Martin's, 1993.

Harris, Robie H. Illustrated by Michael Emberley. *It's Perfectly Normal: Changing Bodies, Growing Up, Sex and Sexual Health.* Cambridge, Mass.: Candlewick Press, 1995.

Hart-Rossi, Janie. *Protect Your Child From Sexual Abuse: A Parent's Guide.* Seattle: Parenting Press, 1984.

Helprin, Mark. *A Soldier of the Great War.* New York: Avon, 1991.

Herdt, Gilbert H., ed. *Rituals of Manhood: Male Initiation in Papua New Guinea.* Berkeley, Calif.: University of California Press, 1982.

Hoff-Sommers, Christina. *Who Stole Feminism.* New York: Simon & Schuster, 1994.

Houff, William H. *Infinity in Your Hand.* Spokane: Melior, 1989.

Jung, C. G., ed., *Man and His Symbols.* New York: Doubleday, 1986.

Kaplan, Louise J. *Oneness and Separateness: From Infant to Individual.* New York: Touchstone, 1978.

Kauth, Bill. *A Circle of Men*. New York: St. Martin's, 1992.

Keen, Sam. *Fire in the Belly*. New York: Bantam, 1991.

Keen, Sam, and Anne Valley-Fox. *Your Mythic Journey*. Los Angeles: Jeremy P. Tarcher, 1978.

Kehoe, Patricia. *Something Happened and I'm Scared to Tell: A Book for Young Victims of Abuse*. Seattle: Parenting Press, 1987.

————. *Helping Abused Children*. Seattle: Parenting Press, 1988.

Kipnis, Aaron R. *Knights Without Armor*. Los Angeles: Jeremy P. Tarcher, 1992.

Kipnis, Aaron R., and Elizabeth Herron. *Gender War/Gender Peace*. New York: William Morrow, 1994.

Kushner, Harold S. *When Children Ask About God*. New York: Schocken, 1989.

Lawlor, Robert. *Voices of the First Day*. Rochester, VT: Inner Traditions International, 1990.

Lee, John. *Facing the Fire*. New York: Bantam, 1992.

Lerner, Richard M., and Graham B. Spanier. *Adolescent Development*. New York: McGraw-Hill, 1980.

Mander, Jerry. *Four Arguments for the Elimination of Television*. New York: Quill, 1978.

Margulis, Lyn, and Dorion Sagan. *Mystery Dance*. New York: Summit Books, 1991.

Maslow, Abraham. *Love and Will*. New York: Norton, 1969.

May, Rollo. *The Cry for Myth*. New York: Norton, 1989.

Miedzian, Myriam. *Boys Will Be Boys*. New York: Anchor, 1991.

Miller, Alice. *For Your Own Good*. New York: Farrar, Straus & Giroux, 1983.

Moir, Anne, and David Jessel. *Brain Sex*. New York: Laurel, 1989.

Moore, Robert, and Douglas Gillette. *King, Warrior, Magician, Lover*. San Francisco: HarperSanFrancisco, 1990.

Moore, Sheila, and Roon Frost. *The Little Boy Book*. New York: Ballantine, 1986.

Moore, Thomas. *Care of the Soul*. New York: HarperCollins, 1992.

Moss, Robert, and Helen Huff Dunlap. *Why Johnny Can't Concentrate*. New York: Bantam, 1995.

Munsch, Robert. Illustrated by Sheila McGraw. *Love You Forever*. Willowdale, Ontario: Firefly Books, 1986.

O'Flaherty, Wendy, trans. *Hindu Myths*. New York: Penguin, 1975.

Olsen, Paul. *Sons and Mothers*. New York: M. Evans Co., 1981.

Orlandi, Mario A., ed. *Cultural Competence for Evaluators:* OSAP Cultural Competence Series 1. Rockville, Maryland: U.S. Department of Health and Human Services, 1992.

Palmer, Pat, with Melissa Alberti Froehner. *Teen Esteem: A Self-Direction*

Manual for Young Adults. San Luis Obispo, Calif.: Impact Publishers, 1995.

Pearce, Joseph Chilton. *Magical Child*. New York: Bantam, 1976.

Phillips, Angela. *The Trouble With Boys*. New York: Basic Books, 1994.

Pierce, Carol, and Bill Page. *A Male/Female Continuum: Paths to Colleague-ship*. Laconia, New Hampshire: New Dynamics, 1986.

Pipher, Mary. *Reviving Ophelia*. New York: Grosset/Putnam, 1994.

Pomeroy, Wardell B. *Boys and Sex*. New York: Delacorte, 1991.

Pool, Robert. *Eve's Rib*. New York: Crown Publishers, 1994.

Rico, Gabriele. *Pain and Possibility*. Los Angeles: Jeremy P. Tarcher, 1991.

Rogers, Carl. *On Becoming a Person*. Boston: Houghton Mifflin, 1961.

Roiphe, Katie. *The Morning After*. New York: Little Brown, 1993.

Rosemond, John. *To Spank or Not to Spank*. Kansas City, MO: Andrews and McNeel, 1994.

Rubin, Lillian B. *Intimate Strangers*. New York: Harper Colophon, 1983.

Sadker, Myra, and David Sadker. *Failing at Fairness*. New York: Scribners, 1994.

Sagan, Carl, and Ann Druyan. *Shadows of Forgotten Ancestors*. New York: Random House, 1992.

Schulman, Michael, and Eva Mekler. *Bringing Up a Moral Child*. New York: Doubleday, 1994.

Scull, Charles. *Fathers, Sons and Daughters*. Los Angeles: Jeremy Tarcher, 1992.

Shelov, Steven P., Editor-in-Chief, American Academy of Pediatrics. *Caring for Your Baby and Young Child: Birth to Age 5*. New York: Bantam, 1993.

Shure, Myrna, and George Spivack. *Problem-solving Techniques in Child-rearing*. Oakland, Calif.: Jossey-Bass, 1978.

Sogyal Rinpoche. *The Tibetan Book of Living and Dying*. New York: HarperCollins, 1993.

Somé, Malidoma. *Of Water and the Spirit*. Los Angeles: Tarcher/Putnam, 1994.

Stern, Daniel N. *The Interpersonal World of the Infant*. New York: Basic Books, 1985.

Storm, Hyemeyohsts. *Seven Arrows*. New York: Ballantine, 1972.

Straus, Murray S. *Beating the Devil out of Them*. New York: Lexington Books, 1995.

Tannen, Deborah. *You Just Don't Understand*. New York: Ballantine, 1990.

Thomas, David. *Not Guilty*. New York: Morrow, 1993.

Thompson, Keith. *To Be a Man*. Los Angeles: Jeremy Tarcher, 1991.

Trueman, Terry. *Sheehan*. Spokane: Siobhan, 1992.

Trungpa, Chogyam. *Cutting Through Spiritual Materialism*. Boston: Shambhala Publications, 1987.

Turner, Victor. *Ritual Process*. Ithaca, N.Y.: Cornell University Press, 1977.

————. *The Forest of Symbols:* Aspects of Ndembu Ritual. Ithaca, N.Y.: Cornell University Press, 1967.

Tyler, Royall. *Japanese Tales.* New York: Pantheon, 1987.

Von Franz, Marie-Louise. *The Interpretation of Fairy Tales.* Dallas: Spring Publications, 1970.

————. *Puer Aeternus.* Boston: Sigo Press, 1981.

Wakefield, Dan. *Writing Your Spiritual Autobiography.* Boston: Beacon Press, 1992.

Wallenstein, Judith. *The Good Marriage: How and Why Love Lasts.* New York: Houghton Mifflin, 1995.

Wallenstein, Judith, and Sandra Blakeslee. *Second Chances.* Ticknor and Fields, 1988.

Weiner, Bernard. *Boy Into Man: A Father's Guide to Initiation of Teenage Sons.* San Francisco: Transformation Press, 1992.

Wexler, David B. *The Adolescent Self.* New York: Norton, 1991.

Williams, Lynne H., Henry S. Berman, and Louisa Rose. *The Too-Precious Child.* New York: Macmillan, 1987.

Williamson, Marianne. *Illuminata.* New York: Random House, 1994.

Wilson, Woodrow. *When a Man Comes to Himself.* New York: Harper Bros., 1915.

Winnicott, D. W. *Human Nature.* New York: Schocken Books, 1988.

Wood, Audrey. Illustrated by Don Wood. *Quick as a Cricket.* Singapore: Child's Play, 1991.

Wright, Robert. *The Moral Animal.* New York: Vintage, 1994.

Yolen, Jane, ed. *Favorite Folktales From Around the World.* New York: Pantheon Books, 1986.

Index

Acknowledgments

If I had not lived the boyhood I lived, this book would be very different, indeed. So to begin it all I must acknowledge my parents, Jay P. and Julia M. Gurian, for taking me all over the world so that I could experience boyhood in other cultures. Among these cultures there are many people to thank, including Aiya and Mahmoud in India and the people of the Southern Ute reservation. Following in my parents' footsteps, I, as a man and a professional, continued the family tradition of traveling and working overseas, enriched by the people of Israel, shown an inspiring lifestyle on Kibbutz Dorot, and later embraced by Turkish communities. Aykut Misirligil, Yusuf Eradam, Necla Aytur, and Audrey Uzmen were special friends and colleagues in my life and research in Turkey.

For clinical insight and assistance, my thanks go to Armin Arendt, Ph.D., of Eastern Washington University's Applied Psychology department, Terry Trueman, M.S., Warren Farrell, Ph.D., Jeff Hedge,

D.O., who both as a psychiatrist and a friend helped me understand elements of human development I would have otherwise missed, Darl Van der Linden, Ph.D., John D'Aboy, Ph.D., who provided me with essential information about genetics, and Michael Mainer, M.D., who let me ask him questions whenever I wanted to.

The Herzog clan deserves special thanks for showing me what "three-family" life could be like in the heart of American life.

Without the help of certain key people in the world of publishing, the book as you will read it would not have come about. My thanks to Laurie Fox and Linda Chester, who worked to find it a home. My thanks to Richard Dalke for immeasurable support. In Alan Rinzler I've been fortunate to have one of the finest editors around, who is also an accomplished clinician and the father of four sons. Many thanks to Irene Prokop and her staff. A special thank-you to Jeremy Tarcher, whose support of my work over the years has been invaluable.

All over the country, adults and children have let me work with them. I thank them for everything I've learned in their communities, schools, campsites, counseling rooms, and homes.

And in the end, as always, my profound thanks for their patience go to Gabrielle and Davita and to Gail, my constant companion.

About the Author

Michael Gurian is a social philosopher, family therapist, corporate consultant, and the *New York Times*–bestselling author of twenty books published in twenty languages. The Gurian Institute (www.gurianinstitute.com), which he cofounded, conducts research internationally, launches pilot programs, and trains professionals.

As a social philosopher, Gurian has pioneered efforts to bring neurobiology and brain research into homes, workplaces, schools, and public policy. A number of his groundbreaking books in child development—including *The Wonder of Boys*; *Boys and Girls Learn Differently!*; *The Wonder of Girls*; and *What Could He Be Thinking?*—have sparked national debate. His book *The Minds of Boys* provides a revolutionary new framework, based in neurobiology, with which to understand and care for the educational needs of our sons.

Gurian has served as a consultant to families, corporations, therapists, physicians, school districts, community agencies, churches, and criminal justice personnel and other professionals, traveling to approximately twenty cities a year to give keynote addresses at conferences. His training videos (also available as DVDs) for parents and volunteers are used by Big Brother and Big Sister agencies in the United States and Canada.

As an educator, Gurian has taught at Gonzaga University, Eastern Washington University, and Ankara University in Turkey. His speaking engagements have included Harvard, Johns Hopkins, Stanford, Macalester College, the University of Colorado, the University of Missouri–Kansas City, and UCLA. His philosophy reflects the diverse cultures (European, Asian, Middle Eastern, and American) in which he has lived, worked, and studied.

Gurian's work has been featured in various media, including *The New York Times*, *The Washington Post*, *USA Today*, *Newsweek*, *Time*, *The Wall Street Journal*, *Parenting*, *Good Housekeeping*, and *Redbook*, as well as on *Today*, *Good Morning America*, CNN, PBS, and National Public Radio.

Visit his website at www.michaelgurian.com.